The United States and China
in the Twentieth Century

The United States and China in the Twentieth Century

Second Edition

MICHAEL SCHALLER

New York   Oxford
OXFORD UNIVERSITY PRESS
1990

Oxford University Press

Oxford   New York   Toronto
Delhi   Bombay   Calcutta   Madras   Karachi
Petaling Jaya   Singapore   Hong Kong   Tokyo
Nairobi   Dar es Salaam   Cape Town
Melbourne   Auckland

and associated companies in
Berlin   Ibadan

Published by Oxford University Press, Inc.,
200 Madison Avenue, New York, New York 10016

Oxford is a registered trademark of Oxford University Press

Library of Congress Cataloging-in-Publication Data

Schaller, Michael, 1947–
    The United States and China in the twentieth century / Michael
Schaller.—2nd ed.
        p.   cm.
    Bibliography: p.
    Includes index.
    ISBN 0–19–505865–8
    ISBN 0–19–505866–6 (paper)
    1.United States—Foreign relations—China.   2. China—Foreign
relations—United States.   3. United States—Foreign relations—20th
century.   4. China—Foreign relations—20th century.   I. Title.
E183.8.C5S323   1990
327.73051—dc 19   89–2885
                                                              CIP

9 8 7 6 5 4 3 2 1

Printed in the United States of America
on acid-free paper

For Sue, again!

Preface

Since the first appearance of this book a decade ago, China has experienced what its current leadership calls a "second revolution." Its modernization program and domestic reforms have not only transformed much of the Maoist system, but have altered, fundamentally, the nature of China's interaction with the United States and the rest of the world. No longer a semi-isolated nation, China has adopted a distinctive brand of "market socialism." Borrowing a phrase from American diplomacy, Beijing's leaders tout a new "Open Door policy" by which China encourages trade, foreign investment, tourism, cultural exchange and participation in world organizations.

The United States, too, has followed new paths in foreign policy. The deterioration of relations with the Soviet Union in the late 1970s, followed by the election of President Ronald Reagan, created both opportunities and tensions in Sino-American relations. After several disputes with Beijing, the Reagan Administration altered many of its ideological objections to closer relations with China. For its part, the People's Republic accepted America's continuing commitment to the security of Taiwan. By the late 1980s, both sides adopted a pragmatic and flexible approach to their relationship that reflected a mutual maturity and shared interest in preserving Asian stability.

In this new edition, I seek to explain the evolution of these developments and assess their significance for the future. Over the past decade, substantial scholarship has added to our understanding of earlier events. I have made certain changes in the text to reflect these new insights.

As this book goes to press, the violent suppression of the spring 1989 student "democracy movement" has jolted China. In the Epilogue, I suggest how this event may alter the course of Chinese-American relations.

Tucson, Ariz. M. S.
June 1989

A Note on Romanization of Chinese Names

Since the publication of the first edition of this book, the "Pinyin" system has become the predominant method of rendering Chinese names, place terms, etc., into the Roman alphabet. Thus Mao Tse-tung and Chou En-lai have become Mao Zedong and Zhou Enlai. Peking is now Beijing. This system more accurately reflects Chinese pronounciation. In many cases I have changed the Romanization to conform to the new standard. In other cases, particularly of some older, historical usages, I have utilized the traditional spellings.

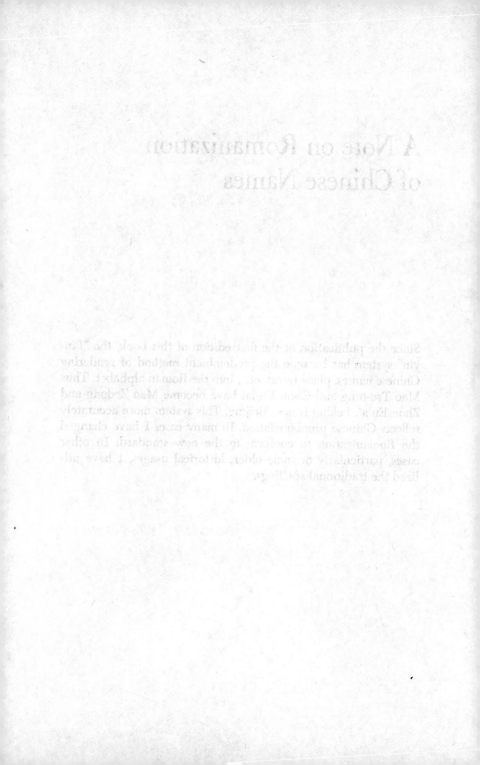

Contents

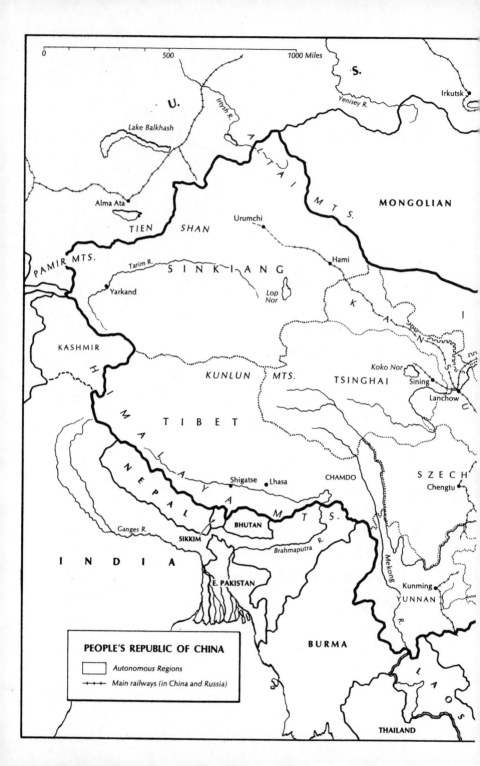

It is said that the ancient Roman triumvir Crassus had both a private fire department and a private arson squad, and that he made many talents out of using the two in judicious combination. To an interesting degree, western powers in China, and perhaps elsewhere, appear to have played the part of Crassus in the last century. Their material interests seemed best secured when the Chinese government had a fire lit under it, the fire of at least partly western inspired domestic rebelliousness; for in such a precarious situation, no matter how much they would ordinarily wish to withhold concessions from foreigners, Chinese rulers would have to make concessions, or confirm them, in order to qualify for the foreign aid which alone could save them at home. For both sides there was one condition to the smooth working of this protection-system: the Chinese government should not become so helpless before its domestic foes that effective foreign aid must overtax the foreigner or over encumber the Chinese client; the former will not dispense more than his stake is worth, the latter will not repay more than he stands to lose.

Joseph Levenson,
Confucian China and its Modern Fate

The United States and China
in the Twentieth Century

1

Images of China

The news from China on October 1, 1949, troubled and confused Americans. Speaking from the Gate of Heavenly Peace (Tiananmen) at the center of the old Forbidden City in Beijing, Communist leader Mao Zedong proclaimed the birth of the People's Republic of China (PRC). During the previous week Mao and other leaders of the Chinese Communist Party (CCP) had addressed a provisional assembly called the "Political Consultative Conference" whose delegates cheered wildly when Mao declared that China would "no longer be a nation subject to insult and humiliation. We have stood up. . . ." Not only were the remnants of Chiang Kai-shek's (Jiang Jieshi) Nationalist army being driven off the mainland, but foreign missionaries, merchants and soldiers joined the exodus. Mao had already declared that the new China would support the Soviet camp against the "imperialist" United States. Even those Chinese educated in the United States became suspect as agents of "cultural imperalism."

By 1949 almost four years of cold war with the Soviet Union had conditioned most Americans to see radical changes anywhere as part of a global Communist conspiracy. Even before Mao formally proclaimed his new regime, the *New York Times* dismissed his followers as a "nauseous force," a "compact little oligarchy dominated by Moscow's nominees." In an official statement in August 1949, Secretary of State Dean Acheson ridiculed the Chinese Communists as mere puppets of Russia whose government could not even pass the first test of legitimacy. "It is," Acheson said, "not Chinese." Former Army Chief of Staff, Secretary of State and Secretary of Defense General George C. Marshall, testifying later, went so far as to agree with a Senator's statement that "what has happened in China is a conquest of that country by Soviet Russia. . . ." In the opinion of *Life* magazine, Mao Zedong had "shattered the illusion cherished by many Americans—the illusion that China's Communists are different." China, most Americans concluded, had somehow been lost behind the iron, or bamboo, curtain. During the next twenty-five years American politics would be wracked by the search for those responsible for "the loss of China." This inquisition, accompanied by a purge of many government and academic China experts, helped propel the United States into both the Korean and Vietnam wars.

To understand the turbulence of Chinese-American relations since the Second World War we must look back in time to an earlier era. In 1937, only twelve years before Mao stood on Tiananmen, another Chinese ruler commanded American headlines. Japan had invaded China and threatened to overrun it completely. *Time* magazine proclaimed Generalissimo and Madame Chiang Kai-shek "Man and Wife of the Year" for their valiant but probably hopeless efforts to resist the Japanese. Japan's armies were portrayed as an avalanche of "ants" driven forward by a primal urge to conquer. The Chinese people, under "one supreme ruler and his remarkable wife," fought for the virtues of Western civilization. If he prevailed, *Time* speculated, Chiang might become "Asia's Man of the Century." Similar reports from many of the 1,500 American missionaries in China proclaimed that Chiang and his wife were the "most enlightened, patriotic, and able rulers" in China's 3,000 year history. These praises, when added to the adulation which followed the Chinese-American alliance after Pearl Harbor, help explain why so many Americans saw Chiang's defeat and the Communist victory as such a fearsome event. In less than a decade China had turned from democratic ally to Communist enemy—or had it?

The dramatic reversals of 1949 were not nearly so startling when seen in the perspective of the previous 150 years. From their initial contacts the Americans and Chinese misunderstood one another, reflecting their radically different cultures and histories. They each saw virtue and progress in terms of their own norms and values. What was different was, by definition, inferior.

As an offshoot of Western European culture, American social values stressed a belief in individualism, Christianity and representative government. The focus of social activity remained within the nuclear family. The capitalist economic system encouraged private economic initiative in a context of government support and regulation. Technological innovations were quickly accepted, transforming the United States into one of the world's leading urban industrial powers. Despite significant regional and ethnic differences, since the Civil War the nation enjoyed unprecedented prosperity due to the integration of a national market. While inequality persisted, as a nation America soon occupied a virtually unrivaled position of wealth and power.

Traditional China presented a very different picture from modern America. Its culture developed in relative isolation several millennia before the birth of Christ. Tremendous regional variations in geography, climate and spoken language divided the society. Life in China was overwhelmingly rural. Even today, after forty years of unprecedented industrial growth, almost seventy-five percent of the people live as peasant farmers in the countryside. In the United States, perhaps four percent of the population remain on the farm. Although traditional China's agricultural achievements compared very well to those of eighteenth century Europe, the technological and industrial revolutions which transformed the West passed it by. Growing population pressures, the deterioration of government, and foreign assaults all placed a growing burden on the peasants who tilled their own land or rented tiny plots. Producing enough food to feed themselves and pay the onerous sums demanded in rents and taxes became increasingly difficult. By the early twentieth century, concluded an eminent historian, "poverty, abuse, and early death were the only prospects for nearly half a billion people" in China.

A rigid political hierarchy governed traditional China. Power radiated downward from an hereditary emperor into the many provinces. The "Son of Heaven," as he was known, ruled through a large bureaucracy chosen by competitive examination. While anyone, in theory, might qualify for this civil service and the road it opened to wealth and power, economic realities minimized this freedom. The examination required rigorous training in classical literature and the written Chinese language which involved years of private study. Written Chinese, composed of innumerable combinations, was not an open door for communications and learning. The complexity of the written language kept the vast majority illiterate and only added to their oppression. Culture became a tool of exploitation, a barrier to upward advancement, not an agent of enlightenment.

The requirements of the competitive examination system gave tremendous advantages to the privileged sons of rural landlords, or "gentry," as they are often called, who monopolized most of the official posts. The gentry class were the guardians of culture, law, morality, order and wealth in rural China. Not surprisingly a strong bond of mutual interest developed between government officials in the countryside and the local property owners who were their natural constituency. The gentry often took responsibility for local security, the collection of taxes and rents, and the maintenance and construction of public works. In return, the officials provided government sanction for the economic and social privileges held by the gentry. This alliance assured political stability and economic security for both groups.

Not religion, but a highly elitist social philosophy known as Confucianism, justified this division of society. Above all, Confucianism stressed conformity to established norms and loyalty to one's "natural superiors." This championed a rigid hierarchy of men over women, age over youth, mental labor over manual labor and gentry over peasant. The emperor sat as head of the whole human family and commanded that obedience to local and central government officers be as complete as that given to one's own father or grandfather. Not surprisingly both the gentry and official bureaucracy enshrined the Confusian classics which sanctioned their own favored position.

The emperor's court and the wealthiest classes did subsidize the creation of magnificent buildings and objects of art. But these luxuries, enjoyed by two to three percent of the population, were acquired by squeezing out of the peasantry whatever tiny surplus they produced. Periodically, the continuing exploitation led to local or regional uprisings. Some revolts even succeeded in toppling a reigning dynasty. Reshuffling the ruling class, however, had little effect on the underlying order. Without a change in values inspired by a new set of political ideas, a new ideology, victorious peasant leaders quickly adopted the institutions of their predecessors.

Even foreign conquerers like the Mongols or the Manchus who established the Ch'ing Dynasty (1644–1912) soon accommodated themselves to the existing system and ruled through Confucian-trained officials and the rural gentry. Real change might come about only when socioeconomic conditions among the peasantry became desperate *and* coincided with the appearance of a new political ideology that offered an alternative vision of society. Ironically, the assault of the West, including the United States, set this great transformation in motion and shattered the cycle of one dynasty decaying only to be replaced by a similar institution.

The Western Impact

Before the late 1700s China had very little contact with the West. Arab trading caravans occasionally braved the trackless desert route through inner Asia. In the thirteenth century Marco Polo followed this path and returned to Europe to write about his journey to miraculous "Cathay." By the early 1600s a dedicated group of Jesuit missionaries convinced the Ming emperors to grant them residence in Beijing. There they indulged in relatively little religious work but offered the Chinese instruction in Western mathematics, astronomy and weapons manufacture. Back in Rome, Vatican intrigues among rival religious orders turned the Pope against the mission and by the late seventeenth century little remained of the Catholic influence.

China, of course, was not totally isolated. Many of the smaller states of Asia which surrounded it, including Korea, Burma and

Vietnam, recognized the supremacy of Chinese power and culture. These states were expected periodically to send "tribute missions" to China carrying gifts and pledges of loyalty. The emperor rewarded tributaries with a reciprocal exchange of favors. In reality the system served as a form of trade and political alliance. To acknowledge acceptance of his Chinese host's superior status, the foreign tribute bearer had to perform a ritual—the *K'e-t'ou* (Ketou), known to us as "kowtow" or "knocking the head"—before a suitable Chinese official. Possessing both predominant power in East Asia and a sense of cultural superiority, the Chinese believed that their country and civilization were truly the center of the world. Their term for China typified this conceit: *"Chung-kuo"* (Zhong quo), or "Middle Kingdom," represented the center of human achievement. By definition, all those outside were barbarians who must embrace Chinese civilization to attain civilized status.

Nearly a century passed between the departure of the Jesuits and the return of a large number of Westerners to the China coast. The interval marked a critical lapse of time, for an industrial and commercial revolution had begun to transform Western Europe and British North America. New ships, better weapons and, above all, a new drive to expand foreign trade swept the West. French, Dutch, Spanish, Portuguese and, most significantly, English explorers pushed the frontiers of their empires further into Asia. The lure of China's potential trade inspired countless voyages. Even Colonial Philadelphia enjoyed a small, though lucrative, trade with China. American merchants, almost immediately after winning independence from England, sent a ship there in 1784. Appropriately, it bore the name *Empress of China.*

However poor the mass of China's farmers might have been, there still existed splendid cities and exotic luxury products which attracted Western merchants. One early American voyager remarked that China was "the first for greatness, riches and grandeur, of any country ever known." The words were those of Amasa Delano who passed down the family fortune and fascination with China to his grandson, Franklin Delano Roosevelt.

Despite its lucrative potential, Western trade with China suffered severe restrictions. The Chinese, clinging to the idea that all foreign contact must be through the tribute system, permitted only a limited number of foreign merchants seasonal residence at Whampoa, a small village near the port of Canton. There they had to conduct trade with thirteen authorized Chinese merchant groups ("hongs"). The Chinese, quite consciously, sought to limit the foreign impact in all ways. Not only did these restrictions prove inconvenient to the foreign merchants, but the actual economic terms of the trade strictly favored China. Westerners purchased expensive luxuries like silk, porcelain, teas and chinaware, while the Chinese bought from them only small amounts of furs, sandalwood and ginseng, a medicinal herb reputed to be an aphrodisiac. The trade imbalance forced British and American merchants to pay for the bulk of their purchases not in goods but in silver, making trade a serious drain on their national treasuries.

As a consequence, Western merchants and their governments hoped to modify both Chinese law and the terms of trade. They hoped to convince the Chinese to establish formal, Western-style trade and diplomatic relations. This would ease penetration of the so-called China Market and afford foreigners better legal protection. But to the Chinese Empire, such a concept was anathema. By definition foreign states were inferior subordinates who should be grateful for whatever trade concessions had already been made. In no event were the Chinese prepared to exchange ambassadors with the West, an act which would imply equality of status.

The British sent an envoy, Lord McCartney, to China in 1793 in an effort to convince the emperor to sign a commercial treaty. The mission failed when McCartney refused to perform a ritual "kowtow" and the Chinese denied his request for an imperial audience. Chinese officials declared they would go no further than to permit trade to continue around Canton on an informal basis. No formal treaties would be concluded. This uneasy stalemate persisted for another four decades, until the commercial and military power of the West began to undermine and then destroy China's self-imposed isolation.

The foreign enclave near Canton, c. 1825. (Metropolitan Museum of Art, Rogers Fund, 1941)

The growth of an international narcotics trade ultimately forced China out of its relative isolation and into the modern community of nations. Although Chinese had long known of the medicinal qualities of opium produced from the milky white sap of the poppy (morphine and heroin were later developed from the same fluid), it had never been widely used as an intoxicant. Early in the nineteenth century, however, some anonymous entrepreneur discovered a startling demand for the drug within China. Though the origins of the demand remain unexplained, its results are clear. Soon, British merchants began hauling opium from India while Americans carried it from Turkey. It proved to be the one foreign product which enjoyed unparalleled popularity in China.

The opium trade proved especially bountiful for the British who had just gained control over India. The cultivation of opium in India was supervised by the semiofficial East India Company, which processed the raw sap into the drug and auctioned it to private merchants for sale in China. Opium profits provided fully one-seventh of the revenues of British India and helped finance the immense British appetite for Chinese tea. By carrying Turkish opium, enterprising Americans were able to corner a ten percent share of this lucrative market.

By 1839 the trade had grown to incredible proportions. That year 40,000 chests each weighing 133 pounds entered China. Vast sums of silver flowed into the hands of British and American traders. The massive use of opium had devastating economic and social effects on China. But whatever moral qualms the Westerners felt, they were mitigated by the staggering fortunes to be made. As one Scottish trader noted in his diary one day, sales were so brisk, there had been "no time to read my bible."

All of this activity defied Chinese law. In 1729 the smoking of opium had been banned and in 1800 additional prohibitions were placed on cultivation and importation. Yet, the weakening and the increasingly corrupt Ch'ing Dynasty interfered with any effort to stop the drug traffic. Opium traders connived with corrupt Chinese officials to bring in the drug, while the British government continued to demand that the entire trading system of China be expanded. Nevertheless, the terrible consequences of the trade led the emperor in 1839 to make a final effort to enforce the law. The emperor personally selected a respected official, Lin Tse-hsu, to serve as a commissioner of opium suppression in Canton.

Lin startled most Western and Chinese merchants by vigorously moving against the opium trade. He quickly blockaded the foreign warehouses in Canton, forcing the merchants to turn over 20,000 chests of opium which he had burned in a public ceremony. In a letter of explanation addressed to Queen Victoria, Lin sought to explain his actions. Since the importation of opium was illegal in Britain, Lin wrote, "then even less should you let it be passed on to the harm of other countries. . . . Let us ask, where is your conscience?"

Unfortunately for China, England had grown far more concerned with the rule of gold than with the golden rule. The destruction of the British and American opium at Canton provoked a wide assault on China's isolation. The British government, to avenge the great wrong done to its citizens, promptly launched a punitive military expedition. The resulting Opium War (1839–42) not only won compensation for the merchants but demolished many of the legal barriers to trade which China had erected. Britain's aim was to force China to throw itself open to Western economic and cultural penetration, to "civilize the Chinese barbarians."

While no American troops took part in the war, leading Americans cheered on the British effort. This pattern persisted for the rest of the century. One of the war's most eloquent champions was former President John Quincy Adams. Despite his stern puritan abhorrence of opium and his fight against slavery, Adams praised England for fighting a just, if not holy, war. China, he explained, had refused to accept the "Christian precept" of engaging in open commerce. The British cause was righteous because the Chinese refusal to accept Western law and trading practices was "an enormous outrage upon the rights of human nature." Hence, the Opium War symbolized a battle between progress and Asian barbarity.

Following three years of sporadic British coastal raids and Chinese military confusion, the war came to a conclusion. The Treaty of Nanking (1842) ushered in a one-hundred-year period of disgrace known to the Chinese as the time of the "unequal treaties," or the "century of dishonor." The previous arrogance was reversed, as the foreign powers now treated China as a barbarous and benighted country. Over the next twenty years, following two more European assaults and an Anglo-French occupation of Beijing, an intricate system of law written by foreigners was imposed on a succession of weak Chinese governments. The system was powerful and durable enough to last until the Second World War.

The Treaty of 1842 gave the British the island of Hong Kong as a colony and compelled China to open five "treaty ports" for trade along the coast. These ports (which eventually numbered around eighty along the coast and rivers) followed a pattern. Each resembled a small European port city, generally on the outskirts of a larger Chinese city. The special zone for foreigners contained warehouses, shops, restaurants and homes. Physical labor on the docks was performed by Chinese workers often directed by a Chinese middleman or "compradore." Inside the foreign settlements were churches, clubs, racetracks and parks (complete with signs proclaiming "no Chinese or dogs allowed")— all the marks of growing foreign power.

Ironically, the treaty which ended the Opium War made no mention of the drug. Great Britain cared far more about compelling China to open itself to general Western commerce—and domination—than securing a legal sanction for the narcotic. This priority was evident in the peace treaty and subsequent settlements imposed on China. In addition to treaty ports, the Western powers imposed a system of rules commonly known as "extraterritoriality." Simply stated, it exempted all foreigners from Chinese law. If accused of committing crimes against Chinese, they were to be tried by courts of their own nations, not Chinese tribunals. (Initially, some Chinese officials favored this system, hoping to avoid legal entanglement with contentious barbarians. They later regretted the loss of control.)

Another component of the unequal treaties was the imposition of a low tariff. Foreign goods could enter China at no more than a five percent charge, stripping away tariff protection from most domestic industries. After 1851, the power to collect even this meager revenue was taken away from the Chinese government and placed in the hands of an international agency whose employees served at the behest of foreign powers.

Further elaborations of the system took place between 1860 and 1895, permitting Christian missionaries to travel and proselytize freely. The missionaries, coming from America, France, England and Germany, sought to extend extraterritoriality not only to themselves and church property, but often to their Chinese converts as well. Following Japan's defeat of China in the Sino-Japanese War (1894–95), foreign businesses were permitted to build and own actual factories in China. Thus, by the close of the century, China's independence had been so compromised that it was more a semicolony than an independent nation.

Americans have tended to commend their forefathers for avoiding a direct role in these assaults. While this was technically true before 1900, Americans were hardly innocent bystanders. As early as 1844 President John Tyler sent Caleb Cushing to secure a commercial treaty from China. So soon after its defeat by the British, the Chinese government had little desire to resist Western demands. The Treaty of Wanghsia (1844) that Cushing negotiated secured not only the same trading rights which the British had won, but also a promise to automatically grant the United States all future privileges given by China to any other nation. During the next one hundred years, whenever the British, French or Japanese compelled China to grant new demands, the same benefits passed immediately to the Americans. In diplomatic language this procedure was known as "most favored nation status." The Chinese called it "jackal diplomacy."

Pressed on all sides by Western power, ideas and culture, Chinese officials initially had difficulty distinguishing Americans as a distinct group. At first, British and American merchants, who spoke the same language, often fraternized, and sought the same commercial advantages, were considered part of the same tribe of "hairy barbarians." Following the first Opium War, Chinese writers began to distinguish the two nations and even hoped to play the two groups off against one another.

By the mid-nineteenth century, as fear of foreign power increased, some Ch'ing officials considered it important to "understand the Barbarians in order to control them." The dynasty created a special bureau for handling relations with the United States and Europe. In the 1870s China made its first concerted effort to "modernize" (the so-called Self-Strengthening Movement), which involved sending students abroad and importing Western technology. In 1872 the leaders of this effort, Zeng Guofan and Li Hongzhang, sent 120 students on an educational mission to America. However, a decade later the reform effort collapsed, in part because of anti-Chinese racism in California and also due to resistance among traditionalists in China who feared the loss of influence to a Westernized elite.

Not all of China's problems, of course, were caused by the foreign assault of the nineteenth century. A population explosion and the deterioration of the Ch'ing administration was going on independently. But the foreign presence and the unequal treaties added greatly to the burden and injured China in subtle ways. The privileged status of foreigners undermined Chinese confidence in their own government. The foreigners, moreover, carried radically new religious, political and economic ideas which began to gnaw away at traditional Chinese beliefs. This set the stage for a crisis of culture and self-confidence. Christian missionaries, including a large number of Americans, played an especially large role in this "cultural subversion" of the traditional order.

The Missionary Movement

In our cynical age we too easily stereotype missionaries as either childishly naive do-gooders or intolerant fire-and-brimstone-ranting Bible pounders. While many individuals may have fit that mold, the movement was more complex. During the nineteenth century religion played a much larger social and political role than today. Christianity represented not just a spiritual belief but a complex set of values intimately related to the Western cultural heritage. Spreading religion, then, meant spreading an entirely new way of life in China.

After 1858 the Chinese government was forced to permit missionaries of all the Western nations to spread the gospel into China's interior. Like the gunboats and troops sent to police the treaty ports, the missionaries, both Catholic and Protestant, formed an invading army. Their "enemy" was the "pagan" religion of China, their task to convert 450 million benighted souls. The war budget for this mass campaign came from large and small donations raised each Sunday at church services in the United States and Western Europe.

Most missionaries were dedicated and well-intentioned men and women. They not only sought to convert the heathen, but to build schools, hospitals and orphanages (though many Chinese must have questioned why so many hospital beds were occupied by victims of the opium trade!). Missionaries pioneered Chinese language study in the West and often praised China's cultural heritage. By its very nature, however, the missionary movement was subversive. Christian beliefs, so unlike traditional Chinese moral thought, demanded that the convert forsake one's ancestors, one's heritage and even the local system of social and political privilege. Not the traditionally educated gentry, but the minister or priest was held up as the paragon of ethical virtue. And as noted earlier, many missionaries tried to extend their own extraterritorial privileges to their converts, placing Chinese Christians beyond Chinese law. Not surprisingly, to many Chinese, Christianity seemed like just another symptom of imperialism.

The "threat" of Christianity as a heterodox, foreign ideology was confirmed by the outbreak of the massive Taiping Rebellion in central China during the 1850s and 1860s. The leader of this revolt, Hung Hsiu-ch'uan, was a failed Confucian examination candidate who had been influenced by Christian religious tracts. For over a decade Hung and his supporters led a largely peasant army in rebellion against the Ch'ing Dynasty, proclaiming their intention of establishing a new, egalitarian order with Christian overtones. Before the rebellion was suppressed, an estimated twenty million Chinese died and entire regions were laid waste. This rather incredible episode is scarcely mentioned in many Western histories, though the much smaller Boxer uprising is prominently featured. Perhaps this is because the victims in the

Taiping Rebellion were almost exclusively Chinese, while several hundred Westerners died during the Boxer troubles.

The number of missionaries grew continually after the 1860s. By the 1930s about 3,000, half of whom were Americans, worked in China. Despite their tireless efforts, not more than one percent of the Chinese people ever converted. Nevertheless, most Americans had an exaggerated idea of the movement's success. Since the cause was righteous, victory was seen to be inevitable. Also, leading American intellectuals, politicians and church leaders throughout the nineteenth and early twentieth centuries held a deep belief in the virtue and necessity of missionary work. Spreading Christianity meant spreading progress and the "American way of life."

Advancing the cause of civilization served as a powerful motivation to justify the presence of Westerners in foreign lands. John W. Burgess, a leading professor of philosophy in the late nineteenth century, expressed the idea this way:

> The larger part of the surface of the globe is inhabited by populations which have not succeeded in establishing civilized states. There is no human right to the status of barbarism. The civilized states have a claim upon them, and that claim is that they shall become civilized.

Crusading groups like the YMCA shared this idea. Its official report of 1895 on missionary activity bore the title "Strategic Points in World Conquest" and discussed the Christian assault on heathenism.

This message was brought before the American public in a variety of ways. Church newspapers, magazines and sermons spoke of it. By the 1920s the new medium of film began to serve religion. Church films entitled *The Cross and the Dragon, The Conquest of Cathay* and *The Missioner's Cross* portrayed missionary work in China and claimed that all Chinese hungered for the opportunity to become Christians.

The missionary movement inspired a countermissionary movement in China almost from its inception. Isolated acts of violence against church property, missionaries and Chinese Christians were common. Occasionally the violence escalated into large-scale riots. To attack a missionary was one of the few ways that ordinary Chinese could oppose the wider foreign assault on their homeland. Contempt for the religious imperialism of the West was even expressed by powerful Chinese. In 1899 a Chinese government representative told a Philadelphia audience that true "civilization" meant more than using military power to get one's way. "A truly civilized nation should respect the rights of other societies, and refrain from stealing other men's property, or imposing upon others unwelcome beliefs."

But like Commissioner Lin's letter to Queen Victoria about opium, this call went unheeded. The missionary movement continued to be a major point of Chinese-American contact and friction right up until the Communist revolution. To many Americans, China's rejection of Christianity and acceptance of communism seemed like the cruelest ingratitude. To most Chinese, the departure of the missionaries marked a reassertion of their pride.

The Myth of the China Market

The impulse to "uplift and civilize," to trade in souls, was not the only compulsion felt by Americans toward China. Ideas of lucrative trans-Pacific trade fascinated business and political leaders almost since the Revolutionary War. American merchants participated fully in the opium trade, but thought of other opportunities as well. They hoped, eventually, to sell American agricultural and manufactured products to a vast market of eager Chinese consumers. Bursts of American territorial expansion toward the Pacific Coast in 1819 and 1846 and later in Panama were partly motivated by the idea of speeding passage to China. Only in the aftermath of the Civil War, however, did Americans fully consider the potential of trade with Asia.

Interestingly enough, by the mid-nineteenth century the lucrative opium trade began to decline in importance. Chinese came to dominate the trade themselves and began to use locally grown opium. The West now turned toward trade in new miracle products: the agricultural and manufactured goods created by technological innovation. The very phrase "China Market" conjured up an image of 450 million consumers able to absorb vast amounts of European and American exports. This idea endured despite economic realities.

The actual facts of the case scarcely warranted such hope. China was a poor, overwhelmingly rural land peopled by farmers living only marginally above subsistence levels. They lacked the money and desire to consume Western products. No modern transportation network existed to market imported goods. Outside the very special conditions of the foreign-dominated treaty ports, there was little opportunity for modern economic development or trade. Chronic instability frightened away most investors. These factors persisted until after the victory of the Communist revolution in 1949. Most leading American companies understood this reality and were reluctant to invest in China. During most of the nineteenth and twentieth centuries, American trade with China remained at a low level, fluctuating between one and two percent of the total volume of exports. Nevertheless, Americans seemed to believe that the *potential* for a vast trade existed and that this required that no other nation—such as Japan, Germany or Russia—be allowed to monopolize China.

Ideas about the China Market became more vivid whenever China appeared threatened by outside powers. During the 1930s, for example, as Japan's armies swept forward, popular books and movies stressed the theme. A bestselling book of the decade, by Carl Crow, carried the blunt title *400 Million Customers*. The 1935 Hollywood film, *Oil For the Lamps of China*, was a masterpiece of this genre. In a climactic scene an oil company executive tells a group of starry-eyed salesmen:

> The company is sending you out to China to dispel the darkness of centuries with the light of a new era. Oil for the lamps of China. American oil. Helping to build a great corporation, helping to expand the frontier of civilization is a great ideal, gentlemen. But you have the youth, the vision and the courage to follow that ideal and with the unbounded faith of Galahads going into a strange land.

With only a few minor changes, the words might have been those of later presidents as they sent off economic advisors and soldiers to remake Asia in the 1950s and 1960s.

The Chinese in America

Describing the Western penetration of China tells only part of the story of Sino-American relations. It says little about how the average people in both societies looked at each other. From Chinese sources we know that most people had only a dim perception of the differences between Americans and Europeans; after all, they arrived together and acted similarly. The epithet of *Ta Pi-tse* (big nose) and *Yang Kwei-tse* (foreign devil) applied to them all. Before 1900 the Chinese government detected nothing especially virtuous in American policy. The United States might not have fought in the Opium War but it certainly was not reluctant to benefit from the spoils.

Direct contacts between Americans and Chinese increased after the American Civil War. Until then, aside from a few merchants, sailors and missionaries, few Americans knew anything at all about China. Most Americans assumed China to be a quaint, somewhat ridiculous society which epitomized backwardness. The great American philosopher Ralph Waldo Emerson summarized it this way: "As for China, all she can say at the convocation of nations must be . . . 'I made the tea.' "

The industrial boom which followed the Civil War sucked in not only millions of immigrants from Europe, but many from China as well. In 1868 Secretary of State William Seward included a provision in the new "Burlingame Treaty" with China to permit the importation of contract laborers. (Roughly, this resembled the "bracero" program in the 1950s which allowed farm owners to import seasonal Mexican farmworkers.) The Chinese were expected to be especially good workers because, as a medical book of the era claimed, their poorly developed nervous system made them immune to ordinary pain!

Within two years nearly 100,000 "coolies" (a term derived from the Chinese words for "bitter labor" and considered a slur) were laying tracks for the transcontinental railroad, while others dug for gold and silver in western mining camps. Despite the fact that millions of European workers had come to America to seek a living, the racially different Chinese seemed particularly threatened. The large majority of Chinese immigrants were single males, which inflamed the suspicions of those who saw nonwhites as a danger to "white womanhood." White workers, many of them recent arrivals as well, began to complain that "cheap Chinese labor" endangered their jobs. Violent anti-Chinese riots swept the western states (where most Chinese lived) from the late 1860s through the mid-1880s. Attacking the "heathen Chinee" went unpunished, even when twenty-five Chinese were brutally massacred in Wyoming in 1885.

The American writer-humorist Bret Harte captured the plight of the ordinary victim of this racism in an obituary he wrote for "Wan Lee": "Dead my reverend friends, dead. Stoned to death in the streets of San Francisco, in the year of grace 1869 by a mob of half-grown boys and Christian school children." A poignant cartoon by Thomas Nast summed up how Americans saw the "Chinese question" in 1880. Nast sketched a Chinese cowering before a crazed lynch mob. Pinned to him were the labels "slave," "pauper" and "rat-eater." The treatment which Harte and Nast described added a vivid phrase to the American vocabulary: "Not a Chinaman's chance."

By 1882 demands for ending Chinese immigration became so powerful that Congress, in violation of a treaty with China, voted to suspend further immigration. The Chinese Exclusion Act of that year placed Chinese in a unique legal category. Along with imbeciles, paupers and prostitutes, they were refused the right to immigrate or become American citizens. This law, with slight changes, remained in force until 1943. Then, with China an ally against Japan, Congress replaced total exclusion with a token quota: henceforth 105 Chinese might enter America each year.

While the most blatant acts of racial violence against the Chinese subsided by the late 1880s, racial prejudice had a much longer life. The willingness of Americans to donate money for missionary work in China was one thing; to accept Chinese as equals at home was quite another. President Theodore Roosevelt spoke for many when he characterized the Chinese as an "immoral, degraded and worthless race." From the turn of the century until the Second World War, the image which most Americans had of China came to them through popular culture—pulp magazines and comic strips, which were then selling

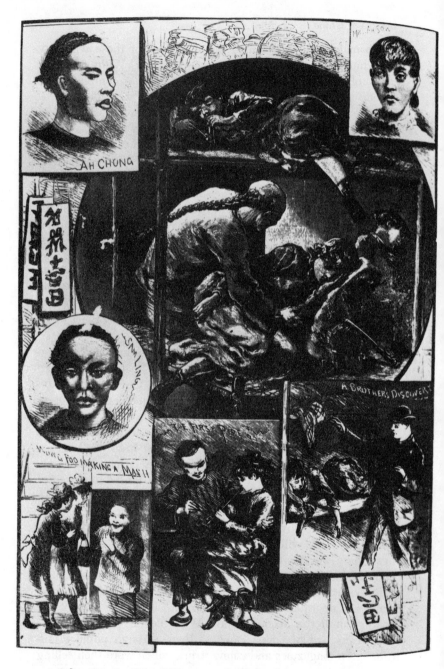

A *Police Gazette* of the 1880s warns of girls lured into opium dens.

20 million copies *a month*. Lurid tales of Chinese madmen were a favorite theme; for example, "Mr. Wu Fang" lusted after the "blonde maiden Tanya" week after week.

On film the Chinese characters were most often portrayed as fiends. The arch villain "Dr. Fu Manchu" was a crowd pleaser and a box office rival to Frankenstein. Fu Manchu personified that most insidious menace, "Chinese torture." This series had a simple theme: blood-thirsty orientals conspiring to violate white women and conquer the world. While some effort was made to find a Chinese cinema hero (the detective Charlie Chan, for example), what was shown had very little to do with the real China or real Chinese.

Americans did take pride in their eagerness to educate the Chinese. After 1900 several American universities established branches in China and thousands of Chinese students were selected to study in the United States. However, the underlying presumption of this plan was to make Chinese accept American values and become more like Americans. Both in film and in real life, a "good Chinese" meant one who converted to Christianity and devoted himself to making over his own culture in the American image.

Selected Additional Readings

Among the outstanding general histories of modern China are John K. Fairbank, Edwin O. Reishauer and Albert Craig, *East Asia, Tradition and Transformation*, Boston, 1973; as well as the following works by John K. Fairbank, *The United States and China*, 4th ed., Cambridge, Mass., 1983; *China's Glorious Revolution, 1800–1985*, N.Y., 1986; and *Trade and Diplomacy on the China Coast: The Opening of the Treaty Ports*, Cambridge, Mass., 1953; also see Jonathan D. Spence, *The Gate of Heavenly Peace: The Chinese and Their Revolution, 1895–1980;* Peter Fay, *The Opium War, 1940–42*, Chapel Hill, N.C., 1975; Mary C. Wright, *The Last Stand of Chinese Conservatism: The T'ung-chih Restoration, 1862–1874*, Stanford, Calif., 1957; Philip Kuhn, *Rebellion and its Enemies in Late Imperial China*, Cambridge, Mass., 1974; and Orville Schell and Franz Schurman, eds., *Imperial China: The Decline of the Last Dynasty and the Origin of Modern China, the 18th and 19th Centuries*, N.Y., 1967.

Aspects of Sino-American relations during the nineteenth century are discussed in the following works: Michael Hunt, *The Making of a Special Relationship: The United States and China to 1914*, N.Y., 1983; Akira Iriye, *Across the Pacific*, N.Y., 1967; James C. Thomson, Jr., Peter W. Stanley and John C. Perry, *Sentimental Imperialists: The American Experience in East Asia*, N.Y., 1981; Harold Isaacs, *Scratches on our Minds: American Images of India and China*, N.Y., 1958; John K. Fairbank, ed., *The Missionary Enterprise in China and America*, Cambridge, Mass., 1974; Paul Varg, *Missionaries, Chinese and Diplomats: The American Protestant Missionary Movement in China, 1890–1952*, Princeton, N.J., 1958; Jonathan Spence, *To Change China: Western Advisers in China, 1620–1960*, N.Y., 1980; Stuart Miller, *The Unwelcome Immigrant: American Images of the Chinese, 1785–1882*, Berkeley, Calif., 1969; Robert McClellan, *The Heathen Chinee: A Study of American Attitude Towards China, 1890–1905*, Columbus, Ohio, 1971; David L. Anderson, *Imperialism and Idealism: American Diplomats in China, 1861–1898*, Bloomington, Ind., 1985; Maxine Hong Kingston, *China Men*, N.Y., 1980; Jonathan Goldstein, *Philadelphia and the China Trade*, Philadelphia, 1978; Marilyn B. Young, *The Rhetoric of Empire*, Cambridge, Mass., 1969; and Ernest R. May and John K. Fairbank, eds., *America's China Trade in Historical Perspective: The Chinese and American Performance*, Cambridge, Mass., 1986.

2

Asia in Disorder, 1894–1936

During the century between the Opium War and the outbreak of World War II, few societies had more dissimilar experiences than did the United States and China. For America it was a time of almost uninterrupted expansion—both territorial and economic—climaxing at the summit of world power. China continued its slide into poverty, rebellion and foreign domination. The ever weaker Ch'ing Dynasty survived only by sufferance of the Great Powers, which extracted concessions from the Ch'ing court and in return let the monarchy administer internal affairs. American merchants and missionaries, who enjoyed the full benefit of the unequal treaties imposed on China, passed through the door forced open by others. The United States government hardly bothered about China, so long as neither the Chinese nor other nations discriminated against Americans or interfered with their activities.

Until the very end of the nineteenth century the U.S. deferred to Great Britain, allowing England to oversee Western access to China. Americans concentrated their own effort on exploring other parts of the Pacific. As early as the 1840s American planters and missionaries dominated Hawaii. Later in the century the U.S. acquired several small Pacific islands, including

Wake, Midway and parts of Samoa. The most daring episode of expansion must have been the naval expedition to Japan in 1853–54 led by Commodore Matthew Perry. Under orders from Washington, the blustery naval officer compelled the feudal Tokugawa regime to open trade with America. As a writer in the *Presbyterian Review* observed: "Christian civilization and commerce has closed upon the Japanese Empire on both sides."

Many Westerners expected—and many Japanese feared—that the island nation's fate would resemble China's after the Opium War. Yet due to a variety of factors Japan escaped the agony of internal decay and gradual reduction to the status of semi-colony. Western economic and military powers never dominated Japan, allowing it an opportunity to mobilize its power far more quickly and effectively than had China. Highly disciplined and adventurous Japanese political and economic reformers enjoyed some time in which to reorganize their society without foreign control. By the 1860s a fundamental political change occurred in Japan, marked by the reemergence of a powerful central government which ruled under the aegis of an emperor revered as a god.

In contrast to the tradition-bound Chinese elite, Japanese leaders set out to study and transplant Western technology in order to speed the modernization of Japan. They fully understood China's mistake in rejecting the material accomplishments of the West in hopes that Confucian values could somehow resist the force of gunboats, steam power and artillery. By the 1890s Japan had successfully transformed itself into a regional power with a strong industrial and military base. Not surprisingly this power would soon collide with that of China and the Western nations.

The Collapse of the Old Order

At the close of the nineteenth century the old balance of forces which had preserved a crude order in East Asia began to strain and then break. Inside China nationalist sentiment, outrage over how the existing rulers and foreign powers had exploited China, threatened the implicit alliance between the Ch'ing Dynasty and the Western nations. At the same time, the industrialized nations of the West and Japan began to compete among themselves for greater economic, political and cultural influence over the less developed areas of the world. For the newly powerful nations, such as Japan, Czarist Russia and Imperial Germany, acquiring more colonies seemed a necessity to catch up to the established powers (Britain and France). Expansionist sentiment grew among American opinion leaders as well, though many Americans thought more in terms of an "informal empire," one of markets for American goods and the expansion of American cultural influence.

Japan's unexpectedly easy victory in the Sino-Japanese War for control of Korea (1894–95) precipitated a race for power in East Asia. A new player had entered the list of Great Powers and demonstrated the woeful shortcomings of half-hearted Chinese efforts at political and military reform during the 1870s and 1880s. In the decade following China's defeat, the European powers and Japan began to divide China's railroads, mines and ports among themselves. The United States, suffering the effects of a severe economic depression in the mid-1890s, began to fear the consequences of being permanently frozen out of China through the creation of such exclusive "spheres of influence."

During the early 1890s interest in playing a more active role in Asia had begun to build. For example, certain American planters and officials in Hawaii conspired to topple the native regime and formally annex the islands, despite opposition from President Grover Cleveland. (Annexation was not accomplished until the end of the decade.) The American navy grew significantly during the 1890s, a prerequisite for establishing influence abroad. In 1898 a group of leading exporters founded the American Asiatic Association, which was designed to lobby for government action on behalf of commercial interests in China. Though no coordinated policy yet existed, a broad concern with East Asia had developed among policy planners and business leaders. The outbreak of the Spanish–American War in April 1898 thrust the United States more directly toward China than anyone had imagined.

The immediate origins of the conflict lay in Washington's demands that Spain grant some form of independence to its re-

"The Miracle Teapot." A Russian cartoon depicting the "Yellow Peril" and foreign troops in China, c. 1901. (Susan Luebbermann, Arizona Historical Society)

bellious Cuban colony. Once war broke out, the United States moved against Spanish forces in widely scattered outposts. The campaign to free Cuba, ironically, began with an order for Admiral Dewey's Pacific squadron to attack the Spanish fleet near Manila, ostensibly to prevent it from sailing to Cuba. Dewey easily defeated his enemy and in the process acquired control of the Philippines. By this act the United States had taken the first step toward becoming a major power in Asia.

Soon after Dewey's victory, the brief war with Spain ended and Washington faced the choice of what to do with the Philippines. Under pressure to demonstrate his concern over the American position in Asia, President William McKinley announced his determination to annex the entire island chain. In the President's words, colonization would be both good business and high morality. America's duty to the Filipinos, he declared, was to "uplift and civilize and Christianize them, and by God's grace do the very best we could by them as our fellow men for whom Christ also died."

When the Senate approved annexation in February 1899, the poor "benighted" Filipinos rose in revolt against their "liberators" who had earlier suggested they would grant the Philippines independence. It required 70,000 American troops and almost four years of bitter jungle fighting to suppress the guerrillas led by Emilio Aguinaldo. Most Americans, however, assumed that the bulk of the natives clamored for the civilizing influence of foreign rule. A typical mixture of metaphors appeared in an 1899 full-page advertisement by the Pears Soap Company. It featured a likeness of Admiral Dewey washing his hands with the company's soap, surrounded by scenes of missionaries handing bars of soap to naked savages. The caption read:

> The first step towards lightening the White Man's Burden is through teaching the virtues of cleanliness. Pears Soap is a potent factor in brightening the dark corners of the earth as civilization advances, while amongst the cultured of all nations it holds the highest place—it is the idea toilet soap.

Despite the decision to annex the Philippines and establish a chain of naval stations across the Pacific, only a handful of

Americans embraced the idea of large-scale territorial conquest. Acquiring strategically situated islands or land areas such as Hawaii, the Philippines, Guam and, eventually, the Panama Canal Zone was one thing; taking responsibility for a vast population and land mass was quite another. Neither political nor business leaders believed that the U.S. ought to directly acquire part of China or fight on behalf of its independence. However, between 1899 and 1901 these policymakers did devise a flexible formula which sought to preserve a measure of independence for China while preserving America's commercial stake in its future.

As Germany, Japan and Russia stepped up demands on the Chinese government to grant them special "spheres of influence" (sometimes ports, occasionally entire provinces), American businessmen with a stake in China, and foreign policy experts in Washington, feared that the resulting partition would eventually result in the exclusion of all American trade and influence in China. Secretary of State John Hay, guided by advisors William Rockhill and Alfred Hippisley, sent notes to all the Great Powers asking that they promise to preserve commercial equality for all nations in any spheres over which they might gain control. Despite the evasive replies he received, Hay declared that the powers had accepted his request. These "Open Door Notes" of September 1899 sought primarily to protect the market for American trade, *not* China's sovereignty. The latter was only a secondary consideration for Hay, who never bothered to consult the Chinese government about his policy.

The rather glib and ambiguous American initiative to prevent the economic partition of China nearly fell apart in 1900 as a mass antiforeign uprising swept parts of China. The Boxer Rebellion was partly a "grass roots" antiforeign, anti-Christian movement and partly an attempt by the Empress Dowager Tz'u Hsi to attack the foreign position in China while winning popular support. The Boxers, a "secret society," took the lead in sponsoring assaults on missionaries, diplomats and merchants. In their appeal for public support—and probably to fortify their own resolve—the colorful Boxers claimed that magic oaths and potions made them immune from bullets and other modern weapons. This claim of invulnerability carried a deeper and more desperate message than many people understood. In their agony and wrath over China's fate these primitive patriots turned to superstition as their only weapon against Western military might.

In June 1900, after killing the German Minister, the Boxers laid siege to the foreign compound in Beijing. Realizing that this attack was doomed, many Chinese government officials and the regular army refused to assist the poorly armed Boxers. After two months of sporadic fighting, an international army, including American Marines from the Philippines, fought its way from the port of Tienjin overland to Beijing. En route the rescuers devastated the countryside, looting and killing in revenge for the Boxers' actions. The German Kaiser had applauded this policy, telling his troops that he wanted the Chinese to tremble "for the next thousand years" whenever they heard German spoken. Though few Westerners shared the Kaiser's blood lust, the fanatic rampage of the Boxers rekindled images of the "yellow peril" and "Chinese hordes."

In September 1901, after suppressing the uprising, the foreign powers imposed a harsh settlement which required China to pay huge cash indemnities and permit the stationing of increased numbers of foreign troops on her soil. In July 1900, anticipating these actions, Secretary of State Hay had dispatched a second set of Open Door Notes to the European powers and Japan urging them not to utilize the Boxer troubles as a pretext to carve up China into formal colonies. Yet again, it was not American policy which saved the dynasty and China's nominal independence, but the fact that the foreign powers remained too jealous of each other to agree on any division of the potential spoils. Nor was the United States quite so selfless as might be imagined. Secretary Hay actually approved contingency plans to seize Chinese territory if the Ch'ing Dynasty fell and the other imperialists began, in Hay's words, "to slice the watermelon." In the end, the powers again chose to permit the dynasty to resume its feeble rule in Beijing. It was the path of least resistance.

The Open Door Notes signaled no clear or consistent U.S. policy toward China. Though Hay's initiative marked an expression of American interest in the preservation of some sort of Chinese independence, neither he nor his many successors clari-

"A Fair Field and No Favor." Uncle Sam protects the Open Door for trade against the European powers. (*Harper's Weekly*, 1899)

fied that interest. China would, it was hoped, be kept open to American cultural and economic penetration. But it was not deemed a vital area for U.S. security right down to the late 1930s. Few Americans, including those most knowledgeable about East Asia, could decide what the U.S. ought to do in or for China, nor was there any agreement about the value of China as compared to its great rival, Japan. Policies during the early twentieth century continually flip-flopped, depending largely on the idiosyncratic mix of interests, personalities and prejudices dominant at a given time. While paying regular lip service to the Open Door, most Americans continued to see China as an abstraction. It became "real" only when threatened by Russian or Japanese expansion that might seal off China or use it as a base for further imperial conquest in Asia.

Early in 1904 Czarist Russia and Imperial Japan collided in northeast China. Both nations coveted control of the resources of Manchuria and believed this area was pivotal for their future power in Northeast Asia. During the Russo-Japanese War of 1904–5, President Theodore Roosevelt encouraged American bankers to loan badly needed funds to the government of Japan. Roosevelt feared Russian expansion more than possible Japanese designs. He believed that America's interest lay in avoiding conflict with Japan. By blocking Russian expansion, he told his son, Japan was playing "our game in Asia." Roosevelt had an especially low regard for the Chinese, as shown by his use of the epithet "chink" to describe people he disliked.

Roosevelt's strategic realism toward East Asian relations was reversed by his successors. Fearful that Tokyo would achieve an economic stranglehold on Manchuria—seen by many as one of the world's great commercial frontiers—President William H. Taft sought to restrain Japan. Taft and his Secretary of State, Philander C. Knox, believed that "today diplomacy works for trade," thus leading to the phrase "dollar diplomacy." Influenced by junior diplomats who overvalued the economic importance of Manchuria to the U.S., Taft and Knox tried in 1911 and 1912 to encourage major private American investments in China. American-owned railroads in Manchuria, for example, would not only be profitable but would enhance the influence Washington could exercise on China, Japan and Russia.

This plan, which also sought to internationalize Russian- and Japanese-owned railway lines in Manchuria, failed for a number of reasons. Russia and Japan, though often rivals, combined to resist American pressure and scared the Chinese away from cooperating with Knox's schemes. Taft's view that "a Jap is first of all a Jap and would be glad to aggrandize himself at the expense of anybody" typified the bluntness with which the administration approached Asian problems. Nor were most American investors very eager to sink funds into a disputed region of questionable value with no promise of firm government protection.

Taft, like many of his successors, misplayed his hand by overestimating the economic significance of China to the U.S. In fact, Europe and Japan itself remained much more important a U.S. trading partners. But to Japan, China was a region of vital economic value and strategic concern, a fact which made it very difficult for the U.S. to influence Tokyo's behavior there. Furthermore, American diplomatic and trade policy was increasingly unable to influence the direction of change within China as events there approached a degree of anarchy defying limited foreign intervention.

As has often proved true, belated reform in a reactionary society inspired revolutionary change. In the aftermath of the Boxer disaster the Ch'ing rulers surprised everyone by initiating a series of major institutional reforms. Instead of turning to the occult and secret societies, Ch'ing administrators sought to upgrade and modernize education by abolishing the Confucian examination system and creating a Westernized school system. Woefully inefficient tax codes were revised to stimulate economic growth and partially representative provincial assemblies were created to allow the local elites a small voice in public policy. These acts, the rulers hoped, would both appease domestic critics and improve China's ability to withstand new foreign assaults. But the reforms were a case of too little too late. The dynasty could no longer count on the mutually jealous foreign powers to sustain its rule. At the same time, more and more politically active Chinese identified the Ch'ing rulers as the source of China's deplorable weakness. While those who favored the overthrow of the dynasty had no unified program or goal, they shared basic ideals of nationalism which would unite China against imperialism. Sun Yat-sen (a Chinese Christian educated in Hawaii) was one of many revolutionaries active in the early twentieth century. He and his followers continually plotted the destruction of the Ch'ing Dynasty and the formation of a republic.

When change finally came in 1911 it followed no revolutionary master plan. Instead, a groundswell of disgust at the monarchy's betrayal of political and economic rights to foreigners cominbed with a series of popular but uncoordinated military revolts which exposed the weakness and isolation of the Ch'ing Dynasty. Many of the recently formed provincial assemblies declared their autonomy from Beijing. Yuan Shih-k'ai, a powerful official and military commander, engineered the peaceful abdication of the Ch'ing emperor in February 1912 and created a republic with himself as president. Over the next four years the new ruler tried to unify the nation by bringing the rebellious provinces back under central control and by winning foreign acceptance.

Yuan's regime received two forms of American support during its short, tumultuous existence. President Woodrow Wilson recognized Yuan's government as legitimate despite many questions about how it assumed and maintained power. At the same time several private American advisors assisted the new Chinese government in an effort to impose national authority. Professor Frank Goodnow, an academic expert on politics, worked closely with Yuan and advised him to abandon the framework of representative government that was established in 1912–13. He reasoned that Chinese needed the symbol and authority of an emperor to remain unified. With Goodnow's encouragement, Yuan Shih-k'ai proclaimed himself emperor in a futile move to win national acceptance by reviving the aura of dynastic power.

The Impact of World War I

China's uneasy passage toward modern nationhood soon foundered on the shoals of World War I, which began in August 1914. With the Western powers preoccupied in the European war, Japan resolved to increase its own power in China. Japan easily seized the leasehold which Germany had held in Shantung province and in 1915 presented Yuan's government with the far-reaching "21 Demands." These sought to extract special economic and political privileges which would have transformed much of China into a Japanese protectorate. Though Chinese and American resistance persuaded Tokyo to back down somewhat, the incident foreshadowed greater Japanese interference in China.

Yuan Shih-k'ai's death in June 1916 destroyed the last vestige of national government in China. For the next twelve years (and in many areas until 1949) China had no real central government. Regional militarists, often called "warlords," used their private armies to hold sway over provinces. They continually fought, often forming alliances of convenience to capture the traditional capital at Beijing. To finance their struggles the warlords resorted to brutal taxation (sometimes collected thirty years in advance!) and frequently accepted bribes from foreign powers. Amidst this chaos, Chinese control over huge areas like Tibet, Outer Mongolia and Manchuria virtually disappeared. The anarchy of the warlord period was a symptom of a deepening social, political and economic crisis. The old imperial order had gone, but no new system had gained general acceptance. This made China fair game for ruthless exploiters, both foreign and domestic.

Ironically, the efforts of President Wilson to restore order to post-World War I Asia stimulated the birth of modern nationalism and anti-imperialism in China. Wilson's idea for a "League of Nations" proposed that all major industrial powers substitute open economic competition and cooperation for war and colonial conflicts. As a method to internationalize the "Open Door," the League would guarantee the industrial nations access to raw materials and markets in less developed countries. Theoretically, the League members would also respect the limited political independence of weaker countries. Wilson believed that in the long run this arrangement would prevent major wars and contribute to the gradual development of poorer countries. It also promised to keep markets and raw materials available to the United States and other industrial nations. Critical to this argument was the belief that the U.S. would prosper by this system as long as the competition for trade remained open and free from artificial restrictions.

Despite his sympathy for many of China's nationalist aspirations, Wilson believed it of even greater importance to convince a reluctant Japan to join the other major powers in the League of Nations. With some misgivings, Wilson agreed to Tokyo's demand that it retain at least temporary control of China's Shantung province, seized during World War I. The Japanese, outraged at the West's refusal to endorse the concept of racial equality, insisted on this as a show of good faith. The sacrifice of Shantung bitterly disappointed thousands of Chinese who had hoped that the League would be a mechanism to protect their country. On May 4, 1919, politically active students—many of whom were prominent in campaigns for cultural as well as political reform—led large demonstrations in Beijing to protest the Japanese-American deal and the groveling, shameful behavior of the warlord regime.*

The May 4th Movement, as it became known, signaled the birth of a modern, mass anti-imperialism in China. Many of the best educated and politically conscious Chinese lost faith both in the United States and in the promises of liberal democracy as a tool of reform. Increasingly, it seemed only a radical and authoritarian political movement might succeed in mobilizing China's masses into a weapon against foreign exploitation. After 1919 Chinese nationalists turned away from the ideals of Western liberalism in their search for an ideology. Although they still sought to use the old strategy of playing the foreigners off against one another, the emerging generation of leaders saw mass action as the key to power.

Chinese Nationalism and Great Power Diplomacy: The 1920s

At the close of World War I both Japanese and American leaders feared the renewal of tension between their two nations. Temporarily, at least, neither nation felt a need to respond to the demands of Chinese nationalists. Since the early twentieth century the U.S. and Japan had been embroiled in a series of disputes over the cruel mistreatment of Japanese immigrants to the U.S., Japan's expansion in the Pacific, and the future of China. American policymakers hoped to devise a formula that might restrain Japanese expansion in China without provoking

* During 1904–5 the U.S. was also the target of Chinese outrage. Protesting against racist immigration restrictions, merchants and students in Canton organized a brief but effective boycott against the purchase of American products. Chinese nationalists had begun to turn toward modern political organization as a weapon, in place of the mysticism of the Boxers.

Tokyo's hostility or a costly U.S.-Japanese naval armaments race.

Leaders in Tokyo and Washington were swayed by the fact that despite lingering rivalries, the two nations complemented each other in important ways. Japanese-American trade was much larger and more significant than American trade with China, although many continued to believe in the myth of the China Market. Taking advantage of the mood provided by this mutually profitable relationship, Secretary of State Charles Evans Hughes sponsored the wide-ranging Washington Conference of 1921–22. At this gathering all the powers with interests in the Pacific, led by the U.S., Great Britain, Japan, France, Italy and the Netherlands, reached a series of political and military accords. The Five Power Treaty imposed naval limitations on battle fleets, reducing fears of an arms race. Another agreement pledged each nation to respect the others' existing Pacific colonies. By the terms of the Nine Power Treaty, the conferees pledged not to interfere with China's political or territorial integrity. This series of agreements fostered goodwill in the major world capitals, but not in China. Much to the displeasure of the Chinese, almost nothing was done to diminish existing foreign domination or the onerous unequal treaties.* Most politically active Chinese demanded that the foreign powers return what they had stolen since the 1840s. A pledge not to take more only added insult to injury.

Amidst their anger, Chinese nationalists of many shades discovered that revolutionary Russia—itself an international outcast since the Bolshevik revolution of 1917—was prepared to help them achieve national unity and power. Vladimir Lenin, leader of the Bolshevik movement, had adapted Marxist theory to apply to the circumstances found in a preindustrial and semicolonial nations. He proposed that a small group of political activists could organize a mass popular movement in China that would unify people under the banner of nationalism. The immediate goal would be to throw out the warlords and the foreign imperialists; a Communist revolution would wait for a later stage. Lenin justified this approach in the belief that wars of

---

* The treaty powers proposed a future meeting to discuss possibly returning to China the right of tariff autonomy.

"national liberation" among colonial and semicolonial peoples would help undermine the strength of the major capitalist nations. In an early gesture designed to impress China, the Communists issued the July 1919 "Karakhan Manifesto," which appeared to renounce all the special treaty and territorial privileges held by the former Czarist government. Even though the Russians neglected to fulfill all their promises, their behavior marked a sharp break from that of other nations toward China. For virtually the first time since 1842 a Western nation had returned something taken earlier. In the succeeding years, Russian influence in China would become a major force.

Agents of the Russian-dominated Communist International (Comintern) traveled to China in the early 1920s and helped reorganize the nearly moribund Kuomintang (KMT, or Nationalist) Party of Sun Yat-sen. Sun, who enjoyed a foothold in Canton, dispatched several of his top assistants, including the young Chiang Kai-shek (Jiang Jieshi), to Russia where they received military and political instruction.* The Russian advisors did not expect the KMT to bring communism to China, but this was not important. The KMT could mobilize a large cross-section of the Chinese people in a popular struggle against the warlords and the foreign powers. An independent, united and anti-imperialist China would indirectly weaken the capitalist nations.

Though assisting the KMT, Comintern agents also sponsored the formation of a small Chinese Communist Party (CCP). While the Communists shared the goal of anti-imperialism, their program also called for fundamental social and economic changes within China. Despite these differences, the Russian agents pressed the CCP and KMT to cooperate against the warlords and the foreign powers. For the short run at least, both parties needed the other's skills and, in 1924, formed a "United Front." Certain Communists, such as the young peasant organizer Mao Zedong, chafed under advice that would have the CCP subordinated to the KMT and that called on the Communists to organize urban, industrial workers. Mao believed the revolution must grow in the countryside. He advocated an alternative strategy based on mobilizing an independent peasant

---

* Chiang had earlier studied in Japan.

army attracted by a revolutionary land policy that was geared to the distinctive conditions in China.

After Sun Yat-sen's death in 1925, Chiang Kai-shek outmaneuvered several rivals to assume leadership of the KMT. Despite his training in Moscow, Chiang emerged as a bitter foe of the Communists and began to limit their role in the United Front. The Russians, who had great hopes for the KMT, ignored this sign and continued to aid Chiang and insist that the CCP do the same. In 1926 the KMT armies and the CCP's political organizers launched the Northern Expedition, a military campaign designed to crush the regional warlords and unify all China. Once Chiang had captured the city of Shanghai—a vital conquest since it gave the KMT access to the port's great wealth— he felt free to jettison his Comintern advisors and CCP allies. In April 1927 Chiang ordered the massacre of thousands of Communists and their sympathizers and ejected the Russians from China. Only a handful of Communists, including Mao, escaped to the countryside. The disastrous advice of the Russians—to remain subservient to the KMT in the United Front, as well as urban-based and unarmed—became a lesson Mao never forgot.

Chiang Kai-shek's purge of the CCP not only brought him supremacy in the KMT, but eased the fears of wealthy Chinese and foreign governments. Earlier he had been thought of as a "Red general." Now he had proven himself a responsible nationalist—both anticommunist and willing to compromise with the rich and powerful in China and abroad. Foreign governments showed their appreciation of this by granting recognition to Chiang's new "Republic of China" proclaimed in October 1928, with its capital at Nanking (Nanjing). He received additional signs of foreign favor when the treaty powers agreed to modify certain aspects of the hated unequal treaties.

During the turbulent 1920s, and especially during the Northern Expedition, signs of chaos and frequent attacks upon missionaries and foreign property had tempted Japan, Great Britain and the U.S. to intervene militarily to preserve their version of law and order. While some intervention occurred, especially involving the Japanese, the foreign powers kept a relatively low profile between 1926 and 1928. This policy proved successful. Chiang convinced the foreign powers that any "outrages" which had been committed were the work of the Communists, now driven underground. The new KMT regime promised to restrain Chinese radicals, protect foreigners and work for gradual revision of the unequal treaties. Chiang seemed determined to build his own power by gaining the support of powerful groups within China and financial backing from the industrialized nations. Superficially, at least, China appeared more unified and stable than it had for almost a half century.

During the 1920s, in spite of successful arms limitation agreements with Japan and pleasure at Kuomintang ascendancy in China, America's official attitude toward Asia remained racist and disdainful. Practice, as well as law, effectively blocked most Asian immigration (by means of the Chinese Exclusion Act, beginning in 1882, and the anti-Japanese "Gentleman's Agreement" of 1907.) In 1924, when Congress again revised immigration law, it stiffened provisions designed to exclude all "Orientals"— a term used pejoratively. Western European states received the bulk of the slots allocated in the quota system of "national origins." People from Eastern Europe were given a far smaller quota. The new law completely barred Chinese and Japanese, as well as most other Asians, from further immigration. This obvious racism led to protests in China and Japan, but Congress did not budge. Some cosmetic adjustment occurred later, establishing nominal Asian quotas, but the system remained largely intact until 1965.

The Manchurian Incident

The Great Depression which began in America late in 1929 soon shattered the tenuous order imposed in Asia by the Washington treaties. For China, the consequences proved devastating. As world trade collapsed and credit shriveled, Japanese exports were frozen out of lucrative Western markets. China, which had long been a major export market for Japan and, more important, a vital source of raw materials, reemerged as the crucial question in Japanese foreign and economic policy. Since 1929 Chiang Kai-shek's regime had grown increasingly assertive in its efforts to push the Japanese and their puppets out of Manchuria—long a virtual Japanese colony. Chiang also expanded his struggle against the remnants of the Chinese Communists who had reorganized in south China. Many Japanese leaders feared that a powerful China, under Chiang's leadership, would threaten both their entrenched position and frustrate any plans to expand economic dominion.

Between 1929 and 1931 various factions in the Japanese government and army (who often bitterly opposed each other's policies) meddled in Manchurian and Chinese politics. They could not agree upon the best course to ensure a "friendly" government in China, or how far they were prepared to go in challenging Western privileges. During the previous decade cooperation with the West on questions of trade, China policy and arms limitations had benefited Japan. Now this Shidehara diplomacy (as it was known in Japan)* seemed an outdated barrier to safeguarding Japan's power and prosperity. By September 1931, as world economic conditions worsened and as the KMT regime sought to assert its control over Manchuria, elements of the Japanese army struck out. Stationed in Manchuria since the early twentieth century, the Japanese Kwantung Army staged an uprising and quickly drove Chinese troops and administrators out of the provinces of northeast China. Following in the wake of its soldier's actions, Japan created the puppet state of "Manchukuo," ruled by a boy emperor (Pu Yi) descended from the Ch'ing Dynasty and controlled by Japan.

Despite some heroic resistance the Chinese forces were no match for the Japanese. Nor could China look toward depression-weakened America or Britain for support. While many Americans regretted Japan's aggression and the violation of several agreements, including the Washington treaties, few proposed that the U.S. intervene. A headline in the influential Hearst press put it simply: "We sympathize. But it is not our concern."

After discussion with President Herbert Hoover, Secretary of State Henry L. Stimson offered the government's formal reaction to the Manchurian Incident, as it came to be known. The Stimson, or Non-Recognition, Doctrine held that America would not recognize the legal existence of Manchukuo or any other

---

* Foreign Minister Shidehara favored a moderate policy in China and opposed military intervention.

territory seized by Japan. That was all. The U.S. would not assist China or impose economic sanctions against the aggressor. Before 1938 most Americans, both in and out of government, saw no reason to do more and risk involvement in a Far Eastern war. They wished China well but felt its government must assume responsibility for its own survival.

America's decision to isolate itself from China's misfortunes was neither totally selfish nor difficult to understand. At the height of the Depression it seemed sheer folly to risk war with Japan. China's confused political situation made it even more difficult for Washington to consider any form of intervention. Not even the small number of Americans who knew something about China could agree upon its meaning. Looking at the uncertain performance of the fledgling Nationalist regime, some declared it appeared like a glass half filled; to others it seemed already half emptied. Between 1931 and 1937 policies adopted by the Kuomintang would have a crucial bearing on future events.

To the Sino-Japanese War

The Kuomintang Party, which in essence was the "government" of the Republic of China, represented a loose alliance of militarists, bureaucrats, landlords and commercial interests. The revolutionary ideals of its early period (Sun Yat-sen had proclaimed a program which included both democratic principles and a policy of national land reform to give peasant tillers control over their own livelihood) largely died with its founder. Even during the mid-1930s, its "golden years," the KMT never really governed all China. Only in two provinces did it exercise firm control, with partial control in eight others. Eighteen provinces remained under the rule of semi- or fully independent provincial officials and warlords. National politics seldom penetrated down to the local level where traditional elites, such as landlords and gentry, continued to dominate rural life. Efforts to make the party a mass vehicle were hollow, for within the KMT, power was dominated by a tiny group. The "Military Council," which Chiang headed, became the center of power and decision making. Eventually, Chiang alone held more than eighty government posts simultaneously.

Chiang maintained this authority by skillfully manipulating the many factions within the KMT. This prevented any combination of rivals from becoming strong enough to challenge him. But it also kept the army and the party too divided to solve any major problems. For finances, the regime largely depended on squeezing profits from the cities and the modern economic sector which it controlled. But these were also the areas most vulnerable to invasion and disruption. China's vast interior, where ninety percent of the people lived, remained largely unaffected by laws adopted in the capital, Nanking. Model reform laws enacted to reduce rents, taxes and usury were routinely ignored by provincial officials and landlords. Chiang had little wish or ability to challenge local vested interests. After all, the KMT itself was likely to be the final victim of any profound social and economic change. Thus most political activity consisted of various KMT factions competing to gain influence with Chiang, not to alter the direction in which he led China.

Chiang's peculiar character had a great impact on the party he headed. Though he was celebrated as personally incorruptible, this meant nothing. After all, commented one cynic, "a man who had everything he could possibly want could afford to be honest." The real corruption was in the nature of the KMT's policy, and in the interests it served. In his 1946 book, *Thunder Out of China*, Theodore White, a perceptive American journalist who studied Chiang closely, noted that as a politician he "dealt in force rather than ideas."

> Any concept of China that differed from his own was treated with as much hostility as any enemy division. In both Party and government, above honesty, experience or ability, he insisted on the one qualification of complete, unconditional loyalty to himself. Since loyalty involved agreement, Chiang became a sage.

What vision did this "sage" have of China's past and future? In 1943 Chiang published his masterwork. Entitled *China's Destiny*, the study blamed virtually all of China's ills on the impact of Western ideas and imperialism. As a cure Chiang proposed to blend traditional Confucian ideas and modern fascism. He seemed unable to conceive of progress in any way other than as the creation of a garrison state. Chiang's politics ignored the demands of China's peasants for basic justice. The book's violent antiforeign tone proved such an embarrassment when read by foreigners that Chinese censors tried to prevent Americans from obtaining copies.

Chiang's failure to understand the plight of or to assist China's poor marked his greatest failing. He proved far more successful in wooing the favor of Americans. Before his purge of the Communists and expulsion of Russian advisors, many foreigners had thought of Chiang as a radical, antiforeign nationalist. His sudden shift in 1927 led to a reassessment. When Chiang remarried that same year, the peculiar circumstances of the wedding won the Chinese leader many new friends abroad. In China the Soong family represented a combination of great political and economic power. T. V. Soong was a powerful, American-educated banker. His three sisters also did much to enhance the family. Soong Ching-ling was the widow of Sun Yat-sen. Soong Ai-ling married another important banker, H. H. Kung. Chiang Kai-shek courted the youngest daughter, Soong Mei-ling. Before winning her family's approval, the ambitious political leader consented to divorce his first wife and become a Methodist. In a deft stroke, Chiang linked the fortunes of one of the richest and most influential Chinese families to his own.

The entire foreign community in China, especially the missionaries, were thrilled by the romance and what it signified. The public conversion to Christianity by China's new leader and his marriage to an American-educated woman represented a rapid advance in the long struggle to convert China. Chiang actively cultivated this belief by inviting many missionaries to assist token educational and health programs. Most ostentatious of these was the Chiangs' pet project launched in 1934. The so-called New Life Movement represented a simplistic, even cynical, blend of Confucian dogma and Christian values. It took the place of real social reform. The movement, complete with missionary advisors, implored Chinese peasants to "correct their posture," avoid spitting on floors, pursue "right conduct" and, most important, respect existing government and social authority. Obedience to party and landlord was the peasant's primary duty. In general, the foreign community and missionaries in China responded enthusiastically to these and similar efforts at KMT "reform."

Unfortunately, moral uplift and conversion were not enough to solve China's internal problems, nor would they deter Japanese imperialism. After a brief hiatus, Japanese pressure against north China resumed in 1936. In that year Tokyo also joined Germany and Italy in forming the Anti-Comintern Pact. Resistance to "communism" began to be heralded as the excuse for Japan to undertake renewed expansion in Asia.

Despite these mounting dangers, Chiang concentrated almost all his attention and strength against his domestic rivals. Between 1931 and 1934 the Nationalist armies launched five massive "Bandit Extermination Campaigns" against the Communist forces who had regrouped under Mao Zedong and had created a small "Soviet" area in the mountains of Kiangsi province. By 1934 the vastly superior KMT armies were on the verge of overrunning the Communist base when Mao and 100,000 troops broke out of the encirclement. The fleeing Communists began what became known as the "Long March," a year-long retreat over 6,000 miles in length. Only about 30,000 of the original force reached the final destination in remote northwestern Shensi province. The incredible hardships endured during the march, including continual battles, hunger and disease, became a legend in the chronicles of revolutionary struggle.*

Even after the Long March ended, Chiang continued to pursue the Communists. Late in 1936 he journeyed to the city of Sian to prod his own reluctant commanders into stepping up the offensive. Several KMT generals, including Chang Hsuehliang in Sian, believed that the internal war against the Communists made China easy prey to Japan. Chang and his supporters pressed Chiang Kai-shek to form a new United Front with the Communists which would rally all Chinese against the foreign aggressor. On December 13, 1936, news reached the out-

---

* The first Westerner to publicize this event was the young American journalist, Edgar Snow, who interviewed Mao. Snow's classic account, in *Red Star Over China* (1938), remains a major source of information even today. Almost thirty-five years later, Snow served as middleman in forwarding Mao's invitation to Richard Nixon to visit China.

side world that the KMT dissidents at Sian had seized Chiang in order to compel him to form a new United Front. During the next two weeks the fate of China dangled by a thread. Throughout the crisis, both the United States and the Soviet Union strongly endorsed a settlement which would save Chiang's life and leadership. Most observers believed his death would lead to greater anarchy and almost certain Japanese intervention. President Franklin D. Roosevelt, who had previously shown little interest in assisting China, informed the American ambassador in Nanking, Nelson Johnson, that Chiang's survival was of grave concern to "the whole world." The Soviet Union echoed this theme, declaring that only Chiang could unite China against Japan—and thus help keep Japan from threatening Russian territory. Admiral Harry Yarnell, commander of the American Asiatic Fleet, declared Chiang's life to be almost sacred. The KMT leader was a "Man of Destiny" who "personified China." If he were killed Japan might easily sweep all Asia.

The fears expressed inside China and abroad were quieted by the resolution of the kidnapping on Christmas Day. Intensive negotiations between Chiang, his captors and Communist representatives at Sian led to an informal agreement that Chiang be freed and the anticommunist campaign halted. The second United Front which developed after Sian was never well defined, but seemed to promise that China might now deter, or better resist, Japanese aggression. Chiang was widely hailed as a hero, savior and "indispensable leader." In the view of many Americans China had ceased to be an abstraction. Chiang Kai-shek had become China.

Selected Additional Readings

Five interpretations of American expansion at the turn of the century shed light on U.S.-China Policy: Walter LaFeber, *The New Empire: An Interpretation of American Expansion, 1860–1898*, N.Y., 1963; Thomas J. McCormick, *China Market: America's Quest for Informal Empire, 1893–1901*, N.Y., 1967; David Healy, *U.S. Expansionism: The Imperialist Urge in the 1890s*, Madison, Wisc., 1970; Marilyn B. Young, *The Rhetoric of Empire: American China Policy, 1895–1901*,

Cambridge, Mass., 1968; and William Appleman Williams, *The Tragedy of Amrican Diplomacy*, 2nd ed., N.Y., 1972.

Specific studies of aspects of Sino-American relations include Michael Hunt, *Frontier Defense and the Open Door: Manchuria in Chinese American Relations, 1895–1911*, New Haven, Conn., 1973; Jerry Israel, *Progressivism and the Open Door: America and China, 1905–1921*, Pittsburgh, Pa., 1971; Paul Varg, *The Making of a Myth: The United States and China, 1879–1912*, East Lansing, Mich., 1968; and Theodore White and Annalee Jacoby, *Thunder Out of China*, N.Y., 1946.

The following works discuss the American response to nationalism: Lloyd Gardner, *Safe For Democracy: The Anglo-American Response to Revolution*, N.Y., 1984; Ernest Young, *The Presidency of Yuan Shih-k'ai: Liberalism and Dictatorship in Early Republican China*, Ann Arbor, Mich., 1977; Akira Iriye, *Pacific Estrangement: Japanese and American Expansionism, 1879–1911*, Cambridge, Mass., 1972; Noel Pugach, *Paul S. Reinsch, Open Door Diplomat in Action*, Millwood, N.Y., 1979; Chou Tse-tung, *The May Fourth Movement*, Cambridge, Mass., 1960; Lucien Bianco, *The Origins of the Chinese Revolution, 1915–1949*, Stanford, Calif., 1971; and Sherman Cochran, *Big Business in China: Sino-American Rivalry in the Cigarette Industry, 1890–1930*, Cambridge, Mass., 1980.

Books discussing American regional policy in Asia after 1914 include Akira Iriye, *After Imperialism: The Search for a New Order in the Far East, 1921–31*, Cambridge, Mass., 1965; Roger Dingman, *Power in the Pacific: The Origins of Naval Arms Limitations, 1914–22*, Chicago, 1976; and Dorothy Borg, *American Policy and the Chinese Revolution*, N.Y., 1947.

American policy toward the Communists and Nationalists during the 1920s and early 1930s is covered in the following works: Edgar Snow, *Red Star Over China*, N.Y., 1938; Harrison E. Salisbury, *The Long March: The Untold Story*, N.Y., 1985; James C. Thomson, Jr., *While China Faced West: American Reformers in Nationalist China, 1927–37*, Cambridge, Mass., 1969; James Sheridan, *China in Disintegration: The Republican Era in Chinese History*, N.Y., 1975; and Lloyd Eastman, *The Abortive Revolution: China Under Nationalist Rule, 1927–37*, Cambridge, Mass., 1974.

The American and British response to Japanese expansion into China is discussed in Christopher Thorne, *The Limits of Foreign Policy: The West, the League, and the Far Eastern Crisis, 1931–33*, N.Y., 1973; and Dorothy Borg, *The United States and the Far Eastern Crisis of 1933–1938*, Cambridge, Mass., 1964.

3

From the Marco Polo Bridge to Pearl Harbor

The year 1937 promised great things for China. Chiang Kai-shek had seemingly clutched victory out of the jaws of defeat at Sian. A leading Chinese newspaper prophesied on January 1 that from this day on, "China will have only the United Front, and never again will there be internal hostility." Within China and abroad many influential persons believed that united, the Nationalists and Communists might finally conquer chaos and show a common front to Japan. The optimism lasted a mere six months. Japanese leaders looked with horror at the spectacle of mobilized Chinese patriotism, for it was a major impediment to Tokyo's plan to create an empire stretching across the Pacific. On July 7, 1937, Japanese troops stationed near the Marco Polo Bridge outside Beijing provoked an incident with Chinese soldiers that quickly escalated. Tokyo insisted that any settlement grant them greater political control over north China. Patriotic fervor in China made it impossible for Chiang to accept defeat as he had done in 1931 over Manchuria. Both sides rushed reinforcements to the battle and soon China and Japan were engulfed in a massive undeclared war.

Japan's invasion of China, which seemed to many Americans a copy of Nazi behavior in Europe, profoundly altered the complacent attitudes of the U.S. After the first year of the new Sino-Japanese War, policymakers in Washington began to view Nationalist China as more than a victim of attack. It became a potentially vital ally in an American strategy to contain Japan and construct a new order in Asia. This alliance between the Kuomintang and the United States not only shaped the course of World War II but affected policy in Asia for a quarter century afterwards.

Despite a few early Chinese victories, the Japanese army succeeded in overrunning the major ports, cities and lines of communication along China's coasts and rivers. After about eighteen months Japan controlled all that it deemed important, roughly the eastern third of China. Rather than sacrifice his strength in what appeared a futile campaign, Chiang settled upon a strategy of "trading space for time." The KMT government and armies gradually withdrew southwest, in China's vast interior. From the provisional capital of Chungking (Zhongjing) (largely inaccessible by river and rail and often shielded from air attack by wretched weather) Chiang would conduct a campaign of attrition, waiting until Japan either overextended its forces or blundered into a war with the Western powers.

Initially, most Americans reacted to this spectacle with a sense of detachment. As with the attack on Manuchuria, there was no rush to intervene as China's savior. Instead, leading citizens and officials pondered how best to avoid involvement in a foreign war. Isolationist sentiment remained strong throughout American society. In October 1937 President Roosevelt broke his own silence during a speech in Chicago that decried the "epidemic of world lawlessness." He told a surprised audience that just as health officials must "quarantine" disease carriers "in order to protect the health of the community against the spread of the disease," America should sponsor some form of international quarantine against aggressor nations spreading the disease of war. But Roosevelt's subsequent statements revealed he had no plan of action, nor would the United States impose trade sanctions against Germany, Italy and Japan. Even in December, when Japanese planes provocatively destroyed the U.S. navy gunboat *Panay* (then escorting Standard Oil barges on the Yangtze River), Washington quickly agreed to accept apologies and compensation from Tokyo. Public opinion polls taken a short time later reflected a belief that the most prudent course for all Americans in China to follow was withdrawal.

During 1938, however, President Roosevelt, his advisors and many influential Americans began to reverse their views about the Sino-Japanese War. By the year's end the idea took hold that the preservation of an "independent" and "pro-American" China was a critical element in protecting America's own security. Increasingly, the United States leadership saw Japan not as a mere regional bully, but as a global menace allied to Nazi Germany and Fascist Italy. The more horrible Japan appeared, the more important China became.

The gruesome human cost of the war in China had a profound effect upon American public opinion. In a world still shocked by modern air warfare, the terror bombing of defenseless Chinese cities and the deliberate pillage, rape and murder by invading Japanese troops seemed especially barbaric. Commentators in American magazines now described the Chinese masses with sympathy. The Japanese, they warned, resembled mad "warrior ants" emerging from a jungle habitat to devour everything in their path. The Japanese were often portrayed as faceless fiends, driven by a "primal urge" to conquer. During the Japanese assault on Shanghai late in 1937, a journalist photographed a severely wounded, abandoned child crying amidst the bombed ruins of a railway station. It was among the greatest of war photographs, and people still referred to it five years later when they sent donations to "United China Relief." One woman from New Jersey sent $3.00 with a note that "it is from my three daughters and it is for the little guy on the railroad tracks somewhere in China." A few weeks after this picture was published, *Time's* cover portrayed Generalissimo and Madame Chiang as "Man and Wife of the Year."

Members of the American diplomatic, military and missionary communities in China who witnessed the war and observed numerous attacks upon foreign property shared the outrage. Japan, they felt, had more in mind than merely defeating China's army. Ambassador Nelson Johnson believed the Japanese in-

A Chinese child amidst the rubble of Japanese-bombed Shanghai, 1937. (UPI)

tended to "eliminate all western influence among the Chinese." Admiral Yarnell warned President Roosevelt that the war in China was really a Japanese challenge to "western civilization." Unless the United States moved to stop Japan, he declared, the "white race would have no future in Asia."

These warnings, sent to Washington in growing numbers,

aroused new fear about Japan's long-term plans for aggression in Asia. The Chinese, though in retreat, still tied down a huge Japanese army. If Chiang surrendered, where might Tokyo send its troops next? Perhaps to the Philippines, Indochina, Malaya, Australia or New Zealand? By mid-1938 this concern was not idle speculation. Japanese officials now spoke of imposing a "New Order" in Asia, one that would incorporate the whole region into a Japanese-controlled "Greater East Asia Co-Prosperity Sphere." Only China, it appeared, stood as a barrier between Japan and the European-American empires of the Far East.

The Origins of an Alliance

As early as September 1937, some members of the Roosevelt Administration expressed the idea that "the peace of the world is tied up with China's ability to win or prolong its resistance to Japanese aggression . . . a Japanese victory increases greatly the chances of a general world war."

For many months this remained a minority view. With time, however, the dominant opinion in Washington changed. In Europe the Nazis first annexed Austria, then democratic Czechoslovakia. Japan's behavior and designs in Asia seemed akin to Germany's. As China's military and economic situation grew increasingly desperate, the prospect of complete Japanese control over so vast an area became chilling. When Chinese officials spread rumors that Chiang might surrender, a few key officials in the Roosevelt Administration sprang into action.

The most influential and active friend of China was Secretary of the Treasury Henry Morgenthau, Jr. An intimate friend to the President, Morgenthau hoped to prod Roosevelt to take a more active stand against both Germany and Japan. Chinese resistance to Japan must continue, he believed, to deter an assault against the entire Far East. Morgenthau felt that Chiang's army and government, if financially backed by American economic aid, could serve as the proxy of the United States in Asia. It could tie down and ultimately overwhelm Tokyo's legions.

Gradually overcoming opposition from more cautious officials in the State Department, Morgenthau developed a plan for the

United States to extend a loan, in the form of commercial credits, to the Chinese government for the purchase of vital supplies in the United States. The first proposed credit, of $25 million, was relatively small in size but large in symbolic value. Stanley Hornbeck, a China expert in the State Department, joined Morgenthau in urging Roosevelt to approve the loan. Economic aid, he said, was a first step in America's "diplomatic war plan" against Japan. Both Hornbeck and Morgenthau feared that if Washington extended no aid, Chinese resistance might collapse or Chiang might be driven into the "hands of Russia" and communism for support.

Opposition to the proposed loan came primarily from Secretary of State Cordell Hull who feared it would antagonize Japan while only marginally helping China. Nevertheless, renewed Japanese threats against Western influence in Asia and timely rumors of a Chinese surrender (circulated by Chiang himself) convinced Roosevelt to approve the credits in December 1938. The most important aspect of the decision was that the President and his closest advisors had begun to see China as a vital link in American security. They looked upon China as the first line of resistance to Japan and a potential base for future American influence in Asia.

Within China, the American decision had a striking effect on sagging Kuomintang morale. The official KMT press hailed the loan as a new American commitment to Chinese independence. Privately, one of the Chinese negotiators cabled Chiang that the United States had granted a "political loan." America had, he said, "thrown in her lot [with China] and cannot withdraw. . . ." The Chinese believed they had found a creditor who would not let their cause collapse.

Between the loan of December 1938 and the Pearl Harbor attack of December 1941, the United States gradually escalated what Stanley Hornbeck of the State Department called the "diplomatic war plan" again Japan. Additional loans were granted to China and restrictions placed on trade with Japan. Often, economic aid was sent in response to new Japanese threats or rumors of imminent Chinese collapse. In 1939 Roosevelt called for imposition of an informal "moral embargo" on the sale of airplane parts to Japan. In January 1940, when the 1911 commercial treaty with Japan lapsed without renewal, the United States government began to impose a selective blockade on the sale of strategic materials to Japan. First aviation gasoline, then high grades of steel, and in July 1941, petroleum and all other products were placed in the prohibited category.

During the three years before the Pearl Harbor attack, Roosevelt and his aides understood that aid to China and trade embargoes against Japan were dangerous weapons which could easily backfire. Japan, so dependent on strategic imports, might react to the sudden imposition of trade restrictions by widening its war. American policymakers walked a very narrow line aimed at maintaining Chinese resistance and weakening Japan through selective trade embargoes while avoiding a general war and, especially, direct American involvement.

Not surprisingly, in its effort to sustain China, the United States became increasingly involved in Chinese politics. American aid proved vital for Chiang Kai-shek's dual struggle to resist Japan and to remain supreme among his many domestic rivals. To ensure both an expanded flow of American support and a monopoly of this aid to his group alone, Chiang promoted the creation of pronationalist lobbying groups in the United States.

In part, Chiang's methods reflected a real need to "sell" China's cause to the Roosevelt Administration. Before 1942, the foreign policymaking apparatus in Washington seemed chaotic. Lines of authority and responsibility were blurred. Roosevelt generally played his advisors off against one another until an acceptable consensus was achieved. Since most military and diplomatic officials agreed that the preservation of European barriers against Nazi Germany outweighed the importance of helping China, the Kuomintang was easily overlooked when it came to the allocation of aid. Accordingly, Chiang saw a need to establish an active arm of his own government in Washington which would work informally to convince American leaders of China's great importance.

In December 1938 Washington approved its first loan to China. Funds were actually granted to a Chinese government "front corporation," the Universal Trading Corporation. In part, this was done to make it appear that the United States was only indirectly subsidizing China, a ploy designed to assuage the Japanese. Universal Trading (succeeded in 1941 by "China Defense Supplies," or CDS) functioned as the Chinese government's purchasing agent in America, buying vital materials for China with U.S. funds. Its activities, however, were not strictly commercial. Headed by Chiang's brother-in-law, T. V. Soong, Universal Trading and later CDS coordinated a political operation in Washington. Soong continually "dipped" into federal agencies and the White House to hire high-ranking employees. Key bureaucrats, familiar with how the American government functioned and able to exercise much personal influence, became paid agents of Nationalist China. Men like Thomas Corcoran, formerly a White House lawyer, worked for the Chinese but kept up their private affiliations with the President and his friends.

Many of those who joined Soong's effort made fortunes in the lucrative sales to China financed by American credits. More important, they forged a personal link between the Nationalist regime and a wide array of government officials. Over the years, especially after 1945, many allegations surfaced concerning bribes paid to influential Americans by KMT supporters. Many CDS employees whom Soong drafted formed anticommunist, pro-KMT organizations in the U.S. after World War II. Tommy Corcoran and Anna Chennault, for example, played a central role in introducing the South Korean secret agent, Tongsun Park, to influential officials in Washington during the early 1970s. Park, like his predecessors, tried to bribe congressmen into supporting the South Korean regime. Commenting on this type of behavior thirty-five years before, Secretary of the Treasury Henry Morgenthau complained how difficult it was to deal with American officials linked to the Chinese. He never knew whether they were working for "Mr. Roosevelt or T. V. Soong, because half the time [they are] on one payroll and the rest of the time . . . on the other."

In addition to establishing these operations in Washington, the Nationalists believed it important to develop special channels of communication between themselves and the White House. Chiang distrusted the regular American diplomatic officials in Washington and Chungking. He doubted (correctly) their sympathies and degree of influence over the President. Thus Chiang and the ubiquitous Soong family selected certain Americans in China and Washington to serve as their personal conduits of information. One of the more important of these contacts was James McHugh, American naval attaché in Chungking. The Chiangs knew McHugh vigorously supported them and enjoyed being taken into their confidence. They frequently supplied him with "secret" information which he would pass on to the Navy Department and White House where it would be taken very seriously. Between 1939 and 1942 McHugh obediently sent messages to the President warning, for example, of a Chinese collapse unless more American aid was forthcoming. More often than not, these cries of panic succeeded in prying a bit more money from the President.

Since the Chiang family had little trust in their own government's representatives in Washington—and little trust of each other—they avoided regular communication channels and instead sent their urgent messages to a half-dozen leading Americans. U.S. officials were never certain if they had received the proper communication or precisely to whom they should respond. Because T. V. Soong "coordinated" this system, and since many of the messages came from or through his three influential sisters, the staff of the Treasury Department composed a sarcastic rhyme entitled "Sing a Song of Six Soongs."

Despite this remarkable confusion, American economic aid grew substantially by the end of 1940. Early in 1941, President Roosevelt introduced Lend-Lease legislation to Congress that permitted the President to purchase and deliver military supplies to any nation whose defense he deemed vital to American security. Britain, the Soviet Union and China would benefit immensely from this program. Still, the importance of American economic aid to China before Pearl Harbor cannot be gauged merely by its size, which probably did not surpass a few hundred million dollars. While the money was important, the psychological and political commitment it represented to Chiang was of greater significance. It seemed a clear sign that the United States would support him against both the Japanese and his many domestic rivals. Ironically, as Chiang became more certain of American support in 1941, he showed an increasing willingness to tolerate an "armed truce" with the Japanese and resume his long-standing conflict with the Communists. Unavoidably, the American aid program soon became a party to this struggle.

The Collapse of the United Front

Even at its inception in 1937, the United Front represented only a limited and temporary truce. While each party hoped to prevent a Japanese conquest of China, both the Communists and Nationalists planned to fight Japan in a way designed to maximize their own chances to eventually emerge supreme. Chiang pursued a strategy of retreat, minimizing large-scale clashes and hoarding American aid for eventual use against the Communists. This reflected his belief that "the Japanese were a disease of the skin; the Communists a disease of the heart."

The Communists, centered in the remote northwestern city of Yenan after 1937, remained a tiny, armed movement in comparison to the KMT. Their strategy stressed combining a program of nationalism with social and land reform to inspire peasants to take up the Communist banner against the Japanese invaders. Eventually, these armed, mobilized and politically radicalized peasant-soldiers could be used against the KMT. In the view of Communist leader Zhou Enlai, the anti-Japanese war would also be the beginning of the end for the Nationalists. More will be said of this later.

Although both Chiang and CCP leader Mao Zedong understood each other's long-term strategy, neither wished to precipitate a full-scale civil war before they were assured of Japan's defeat. They preferred to defer a showdown while continuing a limited struggle to expand their own bases at the other's expense. Though a few token United Front representatives were allowed to reside in each other's capital, this represented the limits of political toleration. The KMT secret police, headed by General Tai Li, were especially brutal in their suppression of all dissident political activities. Chiang even assigned a crack army of half a million troops to blockade Yenan in an effort to limit Communist military and political expansion. While the two political parties nominally cooperated against Japan, Chiang labored especially hard to ensure that no outside aid reached his "allies."

Before late 1940, Chiang's desire to settle the final score with Yenan was constrained by the fact that the KMT, not the CCP, received substantial military aid from the Soviet Union. Joseph Stalin, Russia's Prime Minister and absolute ruler, shared Roosevelt's belief that the best way to deter Japanese expansion was to keep Tokyo's armies tied down in China. Also, like the Americans, Stalin had more faith in the existing Nationalist regime than in the small, unproved Chinese Communist movement that was not under his personal control. Yet, even though the CCP had only loose ties to Moscow, Chiang was hesitant to risk offending the Soviet Union by attacking Yenan. Stalin, he feared, might respond by ceasing to aid the KMT.

During 1940 two factors removed these restraints. In order to meet the growing German threat in Europe, Stalin was forced to reduce his aid to the Chinese Nationalists. At almost the same time, however, the paltry level of American assistance began to increase. Chiang had told many Americans, including Ambassador Johnson, that he would move more forcefully against the Communists if assured of continued American support. In November 1940 he claimed that he no longer had any great fear of Japan, but he did require American aid to suppress the "defiant Communists." An increase in aid from Washington would permit him to cease "appeas[ing] the Communists."

In fact, Roosevelt and his advisors opposed Chiang's idea of moving against Yenan, especially while Japan occupied much of China. Better, they reasoned, to postpone civil war and attempt a compromise solution in the short run. Nevertheless, at this time Roosevelt felt compelled to meet Chiang's demands for increased aid. Japan had recently signed a military alliance with Germany and, in November, Tokyo extended recognition to the puppet regime of Wang Ching-wei as the "true" government of China. Wang, an early KMT leader, enjoyed a substantial following in China, and Washington believed it important to demonstrate its continued support for the Nationalist regime in Chungking. Roosevelt, who pushed for approval of a $100 million loan to China within days of Japan's action, scarcely realized how this demonstration of support would affect Chiang.

In January 1941, only a few weeks after this loan, the KMT armies attacked and destroyed the Communist New 4th Army, then occupying disputed territory along the Yangtze River. The outbreak of large-scale internal warfare not only threatened to demolish the remnants of the United Front, but undermined Roosevelt's idea of China as a bastion against Japan. Since mid-1940, when the Nazi blitzkrieg in Europe had crushed France and Holland, the Japanese had increased their pressure on the colonies of French Indochina and the Dutch East Indies. Tokyo hoped to gain control of these mineral-rich areas, freeing itself from dependence on the purchase of foreign—large American—metals and petroleum products. If civil war in China freed many of Japan's troops, Southeast Asia would become much more vulnerable. Thus Washington began its first effort to patch up the United Front in China and compel Chiang to reform his own unpopular regime. This involvement in China's domestic politics continued through the end of the Second World War.

A major difficulty in the effort to preseve China's internal unity was that few Americans knew very much about the Chinese Communists, whose political program and degree of allegiance to Moscow remained unclear to foreign observers. One of the more knowledgeable Americans in China, military attaché Joseph Stilwell (who became the American army commander in China during World War II) thought the Communists were "good organizers" but doubted that communism had any real appeal to China's "individualistic peasants." An adventurous private citizen, journalist Edgar Snow, had broken through the KMT blockade in 1936 to interview Mao and other CCP leaders. His classic account, *Red Star Over China* (1938), portrayed the Communist movement in an extremely favorable light, contrasting it with the corruption and despair prevalent under the KMT. Communist leaders, he noted, professed their independence from Russia and a desire to cooperate with America against Japan.

But Snow's reports (and those of Marine Captain Evans Carlson who traveled into the Communist zone on Roosevelt's behalf in 1938) remained cries in the wilderness. Few "experts" in the State, War or Treasury departments seriously accepted the idea that the Communists had organized a popular peasant army worthy of American support. In addition, the aura of popularity surrounding Chiang Kai-shek made it hard to contemplate extending aid to his rivals or abandoning his regime.

Nevertheless, the outbreak of civil war would have dire consequences vis-à-vis the United States and Japan. This prompted Roosevelt to seek at least a temporary solution to the crisis. For the long run, the President hoped to steer Chiang's regime in a more democratic direction. A reformed, popular KMT, it was hoped, would undercut the appeal of the Communists. For the moment, however, Washington's need was to discover a formula for increasing aid to Chiang while restraining him from using that aid to start a civil war. Early in 1941, with the prospect that extensive Lend-Lease aid to China might soon begin—and as the United Front crumbled—President Roosevelt dispatched his aide Dr. Lauchlin Currie to Chungking for a sensitive political mission.

Currie, who had played an important part in formulating many New Deal economic reforms, now sought to carve out China as his own special area of expertise under the President. Roosevelt, impressed by his aide's earlier achievement, hoped Currie could quickly "fix" the tangled China policy of 1941. After spending several weeks in February and March 1941 as Chiang's guest, Currie returned to Washington with recommendations which became the informal basis for Roosevelt's actions over the next three years.

Rather than attacking the Communist "problem" with force, Currie suggested that Chiang follow "Roosevelt's example" of promoting liberal economic and political reforms to undercut the radical opposition. Roosevelt could steer Chiang toward democracy by sending "liberal advisors" to supervise the KMT administration, and by playing up Chiang in the American press through "inspired stories from Washington" which said "nice things about him." Since, according to Currie, Chiang looked upon FDR as the "greatest man in the world," Roosevelt enjoyed a unique leverage to influence the most populous nation on earth.

In his report, Currie laid out for the first time the broad outlines of what became Roosevelt's China policy. The Nationalist regime, he argued, should be treated as a "Great Power." Chiang should be given additional economic and military support and encouraged to reform. America's overall goal should be to encourage a political compromise in China, averting both civil war and a Communist victory. These recommendations served as an agenda during the war, locking official policy into an increasingly rigid mold. Unfortunately, Currie's report grossly underrated the depth of China's social and economic problems while magnifying the popularity and strength of the Nationalist regime. The Kuomintang, however "reformed," was intimately linked to the defense of the status quo in China. Moreover, Chiang was an intensely proud man and a sincere—if misguided—patriot. He would never surrender his power or judgment to foreign "advisors." During 1941, when Roosevelt sent Chiang a group of financial, transport and political advisors, they and their recommendations were ignored. (Currie, ironically, was accused of being *procommunist* during the McCarthy period and left the United States in the early 1950s.) Finally, Currie ignored the domestic risks of wildly inflating China's and Chiang's importance to America. The Washington-inspired adulation accorded the KMT convinced many Americans that Chiang was, in fact, the undisputed leader of a vital ally. This mistaken belief would have dire consequences as the two allies drifted apart.

Whatever the long-term results, Currie's visit and the passage of the Lend-Lease aid program solidified the Chinese-American connection. By the summer of 1941 China had powerful supporters in the White House who promised delivery of sufficient weapons to arm thirty Chinese divisions. Despite many recurring bottlenecks, a substantial military aid program took form in middle to late 1941. The more aid that was sent, the greater the American stake there seemed to be. The greater the stake, the more pressing the need to protect it. The situation became, in the words of one historian, "a silver cord attaching America to the Nationalist government. There is no more entangling alliance than aid to indigent friends." This "silver cord" pulled the KMT and the United States further along the road of joint military operations, which had an important impact on the outbreak of war between Japan and America.

A Secret Air War Plan and Pearl Harbor

Ever since the end of the Second World War both the Soviet Union and United States have used "covert" or secret military tactics against a variety of enemies. (American activity against Cuba, Chile and Nicaragua, and Russian policy in Africa are examples.) Most Americans assume that the need for and behavior of the Central Intelligence Agency (CIA, founded in 1947) evolved in response to "communist subversion" after 1945. But, increasingly, historians trace the birth of covert warfare to the period of the early Second World War. In order to strike blows against the Nazis and Japanese even before the United States formally entered the war, the Roosevelt Administration at that time supported a number of covert military operations in Europe and Asia. Among the most elaborate was a plan for "private" American pilots, employed by a Chinese company, to initiate an air war against Japan. The object was threefold: to boost Chinese morale, to weaken Japan and to deter its leaders from risking a more direct confrontation with the United States.

Advocates of a secret attack plan stressed the likelihood of winning great gains with a small investment. The bulk of American war supplies in 1941 were destined for Britain, but the careful utilization of American fighters and bombers against Japan might more than make up for the lack of substantial aid. Moreover, by attacking Japan "indirectly," under a Chinese flag, the United States would assume no formal responsibility and this would minimize the chances of provoking war before the U.S. could substantially strengthen its own naval, air and land forces in the Pacific.

This strategy was born in the mind of Claire L. Chennault, a retired army air force pilot. After his resignation in 1936, Chennault accepted work in China as a private military advisor to the Chiangs. He was a devoted supporter of the Generalissimo and Madame Chiang, believing the latter to be a "princess." After the outbreak of the Sino-Japanese War in July 1937, the Chinese government hoped to use Chennault to win American support for an ambitious military strategy. Chennault and T. V. Soong were sent back to Washington in the summer of 1940 to lobby for the creation of a secret Chinese-American air force.

In late November 1940, they submitted to Treasury Secretary Morgenthau a plan to create a five-hundred plane force supplied by the United States and flown by "private" Americans working for a Chinese company. This "Special Air Unit" would "attack Japan proper," Soong explained, thus lowering morale and destroying industrial plants. Morgenthau, then the key figure in the administration's China aid program, urged approval of the plan in his discussions with the President and with the State, War and Navy departments. Encouraged by his colleagues' initial response, Morgenthau told Soong that while five hundred planes were not available, "What did he think of the idea of some long-range bombers with the understanding that they were to be used to bomb Tokyo and other Japanese cities?" Both men agreed that such an attack would "change the whole picture in the Far East."

By early December the plan had progressed far enough for Morgenthau to hold discussions with Chennault and Soong about specific targets and weapons. The Treasury Secretary hoped they would use incendiary bombs

> inasmuch as the Japanese cities were all made of just wood and paper. Chennault said that a lot of damage could be done using this method, and that, even if the Chinese lost some of the bombers, it would be well justified.

As Morgenthau and Chennault discussed the terror bombing of Japanese cities, they seemed to give little thought to the likelihood of a Japanese counterattack. (Soong was probably well aware of this possibility—which made the idea even more attractive since it would bring the U.S. into the war.) Nor were they troubled by any moral or ethical qualms about a "sneak attack" on Japanese civilian targets. The Americans hoped the plan would deter future Japanese expansion and relieve pressure on China and Southeast Asia. The ends justified the means.

The plan was aborted, however, when Secretary of War Henry Stimson and Army Chief of Staff General George Marshall vigorously opposed it. They did not want to send scarce bombers to China, opposed the idea of setting up military operations outside the "normal" chain of command, and feared the whole scheme would provoke an immediate Japanese counterattack against the United States. The President, responsive to these complaints, urged a compromise solution. Instead of bombers, one hundred fighter planes were slated for shipment to China. Because of their limited range and armament, these could not be used against the Japanese home islands, but only to fight the Japanese in China itself.

Since China lacked personnel to carry out the mission, Chennault worked out a solution with Morgenthau, Currie in the White House, and Navy Secretary Knox. They convinced the President to issue a secret Executive Order permitting American military pilots to resign their commissions and sign contracts with a private company (Central Aircraft Manufacturing Corporation) whose operating funds were provided through Lend-Lease. The pilots, who formed the "American Volunteer Group" (AVG), would then fly the military planes given to the Chinese government as Lend-Lease.

By May 1941, the center of China policymaking had moved from Morgenthau's Treasury Department to the White House, which distributed Lend-Lease aid. Currie, who had just returned from a trip to China, worked closely with Soong and Chennault in Washington and became enthusiastic about their air war theories. Currie revived the bombing plan of the previous winter and again urged Roosevelt to accept it. An air war, he claimed, would be of immense value for "our men to acquire actual combat experience." Air attacks on Japan would psychologically bolster the Chinese Nationalists and might deter the militarists in Japan from moving against the European colonies of Southeast Asia and the Philippines.

As the Roosevelt Administration pondered Currie's recommendations for the creation of a Sino-American bomber force to be flown by the AVG, the world military situation deteriorated. In June 1941 the Nazis attacked the Soviet Union, further diminishing its ability to restrain the Japanese. Japan was about to occupy southern French Indochina and perhaps the Dutch East Indies, which was significant because of its oil supplies.

These prospects made the idea of striking a quick, deep blow against Japanese shipping, industry, cities and troop concentrations very appealing.

Late in July 1941, as the Japanese moved into southern Indochina, Roosevelt made two major decisions. On July 26 he publicly announced an embargo on all trade with Japan, leaving Tokyo with only a 12- to 18-month stockpile of oil which was vital for military operations and the economy as a whole. Secondly, in secret, Roosevelt signed a July 23 order which would permit American bombers to be sent to China and to be flown by the AVG against Japan. American officials hoped this two-pronged policy of trade embargo and secret attack might compel the Japanese to postpone an advance on the rest of Southeast Asia and might even convince Tokyo to withdraw its forces from China and Indochina.

The secret attacks never occurred, for war broke out in the Pacific before the necessary planes could reach China. Even so, the entire operation set a major precedent for United States military planning, not merely in style but also by creating a core of personnel and an organizational structure which could function on a continuing basis.

Chennault and his pilots did fight in China during the war as part of the 14th Air Force and afterwards resurrected the AVG as Civil Air Transport (CAT). In 1946 CAT received American planes as "war surplus" and flew military missions for the Chinese Nationalists in the Chinese civil war of 1945–49. After 1949 CAT became Air America, another "private airline" which was actually a secret arm of the CIA in the Vietnam War. In 1941, of course, no one foresaw the political and military implications of creating a secret air force. Then it seemed a clever way to strike Japan at little risk or cost to America. In fact, it created yet another deep bond between the Kuomintang and the United States.

By the time Roosevelt approved the bombing proposal and the oil embargo in July 1941, war with Japan had become almost inevitable. American hopes that the limited air attacks might deter Japan were irrational. The Japanese desperately needed access to oil and would not have permitted covert U.S. air attacks on their home islands to go unpunished. (Tokyo had at least some knowledge of Chennault's plans, though we do not know how much.) The American position after July 26 was that trade in strategic articles could only resume after Japan withdrew from all its earlier conquests and pledged no further expansion. Neither side could conceive of accommodating the other. U.S. policy toward Japan had evolved into a combination of desperation and intransigence.

During the remainder of the year futile negotiations continued in Washington between Secretary of State Hull and Japanese envoy Admiral Nomura. Even the most moderate proposal offered by Tokyo (that Japan gradually withdraw from Indochina) included a demand that the U.S. cease aid to China, permit Japan to impose a peace settlement on Chiang, and guarantee it oil deliveries from the United States and the Dutch East Indies. To the American government, Tokyo's position still seemed to be an attempt to force its domination over the entire Pacific region. To the Japanese civilian and military leaders, America was responsible for the continued costly war in China, sought to deny their nation its just influence in Asia and now threatened to destroy their military and civilian economy through the embargo. Neither side had any faith in the intentions or honor of the other. Though not eager to precipitate a war in 1941, the President and his major advisors did not wish to reach any settlement with Tokyo that did not include provisions for a roll back of Japanese forces. The only way Japan might prove its good faith was to renounce its alliance with Germany, pull its forces out of China and Indochina and pledge to accept the status quo in the Pacific. This Japan would not do.

In November a handful of American military and civilian leaders suggested that the U.S. ought to "buy time" to strengthen British and American forces in the Pacific through a short-term *modus vivendi* with Japan. Taking a different approach, Assistant Secretary of the Treasury Harry Dexter White devised a fanciful plan by which Tokyo might be induced to actually become an American ally against Germany. The U.S. would resume trade with Japan and extend economic aid if Tokyo agreed to leave China, sell the U.S. most of its military production and join a coalition against Germany!

These schemes did no more than momentarily sway Roosevelt. Almost as soon as they were voiced, distorted accounts reached Chiang and his American supporters who reacted in a panic. The Chinese publicized the fear that any compromise with Japan would cause China's collapse. Chiang warned the American government on November 25 that any softening of the total embargo would be interpreted in Japan as the "sacrifice" of China by the United States: "the morale of the people will collapse . . . the Chinese Army will collapse and the Japanese will be enabled to carry out their plans. . . . Such a loss will not be to China alone. . . ." When numerous American officials such as Treasury Secretary Morgenthau lashed out against a "sellout," Roosevelt dropped the idea of a *modus vivendi*.

Beside the normal diplomatic interchange with Japan, American policy toward the crisis in East Asia reflected a major technological breakthrough. During 1941 navy cryptoanalysts had "broken" several Japanese diplomatic codes. The so-called MAGIC intercepts permitted American officials to learn what diplomats in Tokyo told their colleagues abroad. From reading Japanese dispatches, American policymakers concluded that Tokyo was not acting in good faith and that military leaders might well defy any compromise settlement reached by Japanese negotiators. This made Roosevelt and his advisors even more suspicious of Japan. Unfortunately, MAGIC did not break Japanese military codes, leaving Washington in the dark about plans for the attack upon Pearl Harbor.

On November 26 Secretary Hull told the Japanese negotiators that the final terms for peace demanded Japan's complete withdrawal from China and Indochina and a pledge not to seize any other territory throughout the Pacific. Only then would Washington and its Anglo-Dutch allies resume trade. Neither China nor anything else would be compromised. With their oil running out, and all other avenues blocked to them, the Japanese responded on December 7, 1941, by attacking the American fleet at Pearl Harbor.

By the end of November 1941, the basic policy of the United States in Asia was to resist any further Japanese expansion while simultaneously preventing the collapse of the Nationalist regime in China. The Roosevelt Administration believed that a key element in containing Japan was their program of sustaining and strengthening Chiang. More than just a military calculation, the

KMT leader had become a symbol of resistance in Western eyes. Roosevelt had begun to envision the creation of a new order in Asia, based on an alliance between the United States and the Kuomintang. This new order would destroy the threat of future armed aggression and steer postwar Asia along the hazardous course of political development. The implicit alliance forged by 1941 drew the United States into a struggle to control the destiny of Asia.

Selected Additional Readings

American policy toward China and Japan during the years before the Pearl Harbor attack is analyzed in the following studies: Dorothy Borg and Shumpel Okamoto, eds., *Pearl Harbor as History: Japanese-American Relations, 1931–1941*, N.Y., 1973; Warren I. Cohen, *The Chinese Connection: Roger S. Greene, Thomas W. Lamont, George E. Sokolsky and American East Asian Relations*, N.Y., 1978; Robert J. C. Butow, *Tojo and the Coming of the War*, Princeton, N.J., 1961, and *The John Doe Associates: Backdoor Diplomacy for Peace in 1941*, Stanford, Calif., 1974; Herbert Feis, *The Road to Pearl Harbor: The Coming of the War Between the United States and Japan*, Princeton, N.J., 1950; Michael Barnhart, *Japan Prepares for Total War: The Search for Economic Security, 1919–1941*, Ithaca, N.Y., 1987; Jonathan Utley, *Going to War with Japan, 1937–1941*, Knoxville, Tenn., 1985; Robert Dallek, *Franklin D. Roosevelt and American Foreign Policy, 1932–1945*, N.Y., 1979; Waldo H. Heinrichs, *American Ambassador: Joseph C. Grew and the Development of the United States Diplomatic Tradition*, N.Y., 1966; Waldo H. Heinrichs, *Threshold of War: Franklin D. Roosevelt and American Entry into World War II*, N.Y., 1988; and Michael Schaller, *The U.S. Crusade in China, 1938–1945*, N.Y., 1979.

4

The Chinese-American Alliance

The startling attack upon the American fleet at Pearl Harbor shattered the illusion that China could be used as a proxy to fight Japan. Now the United States, and its allies, faced the Axis Powers along two global fronts. Stunned by the success of Japanese forces in Hawaii and throughout the Pacific, many Americans found relief in their own nation's alliance with a "battle-tested" Chinese army. In an editorial appearing two days after the war began, the *New York Times* optimistically wrote:

> We are partners in a large unity. . . . We have as our ally China, with its inexhaustible manpower—China, from whose patient and untiring and infinitely resourceful people there will now return to us tenfold payment upon such aid as we have given.

Sometime later an army propaganda film entitled *The Battle of China* expressed a similar belief:

> The oldest and the youngest of the world's great nations, together with the British Commonwealth, fight side by side in the struggle that is as old as China herself. The struggle of freedom against slavery, civilization against barbarism, good against evil. . . .

In fact, Chiang and his cohorts privately greeted news of the Japanese attack with unbounded glee. Han Suyin, then married to a KMT officer, chronicled the reaction she witnessed in Chungking to word that the U.S. was at war.

> Almost immediately there were noises in the street . . . people surging out of their houses to buy the newspapers, crowding together . . . the military council was jubilant. Chiang was so happy he sang an old opera aria and played "Ave Maria" all day. The Kuomintang government officials went around congratulating each other, as if a great victory had been won. From their standpoint, it was a great victory. . . . At last, at last America was at war with Japan. Now China's strategic importance would grow even more. American money and equipment would flow in; half a billion dollars, one billion dollars. . . . Now America would *have* to support Chiang, and that meant U.S. dollars into the pockets of the officials, into the pockets of the army commanders, and guns to Hu Tsung-nan for the coming war against Yenan.

As different as these realities were, the importance of the Pacific War transcended the initial understandings of most Americans and Chinese. The Japanese troops who overran the Dutch East Indies, French Indochina, Burma, Malaya, Singapore and the Philippines and threatened India shattered the grip of Western colonial power and sounded the death knell to the age of empire in Asia. Throughout the conquered lands, vigorous nationalist movements arose determined to oppose both the new invaders and the return of the former colonial masters. In China the pattern varied only slightly. Japan's invasion swept away the privileged position of the Western powers and thoroughly discredited the Kuomintang. From out of the cauldron of the war of resistance, the Chinese Communists emerged carrying a dual banner of nationalism and social revolution, a banner which they carried on to victory.

Until his death in April 1945, President Roosevelt struggled valiantly to forge an American policy accommodating the powerful forces of nationalism unleashed by the war. FDR understood the many ways in which postwar Asia would be transformed. When defeated, Roosevelt predicted, Japan would be stripped of its empire and reduced to an island nation again. Undoubtedly, the Soviet Union would play a more powerful role in Northeast Asia. The British, Dutch and French colonial empires, dominant for almost two centuries, would crumble as nationalists seized power. And China, with a quarter of the world's population, would emerge united and regenerated, once again asserting its historical power in East Asia. The great task before America was to devise a policy steering these forces of change in the most friendly direction.

Roosevelt hoped that China and the other emerging states of Asia would be governed by "moderate" nationalists sympathetic to American views of proper political and economic relations. Moderate reform and free enterprise, not revolutionary social upheaval, should be the path of progress. A stable, united, pro-American China could be the linchpin for all of Asia. Furthermore, China would be useful as a buffer against possible Soviet expansion in Northeast Asia. While still fighting Japan, America's policymakers faced the great challenge of creating this new China from the existing chaos. Although military experts soon realized China was not likely to be of much help in winning the war, Roosevelt expressed a vital interest in its future. He told British leaders how China, with its vast population, would be "very useful twenty-five years hence, even though China cannot contribute much military or naval support for the moment." At the very least, China could assist the present war effort by tying down several million Japanese troops. This fact alone seemed to justify extending military and economic aid.

Roosevelt did not divorce China's future from his general scheme of wartime diplomacy. He hoped that the Grand Alliance—the United States, British Commonwealth, Soviet Union and Nationalist China—would emerge from the war as partners determined to construct a lasting peace. There would be, of course, conflicting interests and desires to dominate particular regions. But, Roosevelt believed, they could find common ground in his plans to revitalize world trade, permit gradual decolonization and formulate collective security arrangements. He even felt that America would have sufficient leverage over the British and Western European powers to convince them to grant independence to their colonies in an orderly fashion. This would prevent the outbreak of numerous colonial wars and the consequent "radicalization" of nationalist movements. In Asia, China

seemed the natural choice to become one of what FDR sometimes called "the Four Policemen" to protect world peace.

Even though the bulk of his attention (as well as American
forces and supplies) were absorbed by the war in Europe, for a
variety of practical and romantic reasons Roosevelt wanted to
include China among the ranks of the Grand Alliance. A circle
of like-minded enthusiasts convinced the President he could join
American power to the Kuomintang and create an effective wartime and postwar ally. A strong, democratic China would replace the influence of Japan and the European empires, while
countering the appeal of revolutionary doctrines among the
masses of the East. Another thought expressed during the war
by Roosevelt and Harry Hopkins, an advisor, clinched the argument: "In any serious conflict of policy with Russia," Nationalist
China "would line up on our side."

Before any of Roosevelt's plans could be realized, however,
the United States had first to succeed in breathing new life into
the Kuomintang. Without a profound change in the nature of the
regime, little could be expected from the "Fourth Policeman,"
now or later. Unfortunately, FDR never fully realized that in
his effort to forge a new order in China he had allied America
to a decaying government, one resembling the Austrian "corpse"
to which Germany found itself tied in the First World War. After
1941, despite massive infusions of American money ($500,000,000
in gold in 1942 alone) and weapons, the KMT's claim to power
and popular support continually diminished. While this occurred, the power of the Communists grew far stronger. Before long the United States became the crutch holding up the
losing side in a renewed Chinese civil war.

Warning signals reached Washington even as the fires smoked
amidst the rubble at Pearl Harbor. General John Magruder, assigned as an observer in Chungking, warned that Chiang intended to hoard whatever aid America gave him, "largely with
the idea of *postwar* military action." Chinese military strategists,
he wrote, lived in a "world of make-believe" and Chiang himself
looked upon his soldiers and equipment as "static assets to be
conserved for assistance in fighting against . . . fellow country-
men for economic and political supremacy." Ambassador Clarence Gauss, a distant, brooding man with long years spent in

China, believed that Chiang "suffered from a touch of unreality derived from a somewhat grandiose or 'ivory tower' conception of his and China's role."

These reports were not likely to please President Roosevelt. Like many men, he desired reality to conform to his plan for it. What impressed him most, and what he used to justify his policy, were ideas expressed by Chiang's American supporters such as Lauchlin Currie who again traveled to China on FDR's behalf in 1942. He told the President:

> We have a unique opportunity to exert a profound influence on the development of China and hence Asia. It appears to me to be profoundly in our national interest to give full support to the Generalissimo, both military and diplomatic. I do not think we need to lay down any conditions nor tie any strings to this support. . . . we can rely on him so far as lies within his power to go in the direction of our wishes in prosecuting a vigorous war policy and creating a modern, democratic and powerful state.

Currie's view of Chiang captured the attention of the President and the American people. Madame Chiang made a triumphant tour of the United States during 1942–43 and the press celebrated China as one of our greatest allies. The Henry Luce publishing empire (*Time, Life*) placed Chiang Kai-shek's portrait on six covers before 1945, more than any other mortal. Who could remain unmoved by Madame Chiang's words before a joint session of Congress? The Kuomintang and the United States, she declared, together fought for a "better world, not just for ourselves alone, but for all mankind."

Few of the increasing numbers of Americans in China after Pearl Harbor shared Madame Chiang's certainty about this "better world." During the war, journalists, diplomats and military officers prepared literally thousands of reports on the actual situation in "free China." Their findings chronicled a regime which perpetrated almost unbelievable cruelty. Tragically, wartime censorship blocked most of the news stories from reaching America; the criticisms leveled by diplomats and soldiers were routinely ignored. Roosevelt and his close advisors were not cruel and insensitive men. But they had outlined a policy which committed the United States to cooperation with the Kuomintang and so became unable or unwilling to alter their course. They became prisoners of their own ignorance and optimism.

The Real War in China

Only by disregarding the inspired news stories from the White House and the *Time* covers of Generalissimo and Madame Chiang could one discover the tragedy of wartime China. Theodore White (later famous for his *Making of the President* series) wrote many of the finest accounts later collected in *Thunder Out of China* (1946). His eyewitness report of the 1942–43 famine in Honan province (censored at the time) speaks for itself.

> The peasants as we saw them were dying. They were dying on the roads, in the mountains, by the railway stations, in their mud huts, in the fields. And as they died, the government continued to wring from them the last possible ounce of tax. . . . The government in county after county was demanding of the peasant more . . . grain than he had raised. . . . No excuses were allowed; peasants who were eating elm bark and dried leaves had to haul their last sack of seed grain to the tax collector's office. Peasants who were so weak they could barely walk had to collect fodder for the army's horses. . . . One of the most macabre touches of all this was the flurry of land speculation. Merchants . . . small government officials, army officials and rich land owners who still had food were engaged in purchasing the peasants' ancestral areas at criminally low figures. . . . we knew that there was a fury, as cold and relentless as death itself, in the bosom of the peasants of Honan, that their loyalty had been hollowed to nothingness by the extortion of their government.

This horror, occurring in many other regions of China during the war, belied Madame Chiang's pious words about the better world for which the KMT fought. Lacking virtually all principles save for anticommunism and a dedication to greed, the Nationalist regime allowed its adherents to indulge in an orgy of selfishness. Nor were its long-term prospects much better. Chiang's dependence on the landlords and rural gentry made it almost impossible for him to answer the peasants' cry for social justice. Yet, only the rosy propaganda about KMT China reached the American public. American political leaders all too easily believed the images they helped to create.

American Military Strategy and the KMT

When Chiang requested that President Roosevelt send a military advisor to Chungking, T. V. Soong (by then the Chinese foreign minister) had suggested that "the officer need not be an expert on the Far East." On the contrary, Chiang hoped Washington would send a "yes-man" whose function would be to endorse aid requests. Ironically, the officer selected was General Joseph W. Stilwell, who knew more about China than practically anyone else in the army. "Vinegar Joe," as he was affectionately known by his troops, was a tough, no-nonsense soldier who had spent years in China as a young officer and military attaché. During the 1920s and 1930s he had learned Chinese and traveled widely in the countryside. A life-long friend of Army Chief of Staff General George C. Marshall, Stilwell seemed an inspired choice to serve as commander of U.S. forces in China and advisor to Chiang Kai-shek. Theoretically, he could take charge of the American aid effort and assist Chiang's armies in organizing an offensive against Japanese forces in China.

Almost three years later, in the fall of 1944, a despondent General Stilwell described how political infighting had undercut all his efforts in China. "American aid," Stilwell complained, "had to take into consideration the domestic side of every move we have undertaken . . . so that that Gimo's [Generalissimo Chiang] own command will get the most benefit from it." All serious military initiative had been sacrificed to achieve Roosevelt's goal of "preserving China's precarious unity" under Chiang's leadership. "The cure for China's trouble is the elimination of Chiang Kai-shek," concluded Stilwell.

These somber judgments had begun to form in Stilwell's mind almost as soon as he reached China in March 1942. Although his actual authority was unclear, the American general immediately attempted to assume command of the Chinese forces fighting in Burma to keep the Burma Road open. This land route was crucial for bringing military supplies into China from India. Chiang,

Generalissimo Chiang Kai-shek and General Stilwell in a lighter moment, 1943. (National Archives)

however, failed to understand why the Americans bothered. Instead, he felt, they could fly supplies into China over the treacherous Himalayan air route known as the "Hump." Though air transportation was costly and dangerous, it did not require that Chiang sacrifice KMT soldiers and weapons in its defense. For the rest of the war, Chiang struggled to avoid using his troops to open a land route into China.

Not surprisingly, the Japanese quickly overran Burma and effectively isolated China in the spring of 1942. The disaster in Burma convinced Stilwell that China could only play an important role in the war if its armies were thoroughly reorganized and used to reopen Burma. This would permit substantial supplies to reach China and allow a still more powerful army to take the field against Japanese forces. For the next two and one-half years Stilwell fought against overwhelming odds to create and command this "new army." "While the wasteful and inefficient system of juggling" of Chinese armies might be necessary to maintain Chiang's power, he wrote, "it emasculated the effectiveness of Chinese troops." But even Stilwell failed to fully realize that his plans for drastic military reform threatened to topple the whole jerrybuilt structure of Nationalist power.

As of 1942 the Chinese army, if it could even be called an army in the modern sense, consisted of about 3,800,000 men in 316 divisions. Only about thirty divisions were considered personally loyal to Chiang. The rest were divided among twelve zonal commanders who were tied to Chiang in a loose coalition. The quality of most of these troops (except for the crack army of 400,000 which was commanded by Hu Tsung-nan and which surrounded the Communist capital of Yenan) can be gauged by a report prepared by American army officials in 1945. The report chronicled the formation of a typical Chinese unit.

> Conscription: Conscription comes to the Chinese peasant like famine or flood, only more regularly—every year twice—and claims more victims. Famine, flood, and drought compare with conscription like chicken pox with plague.

> The virus is spread over the Chinese countryside. . . . There is first the press gang. For example you are working in the field looking after your rice . . . [there come] a number of men who tie your hands behind your back and take you with them. . . . Hoe and plow rust in the field, the wife runs to the magistrate to cry and beg for her husband, the children starve.

The report then described how prison officials made money by selling convicts into army service. Together all the conscripts

A group of Chiang Kai-shek's top officers. (National Archives)

were marched hundreds of miles to training camps. Those who could fled along the way. Those caught were beaten and forced to march on. Disease took an increasingly heavy toll. Soon the true "value" of the new conscripts emerged. Officers could "pocket a conscript's pay and his rations can be sold. That makes him a valuable member of the Chinese Army and that is the basis of the demand for him."

If somebody dies, his body is left behind. His name on the list is carried along. As long as his death is not reported, he continues to be a source of income, increased by the fact he has ceased to consume. His rice and his pay become a long-lasting token of memory in the pocket of his commanding officer. His family will have to forget him.

This official report (which also compared Chinese army hospitals to Nazi concentration camps) seemed as if it were meant to condemn the Germans and Japanese rather than America's ally.

No American was more horrified by these conditions than General Stilwell. He quickly developed a policy aimed at reforming the Chinese army by reducing its overall size and selecting thirty divisions for special training. These new divisions, commanded by a Chinese officer chosen by Stilwell, would lead the proposed Burma campaign and form the nucleus of a powerful military force in China.

What Stilwell never sufficiently accounted for was that his plan to restructure the Chinese army and distribute American arms to selected divisions led by hand-picked commanders involved many more political than military questions. In his diary Stilwell wrote, "Why doesn't the little dummy [Chiang] realize that his only hope is the 30 division plan, and the creation of a separate, efficient, well equipped and well trained force?" But Chiang, in his own way, did fully understand what Stilwell's reforms envisioned. They would cut out the heart of Chiang's power structure. No longer would he alone be able to control the contentious KMT factions through selecting commanders and distributing aid to those personally loyal. Instead, the Americans, and *their* Chinese commanders, would become the masters of China's KMT armies. Chiang would become extraneous and expendable. Understandably the Generalissimo did everything possible to prevent this by delaying approval of Stilwell's plans and trying to convince Roosevelt to recall the troublesome American.

Stilwell grew increasingly infuriated by Chiang's refusal to initiate a Burma campaign or support the army reform program. "The stupid little ass fails to grasp the opportunity of his life," Stilwell complained. "The Chinese government," he concluded, was "a structure based on fear and favor, in the hands of an ignorant and stubborn man. . . ." Dismissing Chiang with the epithet "Peanut," Stilwell concluded: "Only outside influence can do anything for China—either enemy action will smash her or some regenerative idea must be formed and put into effect at once." By the end of 1942, Stilwell believed he himself embodied

that regenerative idea and he began to compete with Chiang for control of China's armies. The weapon Stilwell sought was Roosevelt's support in the form of an order to Chiang: let the American general distribute aid as he saw fit and lead all Chinese forces in combat. In short, let Stilwell act as commander of China. Such an order did not come until September 1944, and was countermanded almost as quickly as it appeared.

From late 1942 until the summer of 1944 Chiang successfully resisted Stilwell. The Generalissimo understood that Roosevelt hoped to utilize China as an American protégé in Asia, a stabilizing influence to take the place of Japan and the European colonial empires and to provide a counterweight to Soviet influence. In the long run, Chiang believed, FDR would not act to alienate or undercut the Nationalist regime which he championed as one of the future "Four Policemen."

The Chinese Manipulation of American Policy

Given his growing dependence on American military, political and economic support, Chiang could not afford to appear totally negative and disruptive. He must appear to offer a constructive alternative military strategy to that advocated by Stilwell. Adopting the old Chinese axiom of "playing the barbarians off against each other," the Generalissimo searched for a way to ingratiate himself with the President. He would do so by cooperating with those Americans who were jealous of or disagreed with Stilwell and who hoped to boost their own careers through working with the KMT. Chiang quickly discovered an antidote to Stilwell in the person of General Claire Chennault, former commander of the AVG and now leader of a small air task force in China.

Chennault deeply resented Stilwell's emphasis on a ground campaign, believing that air power held the key to victory in Asia. (His disciples helped devise America's air strategy in Vietnam twenty years later.) Furthermore, the flier knew that only by winning more support for air warfare could he rise from his subordinate role in China. Chiang proved eager to accept Chennault's strategy because it served three basic needs at once. If the very limited air freight capacity of the Hump transport route was filled with supplies (fuel, ammunition, spare parts, etc.) for Chennault's air force, Stilwell would not be able to accumulate stockpiles for his proposed Burma campaign. Building up Chennault's power and prestige posed no threat to Chiang since, unlike Stilwell, the flier virtually worshipped the Generalissimo and Madame Chiang. Finally, permitting Chennault's warplanes to spearhead attacks against the Japanese in China would cost Chiang no troops or resources but would still create the popular illusion that China was the place where the Japanese were really being fought. In return, the American people would reward China with more aid.

Chennault lost no time in his effort to vault over Stilwell and capture Roosevelt's attention. Distrustful of the War Department (where Chennault was considered a publicity hound), the flier communicated directly with the President through a group of carefully chosen intermediaries. Among the most important was an aide to Chennault named Joseph Alsop, who happened to be a distant cousin of the Roosevelts. Alsop and T. V. Soong deluged the White House with advice on how to fight the war in China. Calling Stilwell's policy a "national disgrace," they claimed that if Chennault were given a handful of bombing planes he could cripple Japanese forces in China and bring Japan to its knees. Never known for his modesty, Chennault asserted confidence that he could "not only bring about the downfall of Japan" but "make the Chinese lasting friends of the United States." As icing on the cake, he promised to "create such goodwill that China will be a great and friendly trade market for generations." Who could ask for more?

Stilwell, naturally enough, despised both Chennault and his ideas. Not only would they undercut his own army reform strategy, but they made no military sense. As soon as Chennault began his air attacks on Japanese forces and shipping, the Japanese would attack his air bases. Since the Chinese army was a shambles, the bases could not possibly be defended. Unfortunately, Stilwell's messages were not appreciated by the President. No one in the White House wanted to hear caustic warnings about the incompetence and weakness of America's ally. Chennault, on the other hand, confided to presidential aide Harry Hopkins and others that if the administration supported an air war "there was no doubt of success" in China. Chennault's supporters continually repeated the claim that an air strategy alone could win the war and magically improve the political atmosphere in Chungking.

All during 1942 and the first half of 1943 Stilwell labored in vain to get Chiang and the reluctant British to begin a military offensive in Burma. But without firm presidential backing, there was no way to compel the Chinese to do anything. In May 1943 the President sought to resolve this conflict of strategies by having both Stilwell and Chennault present their cases directly to him in Washington. The questions FDR asked the two competing generals were more concerned with politics than military affairs. What did Stilwell think of Chiang? "He's a vacillating, tricky, undependable old scoundrel who never keeps his word." Chennault disagreed. "Sir, I think the Generalissimo is one of the two or three greatest military and political leaders in the world today."

The President had little interest in reading or analyzing the detailed reports which Stilwell offered explaining the fallacies of an air strategy. Chennault promised easy, cheap and quick success; Stilwell spoke of a protracted, difficult campaign which involved many military and political pitfalls. Not surprisingly, Roosevelt resolved the dispute in favor of Chennault and decided to allocate the bulk of the precious supplies being flown over the Hump to an air campaign. The President would even have recalled Stilwell from China had not General Marshall and Secretary of War Stimson continued to express their strong support for him.

The Rise and Fall of Air Warfare in China

The decision to indulge Chiang by shifting support to Chennault reflected Roosevelt's belief that such actions were a wise investment in future goodwill. Chiang should not be forced to reform by threats, he told General Marshall in March 1943. It would be counterproductive to bully Chiang, a man who had created in China "what it took us a couple of centuries to attain." The Generalissimo was the "undisputed leader of 400,000,000 people" and could not be dictated to as Roosevelt might "the Sultan of Morocco."

By then Marshall understood why the President had been seduced by Chennault's absurd claims. It was not that anyone with a grain of military sense believed that air power alone could defeat Japan, but that Chiang wanted Chennault. As Marshall put it:

> Since the Chinese wanted what Chennault wanted, and Roosevelt wanted to give the Chinese what they wanted, all these things fit together very neatly and required no further presidential effort or analysis.

At a deeper level the President's actions in regard to China demonstrated how far American political leaders were divorced from the reality of the situation. In contrast to Roosevelt's sophisticated views of European rivalries and politics, he, and most of those around him, had only the dimmest comprehension of Chinese conditions. They failed to realize that Chiang's military policy overlay a deeper political crisis in China, that these problems could not be solved by indulging Chiang's whims. Furthermore, their unbounded (and unwarranted) faith that China's glorious future justified postponing the day of reckoning with Chiang ensured that the KMT would undertake no reforms and thus hasten its own destruction.

Fully aware of how he had been cut adrift by Washington, a very bitter and disappointed Stilwell returned to China in the summer of 1943. His diary reflected overwhelming resentment toward Roosevelt, Chennault and Chiang. "Back again on the manure pile after that wonderful trip home. . . . Back to find Chiang the same as ever—a grasping, bigoted, ungrateful little rattlesnake."

For the next twelve months, until the spring of 1944, Stilwell bided his time, doing what little he could to reorganize his thirty Chinese divisions with the few resources that remained available. Chiang continued to interfere with all of Stilwell's training programs and came perilously close to beginning open warfare with the Chinese Communists. As much as possible, both Chiang and Stilwell labored to undercut each other's power base. The

Generalissimo continued to complain to Washington about Stilwell, while Stilwell tried hard to channel American supplies to
Chiang's many rivals within the KMT. He even dabbled in several plots to overthrow the KMT leader.

Meanwhile, Chennault gradually built up his forces until he
was able to begin an air offensive late in 1943. The results
proved devastating, but not exactly in the way Chennault had
promised. As soon as the air attacks began to hurt the Japanese,
they counterattacked and quickly overran Chennault's forward
air bases. The Chinese armies supposedly protecting them dis-
solved into a rabble. The Japanese assault on previously unoccupied east China was so rapid that by the spring of 1944 it
appeared that all China might be overrun. Thus Stilwell had
been proved correct in his predictions. The Japanese advance
had finally exposed the military and political bankruptcy of the
Chiang-Chennault strategy. In the process, however, it looked
like all of China might fall.

The devastating military events sweeping over China in the
spring and summer of 1944 had a great impact upon President
Roosevelt. They not only confirmed Stilwell's predictions, but
forced Roosevelt to question his own faith in Chiang Kai-shek.
In fact, FDR had begun to reassess his policy the previous November when he met the Chinese leader face-to-face at the
Cairo Conference. During several tense meetings, Chiang ha-
rangued FDR with demands for more economic aid—he wanted
a billion dollars this time—and additional weapons. Incredibly,
Chiang still refused to commit himself to a Burma campaign.
The reluctance of both the British and Chinese to pursue the
war in the Pacific with sufficient vigor (the British pushed a
strategy designed to reconquer their own important colonies
first) infuriated the President.

In marked contrast, when FDR went on to Teheran, Iran, in
November 1943 to confer with the Soviet leader, Joseph Stalin,
the Russians promised to enter the war against Japan after
Hitler's defeat. The promise of Russian assistance, as well as
mounting evidence that China would not offer any real help
against Japan, caused Roosevelt to step back, at least temporarily, from his posture of offering Chiang all out support. At
Cairo, FDR even quipped to Stilwell that if Chiang were de-

posed in a coup, the U.S. would support whoever was "next in line."

The President showed his rising ire by blocking new economic aid for China. Treasury Secretary Morgenthau had uncovered evidence of massive embezzlement by Chiang's family and insisted that before he would give China "another nickel" the crooks could "go jump in the Yangtze." The President and his advisors had begun to shed their illusions about Nationalist China. The process accelerated in April 1944 when Stilwell and a few of his new Chinese divisions which had been trained in India began fighting in Burma. Despite furious Japanese resistance, Chiang refused to permit the bulk of the new divisions in China to enter Burma. On April 10, FDR ordered that Chiang be threatened with a cutoff of aid unless he assisted Stilwell in Burma. Chiang quickly sent his troops into battle.

By May and June the Japanese were still on the offensive in China proper and the KMT armies were crumbling. Yet Chiang continued to hold large forces in reserve, claiming they must guard the Communists. Roosevelt used this excuse to initiate a new policy.

Roosevelt and Chiang: Ultimatum and Retreat

By June 1944 Roosevelt was convinced that unless Chiang were actively forced to enter the war against Japan, America's wartime and postwar strategies were doomed. Increasingly, it became clear that the only hope of unifying China was to revitalize the United Front, thus depriving Chiang of any excuse that he needed to guard the CCP and permitting America to tap the military strength of the Communist armies in north China. It was hoped that wartime unity might be carried past Japan's surrender and prevent the outbreak of civil war in China. With these concerns in mind, FDR sent Vice President Henry Wallace to China in June 1944 with instructions to press Chiang to seek a negotiated settlement with the Communists. America, he implied, would help mediate the discussions.

Furthermore, Roosevelt insisted that an American observer mission be allowed passage to the Communist capital, Yenan.

The Burma road into China. (National Archives)

Among the President's motives, it seems, was a desire to put a little fear in Chiang's mind, to let him know that Washington realized there were alternative political leaders and groups in China. Also, if the U.S. could successfully mediate in China, Chiang could no longer use the excuse of a Communist threat to postpone fighting the Japanese. Wallace's report to FDR testified to the administration's growing disillusionment with the KMT.

> Chiang, at best, is a short-term investment. It is not believed that he has the intelligence or political strength to run post-war China. The leaders of post-war China will be brought forward by evolution or revolution and it now seems more like the latter.

As the military situation in China continued to deteriorate, Stilwell seized the moment to suggest again that Chiang be ordered to give him full command powers. Stilwell wanted complete freedom to direct China's war effort and even to utilize Communist units. On July 4, 1944, the President approved a telegram to Chiang which warned that "the future of all Asia is at stake. . . ." Air power had failed and now Stilwell must be given "command of all Chinese and American forces . . . including the Communist forces."

As he had always done, Chiang struggled to survive by playing his rivals off against each other. Rather than refuse the President's orders—and risk the loss of American aid—he gave his conditional agreement. Stilwell would soon be given the power to command, but first the President should send a personal emissary to smooth relations between Chiang and Stilwell.

When General Marshall heard that FDR was prepared to accept Chiang's suggestion, he moved quickly. Marshall wanted to ensure that the emissary would support Stilwell and not be a hatchet man like previous Roosevelt emissaries. Secretary of War Henry Stimson joined Marshall in proposing Patrick J. Hurley for the mission. Hurley, a Republican, former Secretary of War, oil company lawyer and Washington gadfly, had enjoyed good relations with Stilwell during an earlier meeting. Moreover, FDR was known to share confidence in him. At the time no one thought Hurley would have any important role to play.

After a brief stop in Moscow, Hurley arrived in Chungking on September 6, 1944. Roosevelt, apparently, had given Hurley verbal instructions to visit Moscow and secure a pledge from the Soviets not to aid the Chinese Communists. The President believed that if the Russians steered clear of China, the CCP would have no hope of outside support and a compromise between them and Chiang could more easily be arranged. Unless such a peaceful settlement were reached quickly, civil war was sure to break out which would devastate China and scuttle American designs for postwar Asia.

During the first week Hurley spent in China, the pace of events quickened. Believing he now enjoyed the President's full support, Stilwell began making arrangements to take over military command and "get arms to the Communists who will fight." After more prodding by Stilwell, FDR and General Marshall sent an ultimatum to Chiang which Stilwell personally delivered on September 19, 1944. The message declared that the time for stalling had passed and unless Stilwell were given complete power to command all Chinese troops, United States aid would be terminated. The end of U.S. support would almost certainly cause Chiang's regime to collapse.

Stilwell's glee in delivering the ultimatum to Chiang was voiced in his diary:

> Mark this day in red on the calendar of life. At long last, at very long last, F.D.R. has finally spoken plain words, and plenty of them, with a firecracker in every sentence. "Get busy or else." A hot firecracker. I handed this bundle of paprika to the Peanut and then sank back with a sigh. The harpoon hit the little bugger right in the solar plexus, and went right through him. It was a clean hit, but beyond turning green and losing the power of speech, he did not bat an eye. He just said to me, "I understand." And sat in silence jiggling one foot.

This victory proved very short-lived, for as Stilwell prepared to lead Chinese forces, Hurley secretly took it upon himself to work with Chiang in getting rid of the tiresome American general. Hurley's behavior over the next year showed his complete belief in the need to sustain Chiang in power. He feared that if Chiang lost power, China would fall victim to the Chinese Communists or the Soviet Union. Thus a man completely ignorant of actual conditions in China took it upon himself to ensure that the United States would sustain Chiang against all challenges.

Hurley's startling behavior and betrayal of Stilwell has long puzzled observers. Many assumed his visceral anticommunist feelings simply surfaced in the crisis. In fact, his motivation may have been more emotional than ideological. In 1982, a group of American journalists and diplomats meeting to recount the events in China during 1944–45 revealed evidence that Hurley may have been mentally unbalanced. Several people in the group offered firsthand accounts of bizarre encounters with Hurley during which he ranted at them incoherently about personal demons, forgot that he was in China, and confused them with his relatives! Unfortunately, journalists like Annalee Jacoby (who worked for *Time*) could not convince their editors to publish reports on such incidents. Decades later, these "old China Hands" still trembled with rage when they recounted their story to scholars.

On September 24, 1944, Hurley joined Chiang and T. V. Soong in sending a message to FDR. All three agreed that the real problem in China was Stilwell. If only he were removed as a thorn in Chiang's side, the Kuomintang would be able to carry out everything Roosevelt desired of it.

When it seemed that FDR might be wavering in his decision, Hurley sent a pair of messages to the President on October 10, 1944. He argued: "There is no other Chinese known to me who possesses as many of the elements of leadership as Chiang Kai-shek. Chiang Kai-shek and Stilwell are fundamentally incompatible." Later that day Hurley cabled Washington that Stilwell's only motive was vindictiveness.

> His one intention . . . [is] to subjugate a man who has led a nation in revolution and who has led an ill-fed, poorly equipped, practically unorganized army against an overwhelming foe for seven years. My opinion is that if you sustain Stilwell in this controversy you will lose Chiang Kai-shek and possibly you will lose China with him. . . . America will have failed in China.

President Roosevelt was forced to choose between two extreme positions—that of sustaining Stilwell or firing him. Yet, Hurley's reports to the President seemed to offer an easy way out. This was important, for in just a few weeks the President faced election for a fourth term. He was running on his proven record as a war leader and planner for peace. To break with China or to be blamed for China's collapse on the eve of election was political dynamite. After all, it was Roosevelt who had done so much to convince Americans that Chiang was a hero. Furthermore, the President and those closest to him had no understanding of how desperately unstable China was. They still harbored a hope that with some additional American support Chiang might muddle through against the Japanese and be induced to accept a compromise with the Communists. Finally, Hurley made the decision simpler by telling the President repeatedly that Chiang would follow through on past promises only if Stilwell were removed. The choice, Hurley told him, was between a quarrelsome general and the "indispensable" leader of China.

Roosevelt made the expedient decision, issuing an order on October 18, 1944, that Stilwell be recalled. His successor was General Albert Wedemeyer, a man Stilwell despised as "the world's most pompous prick." In turn, Hurley was elevated to ambassador, replacing the career diplomat Clarence Gauss who had been critical of Chiang for years, to little avail. American aid would continue but the Chinese would not be required to appoint an American commander.

A final note of caution is worth mentioning in our discussion of General Stilwell. It is easy—too easy—to see him as a selfless hero and potential savior of China. When compared to Americans like Chennault and the U.S. naval officers who assisted the KMT secret police,* Stilwell seems almost saintly. His earthy, caustic diary makes wonderfully entertaining reading to a later generation. But there were grave problems in Stilwell's program, problems distinct from those caused by Chiang.

Beyond his idea of developing a strong, efficient, American-oriented Chinese army, Stilwell had little to offer China. He knew the depth of China's poverty, understood the misery in which the average Chinese peasant lived and died. Yet, as a

---

* During the war a secret U.S. navy group in China, not under Stilwell's control, worked with KMT Secret Police Chief, Tai Li, to train anti-communist guerrillas. The naval officers bitterly opposed Stilwell and other Americans who sought to cooperate with anti-Chiang groups.

military officer, he had scarcely thought about how to help China in other than military ways. Even his army reforms focused on identifying and promoting efficient Chinese soldiers, soldiers who had a Kuomintang and class background like Chiang's. There is little reason to expect that the new Chinese army Stilwell planned to create would have any desire or ability to cope with China's profound social problems. In some ways, a "better" army might even have retarded the process of change since its officers could more successfully defend the selfish interest of the existing elite.

Twenty-five years later, in Vietnam, President Richard Nixon would announce a similar strategy. Now called "Vietnamization," it proposed to train a client army under close American supervision. The policy proved both a military and political disaster in Vietnam. There is no reason to suspect it would have worked any better in China. Neither Stilwell nor many of those around him understood that real change in China could not be brought about by foreign control, advice or reform. China was a volcano about to explode in a revolution which would dwarf the violence of the Japanese invasion. The forces represented by the Kuomintang and Communists were far too large and complex for Americans to control. The Chinese had to find their own solutions. The United States either had to accept this or fight against China.

Selected Additional Readings

The intrigue and drama of Sino-American relations, especially with the Kuomintang regime, are chronicled in both formal histories and personal memoirs. See Joseph W. Stilwell, *The Stilwell Papers*, N.Y., 1948; Theodore White and Annalee Jacoby, *Thunder Out of China*, listed in Chapter 2; Graham Peck, *Two Kinds of Time*, Boston, 1967; Theodore White, *In Search of History*, N.Y., 1978; Han Suyin, *Birdless Summer*, N.Y., 1968, and *Destination Chungking*, Boston, 1942; Gordon Seagrave, *The Soong Dynasty*, N.Y., 1985; John W. Dower, *A War Without Mercy: Race and Power in the Pacific War*, N.Y., 1986; Christopher Thorne, *Allies of a Kind: The United States, Great Britain and the War Against Japan, 1941–1945*, N.Y., 1978; Herbert Feis, *The China Tangle*, Princeton, N.J., 1953; Barbara Tuchman,

Stilwell and the American Experience in China, 1911–1945, N.Y., 1971; Robert Dallek, *Franklin D. Roosevelt*, listed in Chapter 3; Lloyd Eastman, *Seeds of Destruction: Nationalist China in War and Revolution, 1937–1949*, Stanford, Calif., 1984; Ronald Spector, *Eagle Against the Sun: The American War with Japan*, N.Y., 1985; and Michael Schaller, *The U.S. Crusade in China*, listed in Chapter 3.

5

The United States Confronts the Chinese Revolution, 1942–94

The tumultuous, often bitter course of KMT-American relations during World War II formed only part of a larger Chinese drama. All along the ill-defined battle fronts of north, south and central China, the KMT and CCP continued their political and military struggle. The Communists, centered in their remote capital city of Yenan where they lived in caves dug out of the sandy hills, spent the war years struggling against Japan and unceasingly building a mass peasant army. In 1937 they controlled only a few thousand square miles, a million people and an army of perhaps 80,000. Compared to the Nationalists their power seemed negligible. Eight years later, when Japan surrendered, the Communists commanded almost a million troops, occupied one-fourth of China and governed 100 million people. In just another four years all China would be theirs.

How can we explain this dramatic reversal of fortunes? Many diverse factors, of course, led to the Nationalist debacle and the

Communist victory. In a typically self-centered way, numerous Americans attributed this colossal event to the alleged "treason" of a handful of American diplomats. But the essential element behind the successful revolution was the opposite manner in which the KMT and CCP responded to the challenge of the Japanese invasion.

After the first year of the Sino-Japanese War (late 1938), Japanese troops occupied the parts of China most important to them, primarily the eastern one-third of the country on a line from Beijing to Canton. Chiang withdrew his government and armies to the remote west, leaving the loyalty and fate of hundreds of millions of Chinese up for grabs. The Generalissimo's strategy seemed simple: he would "trade space for time" and wait for an American victory to rescue him. Meanwhile the Nationalists hoarded American money and weapons for eventual use against the Communists. But this strategy contained a fatal flaw. Communist organizers poured into the vacuum created by the Nationalists' retreat. They moved through the countryside, behind Japanese lines, and organized a peasant-guerrilla army which eventually swept on to victory over the KMT.

Chiang's flawed strategy was no simple oversight, but directly connected to the nature of the KMT regime. Successful guerrilla warfare required mobilizing and arming the rural masses. A guerrilla army would threaten not only the Japanese but the landlords and gentry, the social classes which comprised Chiang's staunchest supporters. Thus Chiang faced an insoluble dilemma: to win the peasants he must lose the landholders. By this refusal—or inability—to move against his traditional allies, Chiang became their hostage, doomed by the very people who had kept him in power!

Precisely those circumstances which paralyzed the KMT helped bring success to the Communists. At countless villages in occupied and unoccupied territory across the face of China, the Communists arrived to organize the peasants against the Japanese. They waved the banner of patriotism, throwing themselves enthusiastically into a campaign which the Nationalists had already largely deserted. A report by U.S. military intelligence summarized the process of what happened when Communist forces entered a village.

Its retinue of propagandists, social and economic workers, school teachers . . . immediately started organizing and training the peasant masses for resistance through guerrilla warfare. Their central idea in all these efforts was that the social and economic level of the peasants had to be improved in order to maintain morale and to instill among the people a will to resist Japan and support their own armies.

At this stage the Communists avoided radical land reform and class struggle, for they wanted to attract as broad a base of support as possible. They did, however, reduce rents and try to redress the most serious peasant grievances against notorious local landlords, usurers and bullies.

But the Communists did something more, something quite revolutionary for China: they treated the peasants as valuable human beings. Theodore White, who spent the war years in China, believed that this was the secret of the Communists' success. As he noted in *Thunder Out of China:*

> If you take a peasant who has been swindled, beaten and kicked about for all his walking days and whose father has transmitted to him an emotion of bitterness reaching back for generations—if you take such a peasant, treat him like a man, ask his opinion, let him vote for a local government, let him organize his own police . . . decide on his own taxes, and vote himself a reduction in rent and interest—if you do all that the peasant becomes a man who has something to fight for, and he will fight to preserve it against any enemy, Japanese or Chinese.

As White described it, once this process began it became a sustained reaction. The Communists could offer to the peasant

> an army and a government that help him harvest, teach him to read and write and fight off the Japanese who raped his wife and tortured his mother. [He] develops a loyalty to the army and the government and to the party that controls them. He votes for that party, thinks the way that party wants him to think, and in many cases becomes an active participant.

Within countless Chinese villages the Communists gained support by working with and for the poor peasants and small landholders. Ignoring the rich and influential gentry, the CCP sponsored local defense groups, agricultural cooperatives, educational programs and political discussions. The peasants became convinced of two things. Not only were the Communists dedicated to the patriotic struggle against Japan, but the peasants themselves had a direct stake in the survival and victory of the CCP. The party became their representative, the voice of their demands for social and economic justice against the landlord class. As a result, many joined the Red military forces as regular soldiers or part-time militia.

The Japanese responded to Communist guerrilla activities by visiting terrible retribution upon villages. The "Three-All Policy" of "Burn All, Kill All, Loot All" was applied to regions suspected of sympathizing with the Communists. But Japanese brutality, like that of the Nationalists who squeezed the last grain out of starving peasants in Honan, only won more converts for the Communist cause. Gradually, more and more areas had two governments: Japanese or KMT by day, Communist by night.

During the Second World War, the Communists began to win China and the Kuomintang to lose it. The Communist Party proclaimed that for China to be independent and great once again it must throw off the shackles of both foreign control and internal oppression. Revolution and nationalism would be harnessed together as one force. Power, the Communists learned, would come from the hundreds of millions of poor peasants, not the favor of the wealthy elite or foreign patrons loaning money. By 1949, the Communists parlayed this new source of political power into control of all China.

Americans Meet the Chinese Communists, 1942–44

American leaders never fully understood or accepted the reality of the Chinese revolution. Washington's policy toward the Chinese Communists, with few exceptions, oscillated between indifference and profound hostility. The tendency either to disregard the importance of the CCP or see it as an agent of a "global" conspiracy had a dire impact on Sino-American relations.

When the United States joined the war against Japan in December 1941, there had been little contact between American officials and the Chinese Communists. A handful of American journalists and adventurers such as Edgar Snow, T. A. Bisson, Agnes Smedley, Evans Carlson and Anna Louise Strong had journeyed to Communist territory and written favorable reports on what they saw. But such activities had little impact on mass opinion or government policy.

Official American views of the Chinese Communists before 1941 were a combination of uncertainty and hostility. Government "experts" on communism and China were baffled by the appeal of a Marxist-Leninist party to Asian peasants. While sometimes calling the CCP a party of "agrarian reformers," these same experts assumed that all Communist movements were directly or indirectly controlled by the Soviet Union and were therefore puppets of Moscow. These rather harsh judgments eroded only gradually after 1941, as a group of extremely talented U.S. Foreign Service officers in the Chungking embassy reported extensively on Chinese communism, and as the CCP itself made friendly overtures to Americans.

Following the Pearl Harbor attack, many more Americans and much more military aid flowed into China. This presented new dangers and opportunities for the Communists. They hoped to prevent Chiang from using this aid against them and even thought it might be possible to win some for themselves. Fortunately for the Communists, one of their representatives in Chungking (permitted under the United Front agreement) was the urbane and talented Zhou Enlai. Zhou had a special affinity for Americans and charmed almost all those he met. He befriended and entertained foreign journalists, diplomats and soldiers, frequently asking them to his tiny apartment which was continually surrounded by KMT secret police. Many Americans came to look upon Zhou and his staff as selfless heroes buried in the KMT lion's den.

Always a congenial host, Zhou Enlai made a special point of inviting Americans to visit Yenan in either private or official capacities. Obviously, the Communists expected Americans to be pleased with what they found in Yenan—not a surprising assumption given the horrendous conditions in the Nationalist areas. The Communists had much to gain by improving their relationship with Washington. Not least of all, it would raise their image from that of regional rebels to an internationally recognized political movement which was part of the allied war effort.

During 1942 and 1943 some junior American diplomats in Chungking were enthusiastic about accepting Zhou's offer to visit them. John S. Service (a member of the embassy staff and an advisor to Stilwell), for example, feared that both the Communists and Chinese "liberals" would come to hate the U.S. for its exclusive support of Chiang. In desperation or revenge, these groups might turn "toward friendship with Russia." Service and some of his colleagues argued the need to send Americans to Yenan to determine firsthand what these Chinese were really like.

> What is the form of their local government? How "Communistic" is it? Does it show any Democratic character or possibilities? Has it won the support of the people? How does it compare with the conditions . . . in Kuomintang China? . . . What is the military and economic strength of the Communists and what is their probable value to the Allied Cause?

Only an American observer team could discover answers to these vital questions, and without answers how could Washington possibly formulate an intelligent policy toward China?

During 1943 and 1944 Service and fellow diplomats John Davies and Raymond Ludden worried that America's alliance to Chiang was not only useless in the present war but might soon involve the U.S. in a conflict with the Chinese Communists. Moreover, American hostility or indfference would probably drive the Chinese Communists into a firm alliance with the Russians. These junior American officials, all of whom had a deep understanding of China, were convinced that nationalism would sweep over all of postwar Asia. Like Roosevelt, they hoped the United States could influence the direction of these movements. But to do so, Davies wrote, the United States must "move with the historical stream rather than fighting it."

These men believed the Communist variety of Chinese nationalism would eventually triumph in China, whether the U.S. liked it or not. It would be folly to support Chiang and oppose the Communists simply because of their revolutionary domestic policy. The U.S. could not prevent Chiang's defeat and would

certainly embitter the Communists against America if it tried
to do so. An alternative might be to step back from the Kuomintang and initiate political contacts with the Communists. Then,
even if the Communists won the expected civil war, they might
not bear resentment against America nor necessarily side with
the Soviet Union, America's potential rival for future influence
in Asia.

General Stilwell and members of the Office of Strategic Services (the OSS was the World War II predecessor of the CIA)
had a separate but parallel reason for interest in cooperation
with the Communists. After experiencing only frustration from
the Nationalists, they were excited by the prospect of joining
with the dynamic Communist guerrilla forces in warfare against
the Japanese. Stilwell felt he had to judge China's political parties by what he saw. In the KMT he observed "corruption, ne-
glect, chaos . . . trading with the enemy" and a "terrible waste"
and "callous disregard for all the rights of men." The Communists "reduced taxes, rents and interest" and "practiced what
they preached." But not until the summer of 1944 could anyone
convince the President to approve contacts with Yenan.

Just as the near defeat of China by Japan in 1938 first prompted
President Roosevelt to aid Chiang's regime, the renewed offensive of 1944 now pushed Roosevelt toward the Communists. As
the KMT armies in east China crumbled (among other problems, Chiang cut off their supplies because he questioned the
loyalty of the commanders!), Roosevelt had to wonder whether
the Nationalists really could become a "Great Power" in postwar Asia. Prudently, FDR considered alternative ways to preserve a vestige of stability. One idea was to bring the Communists into the regime as a "junior partner" while limiting Russian
involvement in China. Moscow, FDR believed, could be brought
along by granting the Soviets special privileges in Manchuria.
Though imposing these policies contradicted his public rhetoric
about treating China as a "Great Power," they promised to preserve at least a modicum of noncommunist power in China. As
early as the Teheran Conference of November 1943, Stalin and
Roosevelt discussed exchanging railroad and port privileges in
Manchuria for Soviet support of Chiang. The Yalta agreements
of February 1945 eventually confirmed the deal.

In pursuit of better relations with the Chinese Communists, two groups of Americans breached the KMT blockade of Yenan during the summer of 1944. A group of journalists arrived first. After three years of witnessing the squalid conditions of "free" China, these Americans found Yenan a remarkable improvement over Chungking. Their articles reflected strong approval of what they saw. Virtually all felt the people were "better fed, huskier and more energetic than in other parts of China." The local government actually helped the peasants, it did not simply tax them. Brooks Atkinson, the *New York Times* correspondent, believed the soldiers of the Communists' 8th Route Army were "among the best clothed and best fed this writer has seen anywhere in China." Another reporter commented that an Allied Commander "would be proud to command these tough, well-fed, hardened troops." In the words of one journalist, Yenan was a "Wonderland City." When we remember that the Communists accomplished this with no foreign aid and in one of the poorest parts of China, the achievement is all the more remarkable. Unfortunately, KMT press censors were so frightened by these reports that they rewrote the copy before it reached the United States. Having learned a lesson, the Nationalists refused to allow any more reporters through the blockade.

The first *official* American observers entered Communist territory late in July 1944, following Roosevelt's unsuccessful attempt to pressure Chiang to reform. Calling themselves the "Dixie Mission" because they were in "rebel territory," this group included about two dozen technical personnel, political analysts and guerrilla warfare experts. Their presence enabled American officials to obtain firsthand knowledge about the Communists and permitted the Communists a chance to question and influence the Americans.

The Dixie Mission quickly took on a life of its own. Diplomat John Service's first dispatch said it all. "We have come into a different country and are meeting a different people." The Communists were similarly excited by the mission. They obviously hoped it would allow them to leap over Chiang's military blockade and secure some form of U.S. political recognition and military aid.

Between July and November 1944 the Communists treated

the Americans in Yenan as valued friends. The top CCP leaders hobnobbed with junior American diplomats and soldiers. Mao Zedong, in particular, questioned Service about American policy and attitudes. According to Mao, the U.S. had nothing to fear from the Communists. "Even the most conservative American businessman can find nothing in our program" to object to, he claimed. During detailed conversations, Mao admitted how vulnerable the Communists were to American policy:

> America does not need to fear we will not cooperate. We must cooperate and we must have American help. This is why it is important to us Communists to know what you Americans are thinking and planning. We cannot risk crossing you—cannot risk conflict with you.

In many conversations during the last few months of 1944 the Communist leaders referred to their own tenuous position vis-à-vis the KMT, the United States and the Soviet Union. While fighting both Japan and the Nationalists, the Communists were also absorbed in developing their strategy for agrarian revolution. Mao's ongoing purge of CCP members with a background of Soviet training confirmed the uneasy relationship between Moscow and Yenan. For the short term, at least, improved relations with the United States seemed vital if the Communists were to face a civil war with no promise of Russian assistance. No one who met Mao could doubt the sincerity of his nationalism nor his determination to make China a "Great Power." Yet this new China could still be a stable nation, a major trading partner and an important counterweight to possible Soviet expansion in Asia. The Communists did not deny their commitment to a Chinese revolution. But they did constantly assert the belief that a Communist China need not threaten American interests.

With their belief that Yenan and Washington had certain parallel interests in China, the Communists steadfastly pursued American favor from the autumn of 1944 through the following summer. Determined to resist both the Japanese and Kuomintang, they maintained hope of receiving military and political assistance from the United States. Under the right circumstances, they declared, they would even be willing to form a temporary coalition with the Nationalists. In the long run, neither the Communists nor the Americans could guess how cooperation might affect their two countries. But in late 1944 it certainly seemed that a radical change from the hostility and indifference of the past could not make matters worse.

As these political discussions took place, several OSS officers in Yenan began to offer the Communists basic instruction in the use of some donated American weapons. These individual acts convinced the Communists that U.S. policy was really beginning to turn around, about to rid itself of dependence on Chiang and consider cooperation with Yenan. By September 1944, reports of General Stilwell's plans to send military aid to the Communists further bolstered this belief.

This cooperation never came to pass. At that very moment Chiang Kai-shek and Patrick J. Hurley, Roosevelt's special emissary to China, were conspiring to convince FDR to fire Stilwell and maintain a policy of aid to the Kuomintang exclusively. Henceforth, both Hurley and the President sought to contain the crisis in China by pressuring the Communists into accepting a minor role in a KMT-dominated government. Simultaneously they cut Yenan off from any support from either sympathetic Americans or the Soviet Union.

This drama was first played out by Hurley soon after Stilwell's recall in October 1944. On November 7, 1944, without any prior announcement, Hurley flew to Yenan. As he stepped off the American plane to be met by the American commander of the Dixie Mission and Zhou Enlai, the CCP leader was shocked to learn that this unexpected visitor was Roosevelt's emissary. "Keep him here until I can find Chairman Mao," Zhou said, and he dashed off to town.

Hurley (who privately referred to CCP leaders Mao Zedong and Zhou Enlai as "Moose Dung and Joe N. Lie") shocked everyone by uttering a bloodcurdling Choctaw Indian war cry as he deplaned. It proved only the first of many bizarre outbursts. Not surprisingly, the Communists soon referred to Hurley as "the Clown." At first the Communists and Hurley got on unexpectedly well. He pleased Mao by promising that if the CCP leader went to Chungking for peace talks, the U.S. would guarantee a generous compromise settlement with the KMT. Politi-

cal power and U.S. aid would be shared. The Communists would
be recognized as a part of a new coalition government. After
Mao and Hurley signed a "Five Point" draft agreement to this
effect, Zhou Enlai accompanied Hurley back to Chungking in
mid-November.

What happened next proved a rude awakening for the Communists. Initially it seemed that Hurley might fulfill the hopes
raised in Yenan by the presence of the Dixie Mission. Instead,
when Zhou met with Chiang Kai-shek he was handed a note demanding that the Communists dissolve their independent armies
and accept some token political appointments to the KMT government. No one familiar with the previous twenty years could
doubt that surrender of their troops would mean mass suicide
for the Communists. Negotiations ended abruptly on November
21, 1944, and shortly thereafter an embittered Zhou Enlai returned to Yenan. The Communists realized that Hurley had lied
to them, for now he too demanded that the Communists forget
the earlier compromise draft agreement and accept Chiang's
suicide proposal.

Hurley responded to this breakdown of negotiations by attacking those Americans who had been sympathetic to Yenan.
If the Communists' American friends were forced out of China,
he reasoned, the CCP would have no hope of relying on foreign
support. They would be forced to accept Chiang's—and Hurley's—terms. Realizing what Hurley intended, and hopeful that
the President might countermand his actions, Mao and Zhou
undertook a daring maneuver: a secret approach to FDR which
would circumvent Hurley's influence.

On January 9, 1945, the Communists asked that members of
the Dixie Mission forward a secret cable to Roosevelt. Mao and
Zhou offered to travel to Washington to meet the President and
make a personal appeal for American support. Clearly, the Communists still believed that at the highest levels American policy
remained flexible, that they could still cooperate with the United
States, both against Japan and in the search for a political compromise.

Nothing worked the way Mao and Zhou hoped. Hurley quickly
learned of the "secret" message and warned FDR against dealing with the CCP. The Communists, he declared, were responsi-

ble for all China's problems and were refusing to reach a fair settlement with the KMT because disloyal Americans had joined them in a "conspiracy" against Chiang and Roosevelt. Hurley's message to FDR gave birth to the charge that American "spies" or "traitors" were somehow in league with the Chinese Communists working to oppose U.S. interests.

Roosevelt, who was already preoccupied with political and military problems surrounding the imminent end of the war in Europe, declined to reevaluate his own or Hurley's actions. Instead, FDR backed Hurley and authorized the removal from China of any American whom the egotistical ambassador considered "disloyal." Hurley defined disloyalty as any questioning of Chiang's wisdom or virtue, or any willingness to support Yenan. Over the next several months Hurley made members of his staff swear their loyalty to his own policy and even threatened to shoot one junior diplomat who had the courage to criticize Chiang. Those who did not toe the ambassador's line were sent home or as some put it, "Hurleyed out of China."

The President's New Policy: Yalta

By February 1945 Roosevelt must have begun to realize that his dream of fathering a "powerful, united and pro-American China" was fast becoming a nightmare. At best, China might be held together in a tenuous KMT-CCP alliance. But civil war appeared likely and this raised the prospect of prolonged instability in the Far East, creating a vacuum which might entice Soviet penetration. To increase the chance of maintaining a Kuomintang-dominated China, Roosevelt finally sought the active cooperation of the Soviet dictator, Joseph Stalin. (By then Stalin, too, had added "Generalissimo" to his impressive string of titles.)

Ever since he emerged as the ruler of the Soviet Union in the late 1920s, Stalin had revealed a curious attitude toward foreign, and especially Chinese, Communists. Beneath the public facade of Russian support for all revolutionary movements was the reality of Stalin's cautious attitude in foreign affairs. The Russian leader assisted Communist movements when they were under his personal control or served what he believed were the best interests of the Soviet Union (for Stalin these were often the same). Stalin followed a very ambivalent policy toward Chinese communism. He realized that although Mao and his followers had built a popular, strongly nationalistic revolutionary movement, they did not accept the Soviet Union as their master or model. The prospect of a powerful, independent Communist China bordering Russia was not necessarily a pleasant vision for the security-conscious Soviet leader. In fact, during the late 1930s, as in the 1920s, Stalin had given substantial military aid to the KMT as the Chinese group best able to resist Japanese expansion. In many ways, the maintenance of a KMT regime with loose or partial control over China would pose less of a potential challenge to the Soviet Union than would a powerful Communist neighbor. American observers in Yenan in 1944–45 carefully noted that only a handful of Russians resided in the Communist capital and they were not on close terms with the CCP leaders.

In February 1945 the leaders of Great Britain, the United States and the Soviet Union conferred at Yalta, in the Soviet Crimea, to arrange the future of liberated Europe. Complicated discussions concerning what type of political order should be established in Eastern Europe and Germany frustrated Roosevelt, Stalin and Churchill. FDR saw little alternative to conceding control of Eastern Europe to the Soviets. But, the President seemed to believe, he could trade this concession for Stalin's commitment to a stable world order.

In their discussion of the Far East and Russian entry into the war against Japan (something very much desired by the Americans) Stalin told Roosevelt he would support Chiang's regime and ignore the Chinese Communists. He did, however, insist that the Soviet Union acquire special rights to share control of the major railroads and ports of Manchuria. Believing this was a relatively small price to pay to keep the Soviets out of China, Roosevelt agreed to press Chiang to concede what Stalin demanded in Manchuria. Although many later observers bitterly criticized the President for the Yalta agreements, FDR gave up virtually nothing that the Russians would not have acquired anyway. Russian troops would certainly enter Manchuria after

Germany's defeat and it seemed prudent to set limits on the scope of Soviet expansion. Moreover, a Nationalist China minus parts of Manchuria seemed a far better deal than conceding nothing and risking Soviet intervention on behalf of the CCP.

Roosevelt's revised policy of supporting Chiang and securing a Soviet promise to do the same might have succeeded if the Chinese Communists had not been the independent group they claimed to be. Mao and his followers would not give up their struggle simply because they had been denied American and Soviet support. They might still be willing to share power with Chiang, but they would certainly not surrender their own armies and enter a coalition as a powerless member as Roosevelt and Stalin suggested. Also, the American failure to restrain the KMT convinced Chiang he could be more recalcitrant and uncompromising than ever. After all, he now appeared to enjoy *both* American and Soviet backing! Although Roosevelt still spoke in favor of a compromise in China, so long as U.S. aid flowed only to the KMT, and Ambassador Hurley and General Wedemeyer openly supported Chiang, no *real* compromise was possible.

By the spring of 1945 the Communists had lost almost all hope of influencing American policy. In March John Service rejoined the Dixie Mission's fast diminishing ranks and heard Mao plead for a reversal of Washington's course. The Communist leader lamented that ever since December 1944 American policy had veered away from compromise. Hurley's hostile actions would ensure that "all that America has been working for will be lost." Mao emphasized the great significance of American aid and pointedly declared: "There is no such thing as America not intervening in China! You are here as China's greatest ally. The fact of your presence is tremendous."

Service and most other Americans in China pleaded with their superiors to reconsider their course and rebuke Hurley. On February 28 (while the unpopular ambassador was en route to Washington) they sent a joint telegram to the State Department warning that current policy would encourage civil war and drag the U.S. in as a KMT ally. The embassy staff hoped to "point out the advantage of having the Communists helped by the United States rather than seeking Russian aid or intervention, direct or indirect." Solomon Adler, a Treasury Department official serving in China, spoke even more directly. America's future in China, he wrote, "should not be left in the hands of a bungler like Hurley."

These warnings, however graphic, were outweighed by the arguments presented by Hurley and Wedemeyer during their visit to Washington in March 1945. The two senior American officials in China denied every criticism of their support for Chiang. They described the Communists as a weak, unpopular and hostile group responsible for China's turmoil. Chiang, they claimed, could easily "put down the communist rebellion" and control all China if only the U.S. would give him more support. Weary and only a few weeks away from his death, President Roosevelt declined to rebuke Hurley and in fact effusively praised his behavior of the past few months. The formal confirmation of the anticommunist policy came on April 2, 1945, when Hurley emerged from a meeting with the President in Washington and in a public news conference denounced the CCP as largely responsible for blocking peace in China. By implication, even Roosevelt had now abandoned an evenhanded policy.

American-Communist Hostility, June to August 1945

The Chinese Communists reacted to these events by lambasting Hurley and other anonymous American "reactionaries" who, they said, plotted civil war in China. When Mao addressed the CCP Congress in Yenan in April 1945 he warned that the Americans and the KMT were jointly planning to attack the Communists in the wake of Japan's defeat. Communist fear accelerated in June when word came from Washington that John Service, the Foreign Service officer, had been arrested on espionage charges for passing classified documents to *Amerasia* magazine. The arrest of the American most trusted by the CCP was interpreted as proof of a growing anticommunist plot in Washington. (Although Service was eventually acquitted of all charges, the complex case left a stain on his reputation and eventually was used by pro-KMT forces in Congress to hound him out of the State Department.) Yenan's reaction to the incident appeared in radio and press messages beamed to America: If the American imperialists did not "withdraw their hands . . . then the Chinese people will teach them a lesson they deserve." These denunciations of American policy grew in intensity as the war in the Pacific drew to a close.

Hurley's actions in China and the growing anticommunist attitude in Washington were part of a general trend in American policy during the late spring of 1945. Roosevelt's death in mid-April accelerated the deterioration of the Grand Alliance. While the U.S. and Soviet Union would certainly have experienced major tensions and disagreements even had FDR lived, his passing removed one of the few American leaders determined to try to get along with the Soviets.

Harry S. Truman assumed the presidency with remarkably little preparation and virtually no understanding of international relations. He knew nothing about the development of the atomic bomb nor did he know very much about the complicated diplomatic arrangements worked out between FDR and Stalin. Understandably, this insecure and inexperienced leader relied upon people he presumed to be the experts. Roosevelt's leading advisors on foreign policy were generally far more hostile to the Soviet Union than the President himself had been. They interpreted Russian demands for security and retribution against Germany, as well as Stalin's insistence on the creation of pro-Soviet regimes in Eastern Europe, as preludes to global communist expansion. Only a tough, assertive policy, they argued, could limit Stalin's grasp.

Turning their gaze toward Asia, they saw Soviet interest in Manchuria and the rise of Chinese Communist power as a copy of the situation in Europe. Most American officials neither understood nor believed that Communist strength in China was the product of local conditions. Influential spokesmen on foreign affairs, such as the future Secretary of State John Foster Dulles, argued vehemently in favor of sustaining the Nationalists. The essence of U.S. policy, he told an audience in early 1945, was a "determination that the 400,000,000 of China shall not become harnessed to the predatory design of an alien power." Chiang had chosen to "rely on the ultimate support of the Christian democracies, notably the United States." To desert him would be akin to sin.

One of the most articulate and influential of the circle of advisors around the new President was Averell Harriman, then ambassador to the Soviet Union. In discussions with the conservative Secretary of the Navy James Forrestal, Harriman identified China as one of several flash points where international communism had resolved to challenge the United States. If the United States wavered in its duty to support Chiang, he warned, "we should have to face ultimately the fact that two or three hundred millions of people would march when the Kremlin ordered." Harriman's vivid imagery confirmed that the highest circle of American leaders had come to view the Chinese Communists as Russian agents totally hostile to the United States. It was not hard to convert this illusion into a self-fulfilling prophecy.

By July 1945 the entire orientation of U.S. foreign policy had taken on an anti-Soviet and antirevolutionary posture. American leaders no longer saw the Soviet Union as a loyal ally against Germany and a future ally against Japan. Instead, the Russians had become the new threat to world peace, a totalitarian and fanatical nation plotting the conquest of Western Europe and Asia.

The Potsdam Conference, held in conquered Berlin late in July 1945, revealed how far apart the Russians and Americans had grown. Each side accused the other of breaking wartime promises on the division of Germany, the payment of reparations and the political future of Eastern Europe. However, since Russian military help against Japan still seemed necessary, Truman's advisors counseled the President against a total break with Stalin.

Then, in the midst of the Potsdam meeting, American scientists successfully detonated the atomic bomb in New Mexico. This new weapon yielded immediate military and political results. Japan might now be defeated quickly, without Russian assistance. Furthermore, if Russia were kept out of the war, it would probably limit Soviet penetration of Manchuria, where millions of Japanese troops remained. As Truman's new Secre-

tary of State James F. Byrnes put it, the atomic bomb might get
Japan to "surrender before Russia goes into the war and this
will save China. If Russia goes into the war . . . Stalin will take
over and China will suffer." Thus, by the end of July 1945,
American leaders hoped to end the Pacific War quickly, perhaps
even before the Russians could enter China and assist the Chinese Communists. As Truman told a group of naval officers in
July, with the atomic bomb "we did not need the Russians or
any other nation."

Despite these overwhelming American fears, Stalin appeared
to have no grandiose scheme in China. While the Russians
hoped to dominate parts of Manchuria and seize Japanese-built
industry there, they seemed unprepared to assist the rise of the
Chinese Communists. Stalin pushed for concessions from Chiang
which would have benefited Russia more than FDR had hoped.
But these benefits would not help the CCP. On August 14, hours
before Japan's surrender, Stalin and T. V. Soong reached an
agreement on a Sino-Soviet treaty to implement the Yalta accords. In exchange for receiving special railroad and port privileges in Manchuria, the Soviets pledged their "moral, material,
and military support to China and solely to the Chinese National Government" led by Chiang. When word of this treaty
reached Yenan, the Communists seemed stunned and despondent, American observers noted. Stalin, like the American leaders, appeared to favor a weak KMT regime to the uncertainties
of a Communist China or one wracked by civil war.

The Japanese Surrender and American Intervention, August to November 1945

The Japanese surrender of August 14, 1945, following the use of
two atomic bombs and a Soviet assault on Manchuria, brought
peace to America and a bloody four-year civil war to China.
The smoldering hostility, only partially restrained by the United
Front since 1937, burst again into flames. A crucial element of
both Communist and Nationalist strategy was to seize quickly
the huge amount of territory and weapons held by the more

than three million Japanese and puppet troops in China. Whichever side acquired these resources would have a major military advantage, a fact which Washington thoroughly understood.

Immediately upon Japan's surrender, President Truman issued "General Order #1," a command that all Japanese and puppet forces in China surrender their positions and arms only to Chiang Kai-shek or his representatives. Truman, by this decision put American support even more directly behind the KMT. Though the Communist leaders denounced this as a betrayal of their wartime role against Japan and declared their intention of ignoring General Order #1, Washington brushed aside all protests.

To assist unreliable or scarce KMT troops, almost 60,000 American Marines were rushed from the Pacific to be redeployed along vital rail lines, ports and airfields in north China. In addition, the American navy and air forces ferried hundreds of thousands of KMT soldiers from south to north China. All of this intervention was justified by the claim that American forces were helping to disarm and repatriate the surrendered Japanese. In fact, both American and KMT forces cooperated with the "surrendered" Japanese in resisting Communist efforts to seize cities and lines of communication. The enemy army of only weeks before was now a valued ally! One disgruntled Marine complained of this in a letter to a Senator:

> We were told when en route to [north China] that we were to assist in the disarming of Japanese troops in this area. Before we arrived, the Chinese had the situation well in hand, and have since gone so far as to re-arm some Japanese units for added protection against Chinese Communist forces. Recently we have been told that the reason for our prolonged visit is to hold the area in lieu of the arrival of General Chiang Kai-shek's Nationalist forces. In other words we are here to protect General Chiang's interests against possible Communist uprisings. Everything we do here points directly or indirectly toward keeping the Chinese Communists subdued.

In addition to the Marines and transportation provided to the KMT armies, the level of U.S. military Lend-Lease to the Nationalist regime actually increased in the six months following Japan's surrender. More aid arrived after the war was over—

several billion dollars' worth—than had been given to Chiang for use against Japan.*

In light of this massive American aid to Chiang and the Soviet Unions' general indifference, Yenan faced a difficult choice. An immediate civil war favored the KMT. It seemed advantageous to postpone battle until the Communists could mobilize and expand their forces. Since the Americans still argued that the Communists should join the KMT in a coalition, in late August Mao agreed to explore again the possibility of a compromise. Whatever his misgivings about the American-KMT alliance, Mao felt that it was crucial to delay full-scale fighting.

The new peace talks in Chungking broke down almost as soon as they began. Chiang, with Hurley's approval, repeated his position that coalition required a virtual Communist surrender—no sharing of power or territorial partition. This "hard line" appealed to Chiang, Hurley and Truman's advisors because the initial developments following Japan's surrender seemed to favor the KMT's military position heavily.

But as fighting spread through north China during the autumn months this optimism began to fade. While KMT forces seized urban centers, Communist guerrilla forces controlled the countryside and began to isolate the Nationalist positions. If America was to help Chiang, it would have to do far more on his behalf than had been anticipated. Washington faced the dilemma of whether to expand the American military effort in China or leave Chiang to his own fate.

While Ambassador Hurley demanded a wider involvement, other American policymakers voiced renewed doubts about his advice and Chiang's competence. From China General Wedemeyer wrote that Chiang had little hope of unifying China without direct American intervention. Truman and his advisors had no sudden fondness for the Chinese Communists. But they were forced to admit that the CCP seemed able to hold its own against all of Chiang's military efforts. The only way they might be defeated was to dispatch a huge American combat force to China, something which the KMT hoped for and almost every-

---

* Soviet forces in Manchuria turned over stockpiles of captured Japanese weapons to Communist troops, though the policy varied and the scope of aid was much smaller than U.S. assistance to the KMT.

one in Washington opposed as reckless. The President, like his foreign policy experts, believed the main problem facing the U.S. was the threat they perceived coming from the Soviet Union in Eastern Europe. This sense sharply affected—as it would through the ensuing decade—American policies and capabilities in China. Reluctantly, by November 1945, the Truman Administration concluded that the deteriorating military situation in China could only be reversed if the United States again sought to mediate a coalition settlement.

The administration's plans were jolted on November 27 when Ambassador Hurley (then in Washington) called a public news conference to announce his resignation. Obviously fearful his own policy would be labeled a failure, Hurley, with his accustomed flamboyance, blamed all China's troubles on the actions of "spies" and "traitors" in the State Department who were linked to the Communists. Although false, these charges eventually took on a life of their own. After 1949, when a scapegoat had to be found to explain the Communist victory in China, the charges of treason were revived against those farsighted diplomats who had warned against supporting Chiang.

The Marshall Mission and the Failure of Mediation

Hoping both to defuse Hurley's slanderous charges and perhaps salvage some American influence in China, President Truman appointed General George C. Marshall to lead a new peace effort. Marshall's mission (December 1945–January 1947) strove to get the KMT and CCP to agree to a cease-fire to be followed by the creation of a coalition government. This basically followed the pattern which Roosevelt had pursued during the war. However, according to the orders sent by the Secretaries of State, War and Navy to General Wedemeyer one day after Hurley's resignation, America would continue to provide "at least indirect support of Chiang Kai-shek's activities against dissident forces in China." Truman and Marshall agreed that if the Communists refused to make "reasonable concessions," the Americans would openly assist Chiang's armies in their movement to the disputed parts of China. The United States could not tolerate "a divided China" or the "resumption of Russian power in Manchuria." To prevent this, Washington "would have to swallow its pride and much of its policy" and continue to assist the KMT, lamented Marshall.

Thus, even in their desire to forestall civil war, American leaders were still reluctant to admit the deeper sources of the Chinese revolution. They had the greatest difficulty in distinguishing social revolution and radical nationalism from Soviet expansion. Truman and Marshall believed that it was necessary to preserve "order" and "stability" in China as a way to block Moscow. They tended to interpret the contending forces as proxies connected to the rivalry between Moscow and Washington. The American goal in China after 1945 became the prevention of revolutionary change linked to global Soviet expansion.

Though they must have been quite wary of its sincerity, the Communists hailed the Marshall Mission as an important "change in American policy." From the Communists' perspective, postponing civil war was clearly preferable to an immediate showdown with the better equipped and larger KMT armies. In December 1945, Zhou Enlai and a Communist delegation returned to Chungking and prepared to begin negotiations with Chiang and Marshall. The tone of the talks, however, was set by what occurred on the airfield as Marshall's plane was about to touch down. KMT police "started to chase the Communist representatives off the field" and the delegates were only rescued by the intervention of American diplomats.

Marshall's initial discussions with the two warring groups disclosed very little room for compromise. The Communists insisted that in any coalition they share real power and maintain their separate army; Chiang declared that the Communists must be disarmed and accept whatever political crumbs he might offer. For his part, within his self-imposed limitations, Marshall strove to be evenhanded. Without promising either side anything, the American mediator arranged for a cease-fire in contested parts of north China and Manchuria. Three-party truce teams were established to enforce the peace. On July 29, 1946,

Marshall placed an embargo on arms shipments to China and hastened the removal of American Marines. Yet, these restraints on the KMT were undercut by the extension of additional aid to Chiang. For example, huge stocks of American military equipment in China and the Pacific area were transferred to the Nationalists as "government surplus." U.S. assistance to Chiang between 1945 and 1949 totaled about $3 billion.

Marshall did achieve at least one notable success—arranging for the mutual withdrawal of American and Soviet forces in north and northeast China. In effect, both Moscow and Washington preferred to avoid a direct superpower confrontation in what remained, essentially, a region of secondary importance. If they chose the path of civil war, neither Mao nor Chiang could count on intervention by their patrons.

Despite this fact, the two factions each came to favor a military solution. By late 1946 the cease-fire fell apart. Despite Marshall's attempt to restrain him, Chiang remained convinced that in any showdown Washington would save his regime from defeat. The Communists, who viewed with growing alarm American hostility toward the Soviet Union and revolutionary movements worldwide, lost faith in Marshall's impartiality or ability to control Chiang. So long as the United States did not intervene directly, Communist leaders decided to pursue a military victory.

In January 1947, as civil war flared across China, Truman called his mediator home to assume the position of Secretary of State. Marshall departed with a verbal blast at both the KMT and CCP. The end of the mediation mission coincided with a major reassessment of foreign policy. The Truman Administration acknowledged that America had no practical solution for China's internal problems. Nor, officials realized, would the outcome of the civil war affect, in any fundamental way, U.S. security. Instead, Washington policymakers refocused their attention on the need to reconstruct the economies of Western Europe, Germany and occupied Japan. By revitalizing these industrial societies, America could assure its dominance over the Soviet Union. To put it bluntly, China was too weak, backward and irrelevant to justify a further commitment of American resources.

Civil War to Liberation

Almost three years passed between Marshall's departure and the creation of the Communist People's Republic of China. Initially Chiang's American-equipped armies seemed far superior to the guerrillas and peasant militia which the Communists had organized during the War of Resistance. But in truth, as one American general put it, the KMT troops suffered from "the world's worst leadership." They were routed from positions which they might have "defended with broomsticks" if they had the will. Not just military tactics but morale and politics dictated the outcome of the civil war. A French military expert concluded that, as much as anything else, the maladministration and corruption of the KMT civil administration destroyed civilian morale which directly affected the quality of the Nationalist armies.

> The Nationalist soldier . . . was generally considered to be the scum of humanity. Except in several elite divisions, such a conception could not be changed and morale remained low despite promised reforms. . . . The soldier of Chiang Kai-shek knew not why he fought. Against the Japanese he could fight for his country and his people; but in this civil war a peasant soldier from Kwangtung had no idea why he should be fighting in Shansi and Manchuria. Poorly fed, poorly paid, poorly clothed, poorly cared for, poorly armed, often short of ammunition—even at decisive moments—unsustained by any faith in a cause, the Nationalist soldier was easy prey for the clever and impassioned propaganda of the Communists.

The Kuomintang not only squandered its military advantage but managed to alienate almost all segments of Chinese society in the years 1945–49. During the reoccupation of China from the Japanese, KMT civil and military officers indulged themselves in an orgy of personal aggrandizement. They seized for personal use public property and land, connived with collaborators, ignored the most fundamental economic problems and disregarded public sentiment calling for a compromise with the CCP which would stop the bloodshed of the civil war. In the countryside the KMT again relied on the landlord class as its agents, further alienating the peasants.

The more selfish and blundering the KMT became, the more flexible and popular the Communist program seemed to become. During the civil war the CCP continued to press two great battles at once: the first against the KMT, the second against the social structure of the Chinese village. As they had begun to do behind Japanese lines, Communist organizers infiltrated villages and aroused the fury of the poor peasant against the rich, the debtor against the usurer, the exploited against the exploiter. This campaign of land and social reform not only created a mass base of rural support for the Communists but served as their recruiting headquarters for new troops. By 1948, in Manchuria and on the north China plain, the military initiative passed to the revolutionary armies. Nationalist garrisons, deserted and isolated, began to fade away and surrender.

As the civil war dragged on, China became an increasingly partisan topic in American politics. In 1947 the Truman Administration came under attack for its supposed "softness" on communism. A group of Republican Senators and Congressmen criticized Truman for having first sponsored the idea of including the Communists in a coalition government and then, after Marshall's departure, for not doing enough to help Chiang defeat the Communists. At the same time many of the most qualified China specialists in the State Department were accused of disloyalty. The same men who had correctly warned of Chiang's weakness and the Communists' strength were now blamed for causing the disaster overtaking the KMT. Here was another example of punishing the messenger who brought the bad news. The charges of disloyalty and subversion, initiated by Ambassador Hurley upon his resignation, were perpetuated by the "China Lobby," an assortment of individuals and groups rumored to be financed by the KMT.

The Truman Administration was forced on the defensive over China partly because it had succeeded so well in selling the doctrine of "containment" to the public. Between 1947 and 1949 Truman sponsored the Truman Doctrine, the Marshall Plan and the NATO military alliance, all designed to shore up Europe against Communist encroachment by extending military and economic assistance. Chiang's supporters in both parties and among the public wondered why the possible triumph of Chinese communism was not resisted as vociferously as the "threat" in Europe. The Truman Administration never directly answered this question, leaving its critics free to snipe and ridicule with impunity.

The make-believe world in which Chiang's American allies resided was demonstrated by their complete misunderstanding of Chinese politics. In May 1947, *Time* ran a cover story featuring Ch'en Li-fu, one of Chiang's most notoriously reactionary aides. According to *Time* Ch'en was a virtual reincarnation of the sage Confucius, struggling to build a new China within the Confucianist framework. Ambitious Congressmen, Senators and journalists discovered that "China" was a hot political issue. Since few people knew much about the real conditions there, almost anyone could claim to be a "China expert." The Republican Party, longing for an issue on which to attack the Democrats who had been in power since 1933, perfected the art of baiting the administration on China.

Many of the most ardent defenders of Chiang in Congress were demagogues who simply exploited the issue. Senators William F. Knowland, Styles Bridges, Owen Brewster, Pat McCarran and Kenneth Wherry, often dubbed as "the Senators from Formosa," fell into this category. Others, like Senator H. Alexander Smith and Congressman Walter Judd (a former medical missionary in China) believed that Chiang was specially ordained to do God's work in heathen Asia. Richard Nixon, then an ambitious Congressman from California, simply saw political advantage in attacking the administration.

A profound ignorance characterized most of the so-called Congressional China Bloc. For example, Senator Wherry explained America's mission this way: "With God's help," he declared, the United States could "lift up Shanghai up and up, ever up, until it looks just like Kansas City." Senator Pat McCarran, at one point, offered a proposal to give Chiang several hundred million silver dollars. The State Department objected, arguing that the Nationalist government needed food and raw materials to supply its hard-pressed troops and suffering population. McCarran, it developed, cared less about the impact on

China than on Nevada. All the silver for the dollars was to be mined in his home state. He quickly lost interest in China aid once supplies were substituted for local coinage.

Even more thoughtful and talented members of Congress saw partisan advantage in baiting the administration. In 1949 Congressman John F. Kennedy delivered a blistering attack against Democratic officials who had abandoned China to communism. He charged Truman and his entourage with deserting China "whose freedom we once fought to preserve. What our young men had saved, our diplomats and President have frittered away." A high-level group of disloyal and incompetent officials, Kennedy suggested, bore responsibility for the "loss of China."

Chiang's influential friend, Henry Luce, turned *Life* magazine into a virtual advertisement for the Kuomintang. In October 1947, shortly after the administration's critics charged that a high-level report by General Albert Wedemeyer, supposedly urging more military aid for China, had been suppressed (in fact, the report combined a call for more assistance with a sharp critique of the KMT), *Life* carried a sensationalist article by former ambassador to Russia, Roosevelt crony and gadfly, William Bullitt. Having changed from a liberal Democrat to an extreme conservative, Bullitt insisted the only important foreign policy issue was keeping China "out of the hands of Stalin." It could "certainly" be done, he asserted, "and at a cost to ourselves which would be small compared to the magnitude of our vital interests in the independence of China."

Like most of those calling for intervention, Bullitt never explained why America had a large stake in saving Chiang. Any anticommunist leader and noncommunist country, he implied, was vital to American security. Bullitt now charged Roosevelt with betraying China at Yalta through some sort of conspiracy. To make amends and save Asia, Washington must now commit itself fully to the rescue of the Nationalists.

He proposed that over the next three years the United States spend more than a billion dollars in China, send military and civilian advisors to supervise reform, and assign General Douglas MacArthur (Occupation Commander in Japan, the Republican's favorite general and a likely presidential candidate in 1948) as "Personal Representative of the President" in China.

MacArthur must have full power to "prevent subjugation of China by the Soviet Union." Solemnly, Bullit warned:

> If China falls into the hands of Stalin, all Asia, including Japan, sooner or later will fall into his hands. The manpower and resources of Asia will be mobilized against us. The independence of the U.S. will not live a generation longer than the independence of China.

Life magazine, it appeared, would rush in where American troops feared to tread. In July 1949 it ran a story on General Claire Chennault's efforts to convince Congress and the State Department to revive the "Flying Tigers" as a "volunteer" combat air force to save Chiang. This "Last Call for China" proposed using the mercenary air force to hold a zone in south China. This "fighting American" assured *Life*'s readers that "a third of the Good Earth and 150,000,000 people can be saved." In October, *Reader's Digest* printed another version of Chennault's plan and gave it the graphic title, "Hold 'Em! Harrass 'Em! Hamstring 'Em!" Although the government rejected this idea for technical reasons, a few months later the Central Intelligence Agency secretly bought a controlling interest in Chennault's airline. Civil Air Transport (CAT, later Air America) soon became a covert arm of American military and intelligence operations in Asia.

In spite of many hysterical and partisan demands by Chiang's American allies, the Truman Administration resisted any major, headlong plunge into the vortex of China's civil war. However great their desire to contain communism, few knowledgeable officials thought the United States could—or should—save the Kuomintang regime. Truman remarked that the Chiangs, Kungs and Soongs "were all thieves, every last one of them." Senator Arthur Vandenberg, a leading Senate Republican, privately admitted in 1948 that despite his impulse to aid the Nationalists, "there are limits to our resources and boundaries to our miracles." In China, he later remarked, "we are facing the conundrum of the ages." Democratic leader Senator Tom Connally spoke more directly: any more aid to Chiang would be "money down a rat hole." Squandering resources in a marginal country, in a lost battle seemed idiotic. Most Americans who knew anything about China—academics, business leaders, missionaries—also counseled restraint. They had lost all confidence in the Nationalist regime and felt that any successor government, even a Communist one, would be preferable to continued civil war.

The Truman Administration pushed Congress to build up an anticommunist barrier in Europe where America could rely on reasonably competent and powerful allies. Nevertheless, many of Chiang's diehard supporters, especially among Republican legislators, threatened to oppose the European Recovery Program, or Marshall Plan, unless some aid were allocated to China. In the end, they extorted a small "China Aid Act" of 1948, which appropriated some $125 million for use "at the discretion of the Chinese Government." Even this gesture proved futile, as Communist armies overran much of the mainland before most of the aid could be delivered.

Truman's decision largely to sit out the final round of China's civil war reflected the judgment of an influential group of State Department advisors. Dean Acheson (who became Secretary of State early in 1949, upon Marshall's retirement), Policy Planning Staff Director George Kennan, John Carter Vincent and W. Walton Butterworth (heads of the Bureau of Far Eastern Affairs between 1948 and 1950) all urged the President to minimize American involvement. United States interest in Asia, they argued, had to be separated from the dying Nationalist regime. While distrustful of both Russia and the Chinese Communists, they doubted that anything short of massive, direct intervention could save Chiang. Not only were American interests insufficient to justify such a policy but any increased aid to the KMT would poison the chance for possible future relations with the triumphant Communists.

These policymakers retained an interest in halting Asian communism, but recommended "drawing the line" outside China. Thus, in 1948–49 they argued successfully for rehabilitating Japan as a pro-American bulwark and initiated the process of providing aid to the French anticommunist war in Indochina. Acheson described the new approach as standing back and "waiting for the dust to settle" in China.

George Kennan typified the group's thinking. To him, China remained a poor, backward nation of little immediate importance in the cold war. Even if China became a Soviet satellite, as a "vast poorhouse," it would tie down the Soviets, not enhance their power. Arguing that "nationalistic" elements within the Chinese Communist movement might eventually split from the Soviet bloc, Kennan and his colleagues thought it vital not to adopt hostile policies which would drive Mao closer to Stalin. Between 1948 and early 1950, this group urged Truman to remain tactically flexible while avoiding any commitment to Chiang. When, in 1949, the KMT government and army fled to Taiwan, Acheson, Kennan and Butterworth convinced the President to retain nominal recognition of the Nationalists while leaving the door open to possible relations with the emerging Communist government in Beijing. During 1949–50, Truman agreed to permit private trade with China, declined to authorize any substantial aid to anticommunist guerrillas still active on the mainland and refused to commit the United States to defending Taiwan from a Communist invasion.

All theories aside, battlefield realities by the end of 1948 confirmed the demise of Chiang's hold on China. The Communists already controlled more than half the country, the economy had all but collapsed and Nationalist troops were defecting to the Reds en masse. Officially, the Truman Administration declined to make any moves which might "deliver the knock-out blow to the Nationalist government." As some officials put it, it was better to keep the "facts from the American people and thereby not be accused later of playing into the hands of the Communists." Privately, however, Acheson told influential members of Congress that Chiang had been doomed by his own mistakes, not Soviet subversion.

In August 1949, the administration decided to take its case to the public by releasing a massive "China White Paper," a review of Sino-American relations during the previous decade. Intended to clear the air by demonstrating the tawdry record of KMT decadence, incompetence and corruption, the document concluded that Washington had done all that was possible but that Chiang had brought defeat on himself.

Hoping to appease Republican critics and counter any claim that the administration was "soft on communism" or had "stabbed Chiang in the back," Dean Acheson appended to the lengthy report a "Cover Letter" which contradicted many of the report's conclusions. The letter described the Chinese Communists as abominable villains who had "foresworn their Chinese heritage and have publicly announced their subservience to a foreign power, Russia. . . ." Administration critics had charged this all along.

To be sure, Mao had, in June 1949, declared that China would henceforth "lean to one side," supporting the forces of "socialism" against those of "imperialism." Reacting to the White Paper's Cover Letter, he published several essays denouncing American policy as a fraud. A few months later, in February 1950, Mao traveled to Moscow where he and Stalin signed a Friendship Treaty pledging mutual support and military aid. These and other actions by the new Chinese government (such as the temporary arrest and roughing up of American consular officials) convinced many Americans of the Communists' unremitting hostility. Communist denunciations of the United States (in part reflecting the nationalist and anti-imperialist fervor of the Chinese people, and in part designed to win support from the Soviet Union) seemed to confirm the arguments offered by American hardliners. All hope of an imminent Sino-Soviet split or of Mao emerging as a new "Tito" (the Yugoslavian Communist leader who broke with Stalin in 1948) appeared dashed.

However, beneath the surface, Communist leaders tried to hedge their bets. During 1949 Zhou Enlai and other Communist officials had made several quiet approaches to American diplomats remaining in China, suggesting that informal negotiations might lead to some improvement in relations. Mao, it seems clear, did not want China to become solely dependent on the Soviet Union or locked in confrontation with the United States. At the same time, many American businesses and missionaries were permitted to carry on their work, so long as they accepted the new regime.

But mutual suspicion and Washington's continued formal recognition of Chiang's government on Taiwan led both sides to restrict contact. Truman and Acheson came under increasing attack from Republicans, such as Senator Joe McCarthy of Wisconsin, who in February 1950 charged that Communist traitors in the State Department were in league with Mao and Stalin.

During the spring of 1950, Washington pulled all remaining diplomats off the mainland and quietly resumed, after a lapse of several months, military assistance to the Nationalists on Taiwan.

Since October 1, 1949, when Mao stood at Tiananmen to proclaim the People's Republic, Sino-American relations had begun a downward slide. Within a year, Chinese and American soldiers would be killing each other on the battlefields of Korea.

Selected Additional Readings

Relations between the U.S. government as well as individual Americans and the Chinese Communists are discussed in the following works: Michael Schaller, *The U.S. Crusade in China*, listed in Chapter 3; Joseph Esherick, ed., *Lost Chance in China: The World War II Dispatches of John S. Service*, N.Y., 1974, John S. Service, *The Amerasia Papers: Some Problems in the History of U.S.-China Relations*, Berkeley, Calif., 1971; John Patton Davies, *Dragon by the Tail*, N.Y., 1972; Janice MacKinnon and Stephen MacKinnon, *Agnes Smedley: The Life and Times of an American Radical*, Berkeley, Calif., 1988; Kenneth Shewmaker, *Americans and Chinese Communists, 1927–1945: A Persuading Encounter*, Ithaca, N.Y., 1971; Tracy B. Strong and Helene Keyssar, *Right in Her Soul: The Life and Times of Anna Louise Strong*, N.Y., 1983; and Stephen MacKinnon and Oris Friesen, *China Reporting: An Oral History of American Journalism in the 1930s and 1940s*, Berkeley, Calif., 1987.

The atomic bomb and end of the war are discussed in Martin J. Sherwin, *A World Destroyed: The Atomic Bomb and the Grand Alliance*, N.Y., 1975; Gregg Herken, *The Winning Weapon*, N.Y., 1982; Lloyd Eastman, *Seeds of Destruction*, listed in Chapter 4; Suzanne Pepper, *Civil War in China: The Political Struggle, 1945–1949*, Berkeley, Calif., 1978; James Reardon-Anderson, *Yenan and the Great Powers*, N.Y., 1980; Steven I. Levine, *The Anvil of Victory: The Communist Revolution in Manchuria, 1945–1948*, N.Y., 1987; William Hinton, *Fanshen: A Documentary of Revolution in a China Village*, N.Y., 1966; and John Melby, *The Mandate of Heaven: Record of a Civil War, China 1945–1949*, Toronto, 1968.

On American policy during the civil war, see E. J. Kahn, *The China Hands: America's Foreign Service Officers and What Befell Them*, N.Y., 1976; Gary May, *China Scapegoat: The Diplomatic*

Ordeal of John Carter Vincent, Washington, D.C., 1983; Robert M. Blum, Drawing the Line: The Origin of American Containment Policy in East Asia, N.Y., 1982; Nancy B. Tucker, Patterns in the Dust: Chinese-American Relations and the Recognition Controversy, 1949–50, N.Y., 1983; Dorothy Borg and Waldo Henrichs, eds., Uncertain Years: Chinese-American Relations, 1947–1950, N.Y., 1980; William W. Stueck, The Road to Confrontation: American Policy Toward China and Korea, 1947–50, Chapel Hill, N.C., 1981; Bruce Cumings, The Origins of the Korean War, Princeton, N.J., 1981; James I. Matray, The Reluctant Crusade: American Foreign Policy in Korea, 1941–50, Honolulu, 1985; Gary R. Hess, The United States' Emergence as a Southeast Asian Power, 1940–50, N.Y., 1987; John L. Gaddis, Strategies of Containment, N.Y., 1982; and Michael Schaller, The American Occupation of Japan: The Origins of the Cold War in Asia, N.Y., 1985.

6

The Red and Yellow Perils

The "loss" of China sent tremors throughout the American political landscape. Americans seemed stunned by the reality of a Communist China allied to the Soviet Union. Conditioned to see the Chinese as eager to adopt American culture and religion, people in the United States were shocked by the new regime's rejection of outside guidance. How could the Communists be so ungrateful as to drive out missionaries, churches and businesses?* What could impel Mao to journey to Moscow and, in February 1950, sign a military alliance and trade agreement with the hated Stalin? To many the answer seemed clear: the nefarious web of Communist subversion had trapped China and betrayed its hapless people.

The terms of the American debate over events in China had relatively little to do with China itself. Essentially, they reflected our own fear of people who challenged American values. By 1950 the cold war with communism in Europe had raged for four years. The enemy, centered in Moscow, ensnared nations

---

* Not all American missionaries and businesses were immediately expelled. Washington chose to publicize the expulsions and pressured all U.S. nationals to leave China, in order to emphasize Communist hostility. Only with the Korean War did the Chinese move against most of the remaining American residents.

by subversion and treason. No people, Americans of that time believed, would ever choose to accept communism of their own free will. Our sense of omnipotence in China was directly challenged by the Communists' success. Failure in such an area of special interest to the U.S. seemed to prove that someone must have betrayed the effort from the inside. For the next twenty years American policy toward Asia sought first to root out this "treason" and then to limit the contagion of what was called "Red China." As the most knowledgeable American China experts were purged from the government, new experts were found who decreed that the United States must become the policeman of Asia.

Strangely enough, in 1950 and for many years thereafter, only a handful of Americans in or out of government questioned whether China was ours to lose. Few inside the Truman Administration and fewer among its conservative critics considered the root causes of the Chinese revolution. Reports of peasant violence against landlords and the expropriation of foreign-owned and church property were interpreted as evidence of Communist madness and a portent of what the Chinese would do to the rest of Asia if only given a chance. American political and opinion leaders could not or would not see the significance to the Chinese of the destruction of the power of the landholding classes and the abolition of the special privileges granted foreigners. Looked at from the perspective of Western liberalism and the ideology of anticommunism, the Chinese Communists' violent rejection of the American model proved the new regime to be a Russian pawn. As such, Communist China must be considered a threat to American security.

Speaking in 1951, Assistant Secretary of State (later Secretary of State under Presidents Kennedy and Johnson) Dean Rusk expressed this underlying view most graphically. He explained China's involvement in the Korean War and the nature of the new regime in this way:

> The peace and security of China are being sacrificed to the ambitions of a Communist conspiracy. China has been driven by foreign masters into an adventure of foreign aggression. . . . The

Peiping* regime may be a colonial Russian government. . . . It is not the government of China. . . . It is not Chinese. . . .

The fixation which Rusk and others voiced was a bizarre distortion of America's traditional interest in China. Before 1937 the official role of the American government in China was relatively small. Washington used its influence to dissuade Russian and Japanese meddling in China and pressed the Chinese not to discriminate against private American activity. The majority of the Americans involved with China had always been missionaries, merchants and philanthropists. After 1937 President Roosevelt reversed this policy, seeking to transform China into a Great Power and postwar partner through American aid and political support to the Kuomintang. By the late 1940s it had become difficult for many Americans to separate their interests in China from the preservation of Chiang Kai-shek and the continuation of KMT rule. A China not ruled by Chiang was, *ipso facto,* not really Chinese. In the mind of the average American this former ally was not only a Great Power, but a sort of Frankenstein's monster controlled by an implacably hostile Communist foe. This vision set the stage for East Asia to become a battleground between the United States and China.

During the first few months of the new regime, American policy remained in a period of flux, waiting, in Dean Acheson's words, "for the dust to settle." The United States refused to establish diplomatic relations with the Communist regime, preferring to continue the fiction that Chiang's rump faction on the island of Taiwan was China's legal government. But, at the same time, the United States made no promise to help defend Taiwan against the expected Communist attack. Apparently, Truman and Acheson planned to allow the Chinese civil war to end with no more direct American interference.

This did not mean that the United States expected to play a

---

* Rusk, in accord with U.S. government policy, refused to call the Communist capital by its original name, Beijing, which means "northern capital." Under the KMT, Nanking (Nanjing) was made the capital and the old capital was renamed Peiping, or "northern peace." This American stubbornness, which continued until the late 1960s, was designed to show that Washington refused to accept the legality of the Communist regime.

minor role in Asia's future. On the contrary, many actions already taken indicated a strengthened American determination to control Asian development. Since 1947, for example, American occupation policy in Japan, under the guidance of General MacArthur, had moved increasingly toward restoring Japan's economic strength and the influence of its more conservative, pro-American politicians. Initially it had been U.S. policy to break up the giant Japanese business monopolies ("zaibatsu") which had been linked to military expansion. By 1948–49 this policy was shelved. Instead American occupation authorities emphasized the rebuilding of Japanese defense forces, the curbing of left wing political and labor groups and other programs to enhance rapid recovery. Japan, it seemed, would become the pivot of U.S. influence in Asia, a role originally slated for Nationalist China.

Within months of the Communist victory in China the State Department and National Security Council began a comprehensive review of American policy in Asia. Secretary of State Acheson made it plain that the review should be premised with the determination to defend the rest of Asia from succumbing to communism. On December 30, 1949, President Truman approved a major National Security Council Study (NSC–48–2) which placed U.S. policy firmly on a course "set to block further Communist expansion in Asia." The document recommended that "particular attention should be given to the problem of French Indochina."* This "problem" would haunt America for the next twenty-five years. Though the administration remained unsure of what to do and where to do it, it was certain that a military barrier must soon be drawn around the People's Republic of China.

Red Scare at Home

The Truman Administration's effort to explain events and formulate a new policy in East Asia became nearly impossible after 1950. Both Congress and the American public lost faith in "official" explanations. The China debate became the haunt of

---

* A French colony which included Vietnam, Cambodia and Laos.

wildly irresponsible demagogues both in government and in the press. The issue of China became only a means to an end—gaining political power by stoking fears of treason and conspiracy committed by career officials and the Democratic Party. Many of postwar America's social and political tensions became wrapped up in the debate over the "loss of China."

Vitriolic accusations concerning the betrayal of China had been voiced as early as November 1945 when Ambassador Hurley resigned. Though given attention then and later, the flamboyant ambassador's reckless charges against allegedly disloyal, procommunist subordinates had failed to persuade most people. Still, enough members of Congress and the Senate and some in the press sympathized with Hurley and Chiang so that the claims of treason were revived in several inconclusive Congressional hearings. But the truly massive search for subversion, the great Red Scare called "McCarthyism," only began in earnest after 1950.

By then political paranoia had a much richer soil in which to grow. Communist China was a reality. Mao had gone to Moscow and signed an alliance with the Soviet Union. One hundred miles off the Chinese mainland lay a vulnerable anticommunist Taiwan, expecting an imminent invasion. In the autumn of 1949 the Russians had ended the American atomic monopoly by exploding an atomic bomb. Within the United States a series of sensational Congressional investigations had attempted to spotlight Communist spies in the federal government. Most notably, Congressman Richard Nixon's House Committee on Un-American Activities had "exposed" former State Department official Alger Hiss as a Russian spy. Though the evidence of Hiss's guilt was far from clear, he was finally convicted of perjury (*not* espionage) after a second trial in January 1950.

But spy mania and fears of treason were not solely the product of professional bigots and Red-baiters. The Truman Administration itself had inadvertently contributed to the Red Scare. In 1947, partly to stifle critics, Truman ordered the creation of a federal loyalty program designed to root out any actual spies or potential security risks working for the federal government. During the next five years almost seven million people underwent security investigations. Although not a single person was charged with any illegal act, the investigation itself fueled fears of subversion.

The government's reaction to the detonation of a Russian atomic bomb demonstrated how Washington promoted sensational fears. While Soviet espionage had certainly penetrated the British and American atomic energy research programs, the development of a Soviet A-bomb was an inevitable fact, only marginally speeded up by stealing secrets. Nevertheless, the American government, and especially the FBI, emphasized the espionage angle and carried on a massive search for atomic spies. During the summer of 1950, almost simultaneous with the outbreak of fighting in Korea, the FBI announced the arrest of Julius and Ethel Rosenberg for allegedly passing atomic secrets to the Russians. The confusing legal battle dragged on for three years before the Rosenbergs were executed. Throughout their trial the prosecution and judge made references to how their "treason" had emboldened the Russian and Chinese Communists against America.

In this atmosphere of grave suspicion, witch-hunters found it relatively easy to turn public attention again toward the branch of the State Department which, they claimed, bore responsibility for the "loss of China." The Far Eastern Division was a small, close-knit and highly respected group of career officials. The China area officers, trained during World War II, were considered among the most tested young diplomats in government service. Their reports from wartime China—the warnings about the KMT's fatal flaws, the analyses of Communist power, the recommendations that the U.S. might support the CCP—still stand the test of time for their uncanny accuracy. Ironically, as we have shown, their reports generally had little influence on the major decisions of the Roosevelt and Truman administrations. But during the war years and on into the cold war these Foreign Service officers were resented for committing a grave human error. They continually transmitted unpleasant news to their political superiors. Time and time again their reports from China spoke of KMT corruption and oppression. They predicted the Communists' eventual victory—which in the popular mind became synonymous with being procommunist and causing Chiang's defeat.

One demogogue in particular rode the anticommunist fury to fame and power. Among the many witch-hunters in national politics, Wisconsin Senator Joseph McCarthy led the campaign to hunt down traitors. From 1950 to 1954 he and his cohorts terrorized and gutted the Foreign Service, driving respected officials out of office and draping a pall over U.S.-China relations which lasted until 1971. McCarthy claimed a desire to expose and destroy

> individuals who are loyal to the ideal and designs of Communism rather than those of the free, God-fearing half of the world. . . . I refer to the Far Eastern Division of the State Department and the Voice of America.

In reality, this cruel and reckless politician used the largely bogus issue of Communists in government to gain fame, notoriety and reelection.

On February 9, 1950, McCarthy "went public" with his accusations. In a speech in Wheeling, West Virginia, he revealed his charges of a massive conspiracy.

> I have here in my hand a list of two hundred and five [names of people] known to the Secretary of State as being members of the Communist Party and who nevertheless are still working and shaping the policy of the State Department.

McCarthy never actually revealed the names of anyone in any way connected with the Communist Party and the State Department. What he did do was to charge that the Foreign Service officers who had so accurately criticized Chiang and predicted his downfall were agents of a "Communist conspiracy." He eventually even claimed that Owen Lattimore, a professor of Asian history at Johns Hopkins University and sometime government consultant, was the "number one Soviet agent" in America.

No one named had been guilty of anything except telling the unpleasant truth. Yet, in this hysterical, anticommunist atmosphere, being accused was tantamount to guilt. Neither Truman nor Eisenhower spoke up to defend the accused diplomats. One by one, during the early 1950s, officers in the China service were driven from their posts as "loyalty" or "security" risks. None was actually charged with willful crime, but with committing absurd indiscretions. For example, Foreign Service personnel who had been stationed with the Dixie Mission in Yenan were criticized for "consorting" with known Communists! By the time President Dwight Eisenhower assumed office, John Carter Vincent, Oliver Clubb, John Davies and John Service had already been or would soon be driven out of the State Department. Some other lesser known diplomats were permitted to stay on provided that they switch areas and steer clear of Chinese affairs. By 1954 virtually no one with expert training or experience in China remained in the Far Eastern Division of the State Department.

Talented junior officials quickly learned to avoid specializing in Chinese affairs because the area was a political minefield. As a result of McCarthyite attacks and the refusal of Presidents Truman and Eisenhower to resist them, an entire generation of government China experts was professionally destroyed. The purge of these diplomats in the prime of their careers ensured that a long time would elapse before the next generation of China specialists emerged. Until then the blind would lead the blind. In a remarkable irony, the United States was ostracizing Americans who had contacts with the Chinese Communists just as the Chinese Communists were punishing their own citizens whom they considered too close to American culture.

The American political inquisition made it both difficult and dangerous for anyone to question the "truth" that China was a vicious enemy—a victim and a tool of world communism. The simplistic division of the world into two camps was not limited to the radical right. In January 1950 President Truman ordered the National Security Council to review overall American defense policy. The study, named NSC–68 when completed in June, predicted a long-term confrontation between the "free world" (led by the U.S.) and the Communist camp (led by the U.S.S.R.). This top secret report (not released until the 1970s) implied a need to increase U.S. defense spending by 300 to 400 percent to confront not only direct Soviet challenges but indigenous nationalist movements attacking colonial or neo-colonial regimes.

NSC–68 served as a "call to arms," a rallying cry for the U.S. and its allies to drastically increase their own military preparedness to resist a perceived Soviet threat. The special State and

Senator Joseph McCarthy smiles after having accused Foreign Service officer John Service of "losing China," June 1950. (National Archives)

Defense Department study group headed by Paul Nitze to prepare the documents described a world in which a Communist victory anywhere meant an equivalent loss for the United States. NCS–68 disallowed any gray areas. It hardly distinguished between Soviet expansion, national Communist movements or insurgents fighting in strictly local conflicts. Because U.S. planners now viewed virtually all threats to the status quo as a prelude to Soviet expansion, Americans had a vital stake in intervening to preserve the existing order everywhere.

The Truman Administration hesitated to proclaim this doctrine of American globalism upon its completion. Congress was expected to balk at the huge outlays for weapons it entailed. Administration supporters believed that only a crisis might persuade Congress and the public to support such a radical increase in the military budget. Truman did not formally approve the plan until September 1950. As one of Truman's advisors put it later: in June 1950 "we were sweating over it and then—with regard to NCS–68—thank God Korea came along."

The Korean War

The outbreak of war in Korea on June 25, 1950, quickly brought American combat forces into Northeast Asia. Within a few days, President Truman committed the United States to the defense of South Korea, the protection of Taiwan and the expansion of aid to French Indochina. The introduction of the 7th Fleet to the Taiwan Strait and Truman's decision, by October, to unify all Korea under an anticommunist regime convinced Chinese leaders that the United States sought to surround and undermine, perhaps even overthrow, the People's Republic. In response, Mao dispatched a Chinese "Volunteer" army to halt the American offensive in North Korea. By November 1950, a half million Chinese and American troops were locked in a brutal war that lasted until mid-1953.

At the end of World War II, Korea (a Japanese colony since the early twentieth century) had been divided at the 38th parallel into Soviet and American occupation zones. Designed as a temporary expedient, the division became permanent as Washington and Moscow fell into the pattern of the cold war. Each superpower established a client regime in its sector. The Communist leader Kim Il Sung ruled with Russian support in the north, while arch-conservative Syngman Rhee formed an American-sponsored regime in the south. Each claimed a right to rule the entire peninsula. Despite (or because of) the explosive potential, both occupying powers withdrew the majority of their own forces by 1949. Thereafter, Moscow and Washington confined their activities to supplying military and economic aid to their respective clients.

Historians now generally agree that the causes of the Korean War lay in the hostility between the two competing regimes. Kim Il Sung probably sought and received Stalin's approval to invade the south, but there is little evidence that the Soviets, or, especially, the Chinese, were heavily involved in planning the invasion. The Chinese Communists had deployed the bulk of their own troops southward, away from Korea, where they could be employed against Taiwan.

While concerned for the security of its South Korean client, the Truman Administration retained numerous misgivings about the mercurial and authoritarian Syngman Rhee. Like his counterpart in the north, Rhee abhorred democracy and pledged to lead an invasion to topple the rival regime. Worried that such an assault would destabilize the region, Washington had sent mostly defensive weapons to Rhee. Nevertheless, since 1947, there had been constant cross-border skirmishes, social upheaval and brutal repression on both sides of the 38th parallel.

The United States responded to the June 1950 North Korean attack by interpreting it as a Soviet-directed challenge against all American allies. Truman, Acheson and other American leaders convinced themselves that Stalin sought to test Washington's "credibility," its determination to resist aggression even in marginal areas. In the aftermath of Mao's victory and the detonation of the Soviet atomic bomb, American leaders believed, Stalin hoped to expose American weakness and destroy the faith of Washington's allies (especially the West Europeans, Germans and Japanese) in U.S. defense guarantees. This, Truman reasoned, made it imperative to intervene on behalf of South Korea, even if that country was itself irrelevant to American security.

Within days of the North Korean invasion, Truman ordered a series of actions to defend the south, protect Taiwan and expand aid to Indochina, all designed to show Moscow, Beijing and American allies that they could count on Washington's security pledge. The President justified these actions by declaring that the "attack upon Korea makes it plain beyond all doubt that Communism had passed beyond the use of subversion to conquer independent nations and will now use armed invasion and war." Not even lip service was paid to the fact that the war sprung primarily from political divisions on the Korean peninsula itself.

The United States easily secured the United Nation's support for a call to dispatch troops to help the south restore the prewar boundary. For some time, the Soviet delegation had boycotted Security Council sessions, protesting America's success in blocking Beijing's membership in place of Taiwan. Now, to China's horror, a U.N.-sanctioned army (consisting largely of U.S. forces) led by General Douglas MacArthur would be landed only a few hundred miles from the Manchurian border. To make matters worse, Truman announced that since the "occupation of Formosa [Taiwan] by Communist forces would be a direct threat to the security of the Pacific area," America's 7th Fleet would shield the island from the mainland. From China's perspective, these actions seemed suspiciously like an attempt to surround the PRC with hostile forces while bolstering the Nationalists for another round of civil war.

American moves to protect South Korea and Taiwan, to re-arm Japan and to assist the French war in Indochina did represent a determination to contain Chinese power in Asia. Not surprisingly, on June 28, Zhou Enlai declared that U.S. intervention in Korea and Taiwan constituted "aggression against the territory of China" and marked a "further act of intervention by American imperialism in Asia."

Even though America's initial war goals in Korea were confined to the restoration of the 38th parallel boundary, both the Truman Administration and its theater commander, General Douglas MacArthur, entertained more grandiose visions. In mid-September, MacArthur's forces crushed the North Korean army by landing behind its lines in an amphibious assault at Inchon. Soon, the south was secured, fulfilling Washington's stated purpose. But the rush of success at repelling a Communist invasion proved intoxicating. The President and MacArthur both resolved to push beyond the prewar boundary in order to destroy the North Korean regime and unify the country. They hardly seemed to notice that Manchuria, China's industrial heartland, lay on the other side of the Yalu River, Korea's northern boundary.

Chinese wariness of American intentions increased during the summer and fall when Douglas MacArthur undertook a series of actions, some of which defied official policy, to assist Taiwan. He visited the island at the end of July, issuing vague statements about coordinated operations against Communist enemies. In August he issued a controversial statement calling for the United States to support military action by Chiang against the mainland. Finally, after Truman's decision to unify Korea, MacArthur proposed a "win the war offensive" which would bring American troops right up to the Manchurian border. Given MacArthur's well-known support for Chiang and antipathy to the PRC, Chinese leaders could not help but wonder if the flamboyant general would stop at the Yalu or press the war into China.

In October, rumors about possible Chinese intervention led Truman to confer with MacArthur at Wake Island in the Pacific. (Already the Chinese press and Premier Zhou Enlai declared that if American troops entered North Korea, China would not stand "idly by." The Americans would encounter Chinese resistance.) The commander assured the President that Chinese forces would not intervene, and, if they did, he would easily defeat them. Apparently reassured that the Communists were bluffing, and not eager to be criticized for tying the hands of a general "rolling back the iron curtain," Truman pinned a medal on MacArthur's chest and flew home.

American—particularly MacArthur's—strategy terrified China's leadership. While not overly concerned about Washington's decision to save South Korea, they looked upon the invasion of North Korea as a direct blow to their own security. At best, an anticommunist regime along the Yalu River would make Manchuria a hostage and interfere with China's economic development program. At worst, they feared an invasion of Manchuria that was coordinated with assaults by Nationalist forces operating from Taiwan. Unless they stopped the American push in its tracks, Mao argued to his colleagues, even "moderates" in Washington would be tempted to see how far they could push China.

By the fall of 1950, several hundred thousand Chinese troops were redeployed to Manchuria. They planned to move across the Yalu and engage American forces at some distance from

China's border. This "forward defense," Mao and Zhou explained, sought to deter more aggressive American action by bogging MacArthur's forces down in the "Korean quagmire." Brought to its senses, the Truman Administration might then negotiate a settlement restoring North Korea.

But flushed with his success at Inchon, MacArthur ignored Chinese warnings and American intelligence reports indicating that Chinese troops would intervene if American forces pushed into North Korea. During October and early November 1950, the Truman Administration grew increasingly alarmed at signals from Beijing. While still favoring Korean unification, Washington feared the consequences of a wider war with China. An expanded war in Asia would prevent the U.S. from protecting either Western Europe or Japan, the real pivots of American security. MacArthur cared more about achieving a dramatic victory over North Korea or China than limiting the scope of the war. The general's wide popularity at this point intimidated Truman and his advisors so much that they declined to restrain him or limit his operations near China. When the administration made some half-hearted efforts to slow the march to the Yalu, MacArthur leaked stories to the press that weak-willed Democrats sought to snatch away from him a great victory over the Communist enemy.

The bubble began to burst early in November 1950 when, true to their word, Chinese "Volunteers" made their first appearance on the Korean battlefield. After defeating several small American and South Korean units they broke off contact. China probably intended this as a final warning to stay clear of the Yalu. MacArthur dismissed it as proof of China's inability to sustain combat and ordered, at the end of November, his "win the war" offensive to the Manchurian border.

The *People's Daily* explained in blunt terms what happened next. Three hundred thousand Chinese "Volunteers" were counterattacking as a last resort to turn American troops around. China would "check them with force and compel them to stop" because there was "no alternative." During December the Chinese pushed the American 8th Army and X Corps back toward the 38th parallel in a remarkable reversal of military fortune.

Only five years earlier Chinese armies had been allies against

Japan. Now "Red Chinese hordes" (in the current phrase) were slaughtering Americans. MacArthur and much of the press reacted as if China's intervention was a total surprise and simple proof of Communist evil. As one contemporary newsreel reported:

> Americans were being routed by Chinese Red Army Legions, treacherously forced into this war by the unscrupulous leaders of international communism. The G.I.'s battle the new elements with everything they have, but the latest Communist perfidy in Korea makes the picture grim.

The "new war" in Korea presented the American government with a terrible dilemma. Truman's advisors, both military and civilian, feared getting "sewed" up in a war against the "second team" (China), while the real danger remained a Soviet threat to Europe and Japan. MacArthur dismissed such ideas, insisting that China had emerged as the central threat to American global security. He and right wing supporters demanded that the administration permit him to widen the war through air and naval attacks on China and by utilizing Nationalist troops in Korea and against the mainland. Unable to sway the Truman Administration, he began making direct appeals to the American public and Republican politicians in favor of expanding the war against China.

MacArthur's challenge was as much a political confrontation with hated Democrats in Washington (he still had pretensions of running for President) as a serious military strategy. He also hoped to shift the blame for his humiliation by the Chinese to political opponents at home. An unrestricted war against China, he reasoned, would allow him to regain the glory lost when he blundered into China's trap.

Not surprisingly, Truman had other ideas. By early 1951, the administration had all but abandoned the grandiose plan to unify Korea by force. Truman now favored armistice talks with the Chinese that aimed at restoring the prewar boundary. The President rejected claims by MacArthur that unless the war were expanded, his troops would be overwhelmed. By January overextended and poorly equipped Chinese forces pushed down to the 38th parallel, but they ran out of steam. They simply lacked the ability to drive the U.N. command from South Korea. Had both sides acknowledged the stalemate, an early armistice might have averted two more years of war. Unfortunately, early attempts at negotiations floundered. China insisted that an armistice in Korea be tied to an American withdrawal of support for Taiwan and to seating the PRC at the United Nations. Washington refused to concede either point, insisting that an armistice could not be linked to China's claims against the United States. When the PRC spurned a U.N. peace proposal more or less along American lines, the United States convinced the world organization to condemn China as the sole aggressor in Korea. This, of course, further enraged Beijing.

While diplomacy stalled, in March and April 1951 MacArthur renewed his public condemnations of both the Chinese and American governments. He called on Chinese and Korean forces to "surrender" to him, denounced Truman for refusing to allow him to win the war by attacking China, demanded that Chiang be given U.S. help to invade China and suggested he had a secret plan for victory, perhaps by using atomic weapons. In April, when he sent a letter containing some of these ideas to leading Republican Congressman Joe Martin, Truman finally sacked the general.

Despite the public outcry and Senate investigation of Truman's action, it helped break the stalemate. General Matthew Ridgway, MacArthur's successor, rallied dispirited American troops to halt China's renewed ground offensive of April–May 1951 without relying upon atomic weapons, the bombing of Manchuria or a Nationalist invasion of the PRC. Shaken by their failure to push the Americans out of South Korea, but relieved by the removal of MacArthur, Chinese leaders agreed to discuss peace terms with the United States.

Armistice talks began during the summer of 1951 and dragged on, along with continued fighting, until July 1953. Numerous issues, such as exactly where to redraw the border and, especially, what to do with Chinese prisoners who did not want to go home, proved extremely difficult to resolve. By early 1953, however, several factors broke the log jam. Stalin's death, in March, brought to power a new group of Russian leaders eager to improve relations with the U.S. following the election of

Dwight Eisenhower as President. American and Chinese negotiators finally devised a voluntary formula for repatriating Chinese POWS. At this time President Eisenhower and his Secretary of State, John Foster Dulles, also made veiled threats to expand the war, perhaps with atomic weapons, unless China and the Soviet Union agreed to an armistic quickly. These and other factors contributed to a settlement. Ironically, Syngman Rhee proved the last stumbling block. Enraged by Washington's refusal to fight for the destruction of North Korea, he threatened to sabotage the negotiations. Before Rhee relented, Eisenhower ordered a plan to depose the American ally for whom the U.S. had sacrificed so much. The final settlement restored, essentially, the status quo.

The Korean War froze Sino-American relations in a pattern of hostility which lasted two decades. About 142,000 Americans were killed or wounded in Korea. Chinese casualties surpassed a million, including the death of Mao's son. Washington had convinced the U.N. to brand China an international aggressor and sponsored a strict economic embargo of the PRC. Not only the United States, but Western Europe and Japan now declined most trade with China. American military and economic aid flowed to Taiwan after 1951, while the island enjoyed a U.S. naval shield. During the Korean War, the Central Intelligence Agency and Taiwan initiated small-scale guerrilla operations against China which, in one form or another, continued until the Nixon Administration took office. Finally, the war proved a catalyst for expanded American involvement in French Indochina. By the time of the Korean armistice, the United States had taken over eighty percent of the cost of the colonial war and already had an American military mission active in Saigon.

The Republicans Take Command

The stalemated war in Korea further discredited a President and Democratic Party already charged with disloyalty and corruption. During the 1952 presidential campaign enterprising Republicans popularized a slogan, "K^1C^2," signifying Democratic responsibility for "Korea, Communism and Corruption." Even more striking was the phrase coined by Senator Joe McCarthy: since 1933, he intoned, the Democrats had perpetrated "Twenty Years of Treason."

Promising to end the stalemate in Korea and fight the "international Communist conspiracy" more vigorously, Republicans Dwight D. Eisenhower and Senator Richard M. Nixon, the vice presidential nominee, rode a tide of victory into the White House. The 1952 campaign was clear warning to American politicians—anyone tainted with the "loss" of a country to communism faced near certain electoral defeat. No one, Republican or Democrat, could risk the charge of compromising with the devil or being "soft." Thereafter, American policy, especially in Asia, became largely a knee-jerk reaction. Any regime, no matter how corrupt or reactionary, could call on American assistance if it was threatened by a revolutionary movement and the Americans would feel required to respond.

This rigid political stance was encouraged by the activities of the China Lobby in the United States. Dedicated to aiding Taiwan and opposing the People's Republic, the China Lobby emerged as an informal watchdog over American foreign policy. The largest and most influential of these groups was the "Committee of One Million," established in 1953 to resist any tendency toward improvement of U.S.-Chinese Communist relations. The China Lobby was particularly influential in Congress, continually pushing that body toward extreme anti-Chinese Communist position. Any politician who suggested a more moderate policy risked incurring the organized wrath of the China Lobby. The group directed its influence and funds on behalf of "friends" and against "enemies." This pressure was often successful.

It is inaccurate to assume, however, that American policy toward Communist China was manipulated solely by lobbyists for Taiwan. A broad range of American political, military, economic, religious and intellectual leaders was convinced that the PRC represented a real danger to the security of the United States. Since these leaders were certain China was actively spreading revolution in Asia, American policy after 1950 centered on the creation of anticommunist bulwarks surrounding China.

The Eisenhower Administration placed the final bricks in the wall around China begun by the Truman Administration. In 1953 Eisenhower appointed John Foster Dulles as Secretary of State. An accomplished international lawyer and elder of the Presbyterian Church, Dulles brought a special moralism to his China policy. The new Secretary, who enjoyed Eisenhower's trust, had observed the power of the anticommunist zealots in Congress to hamstring the previous administration. Partly to avoid criticism from that contingent, Dulles exhibited the behavior and rhetoric most likely to placate the McCarthyites. He accepted their allegations that disloyal diplomats had subverted American policy in China and announced that, henceforth, mere loyalty to U.S. policy was insufficient: diplomats would have to demonstrate "positive loyalty"—whatever that meant. One thing it did mean was that the few remaining China experts in the State Department who had been critical of Chiang, such as John Carter Vincent, were forced to resign. Furthermore, Dulles appointed a special assistant, Scott McLeod, whose duty was to oversee the Foreign Service and root out "subversives."

Dulles's view of China throughout the 1950s was similar to that expressed by Rusk in 1951. Between Republicans and Democrats after the outbreak of the Korean War there was little difference over China. As one of his aides put it, Dulles continued to dream "his fancy about reactivating the civil war in China." He deeply believed the People's Republic of China was a "godless," illegal regime which did not "conform to the practices of civilized nations." The U.S., he insisted, must never recognize or do business with Beijing. Instead, it must promote conditions leading to the overthrow of the regime. In 1957 Dulles declared, "We owe it to ourselves, our allies, and the Chinese people to do all that we can to contribute to that passing."

The compromise which ended the Korean War in 1953 (though American combat troops remained in the south) was a policy of expedience and did not signal acceptance of the PRC. Both before and after the Korean armistice, Washington maneuvered to contain China. Early in 1952 the United States ended the formal occupation of Japan. John Foster Dulles, then serving as special advisor to the Truman Administration, had drafted a mutual security treaty with Tokyo that linked the two nations in a mili-

-> professional foreign service weakened ⎫ undermined using one
-> political myth of "int'l. communism" ⎬ c.f. u. another

tary pact aimed against China and the Soviet Union. The Japanese pledged to recognize Chiang's regime on Taiwan as the legitimate Chinese government and permitted American military forces to remain in Japan. Defense pacts with Australia and New Zealand (the ANZUS Treaty) supplemented this arrangement.

Following the Korean armistice, the Eisenhower Administration continued to oppose any substantial relaxation of tensions with China. In fact, it devised more comprehensive containment schemes. Shortly after taking office, Eisenhower placated Taiwan's supporters by "unleashing" Chiang, or removing American restrictions on Nationalist operations mounted from Taiwan against the mainland. In September 1954, Dulles fathered the Southeast Asia Treaty Organization (SEATO), a bloc of anticommunist states on China's periphery organized under American sponsorship as a regional defense alliance. In December of that year the United States and Taiwan entered a mutual defense treaty which pledged American support for Taiwan against any attack from the mainland. United States agencies also regularly utilized the island as a base of military and intelligence operations.

In addition to these military arrangements, the Eisenhower Administration maintained a strategic trade embargo on economic contacts with China. A comprehensive arrangement among the American, Western European and Japanese governments ensured that China could not obtain a wide variety of products and technology. This effort to restrict trade contact represented part of an overall approach sometimes called the "Closed Door policy." Dulles and Eisenhower hoped that by isolating China from all Western contact, Beijing would become increasingly dependent on the relatively backward Soviet bloc. This, they guessed, would lead to resentment and frustration as the Soviet Union failed to meet China's development needs. Ultimately, the People's Republic might break with Moscow, change its stripes, and come crawling back to America for help.

The Western blockade extended to human beings as well as material items. During the 1940s several thousand Chinese students and scientists had come to America for study. After 1950 many opted to return to China rather than Taiwan. The United

States government denied them this right of return until the mid-1950s. Lest the American people be duped by Communist propaganda, Secretary of State Dulles forbade all travel, by tourists, scholars or journalists, to China. Similar restrictions were imposed on Chinese nationals wishing to visit the United States.

While many of these policies were more spiteful than dangerous, America undertook other actions of an aggressive nature. During the 1950s and 1960s, Washington sponsored a limited secret war against China, largely under CIA and Taiwanese control. Beginning during the Korean War, the CIA cooperated with the Nationalists in staging frequent raids against the mainland. These included assaults across the Taiwan Strait, attacks from Nationalist-held islands, some of which were only a few miles from the mainland, and border raids staged by KMT armies which had retreated from China to Burma in 1949.*

One of the more peculiar operations carried on during the 1950s took place in Colorado. There the CIA trained Tibetan guerrillas in mountain warfare for later airdropping inside Tibet. These specially trained forces were supposed to form the nucleus of an anti-Chinese uprising. During the 1950s and 1960s, reports of the Colorado operation were dismissed by the American press and government as "Communist propaganda." In truth, most of the military operations were small-scale attempts to disrupt and confuse the enemy. Few were large enough to pose a serious threat to Communist rule.

More upsetting to China was America's stated support for Chiang's professed intention of "recapturing the mainland." Since the United States had a military alliance with the Republic of China on Taiwan, the leaders in Beijing feared that, by design or accident, Washington might support a full-scale Nationalist invasion. Even though Dulles and Eisenhower had "unleased" the Generalissimo, they privately told him *not* to expect American backing for such an operation. Nevertheless, the Commu-

---

* The KMT forces in the "Golden Triangle" of Burma, Thailand and Laos supplemented their military missions by becoming major producers of opium and heroin for the American market. In exchange for their help in destabilizing China, the CIA and its airline, Air America (sometimes called Air Opium), either assisted or tolerated the drug operations.

nist regime witnessed the thoroughness of the American effort to isolate their country and Washington's direct support for at least small-scale military aggression.

Indeed, considering U.S. behavior, it is not hard to understand China's intense hostility toward America. From Beijing's perspective, it was encircled by American-sponsored anticommunist alliances, prevented by the U.S. navy from invading Taiwan, kept out of the U.N. and world trade by an American embargo, and constantly needled by U.S.-assisted guerrilla operations. Most Americans either ignored or rejected this evidence. They saw China as an illegitimate regime committed to aggression.

China's policy, at least superficially, confirmed part of the American view. Once the Korean War began, China initiated a mass campaign among its people to "hate" America. Mao proclaimed support for revolutionary struggles around the world and provided assistance for the Viet Minh fighting the French in Indochina. The PRC described itself as a firm ally of the Soviet Union and condemned "American imperialism" as the world's greatest enemy.

During most of the 1950s, China had nowhere else to turn but toward the Soviet Union for support. Only Stalin could supply (actually, he sold) the weapons used by the People's Volunteers fighting in Korea. Cut off from the West and Japan, China became dependent on Soviet credits, technology and trade for its ambitious development projects. Thousands of Chinese studied in Russia, and economic planners adopted Soviet models of central planning and social control. Following Moscow's lead was part of the price the PRC paid for assistance and Soviet military protection. U.S. policy pushed China toward the Soviets and then condemned the Chinese as Soviet lackeys.

China's actual behavior, in contrast to its rhetoric, often appeared more moderate. Despite Beijing's verbal support for world revolution, it remained a poor and backward nation, desperately trying to overcome a century of political, military and economic chaos. Its leaders spent most of their time struggling to create a new agricultural and industrial order, an enormous task. Age-old traditions of elitism and superstition had to be overcome, often by harsh regimentation. Peasant hatred against landlords was a useful tool which the Communist Party could use to mobilize apolitical and long-suffering peasants. At times, the outpouring of emotion led to the slaughter of landlords.

Eager to shake off the legacy of imperialism, the new regime expelled most missionaries and foreign businesses. China provided some small, but important, military support to Communist insurgents fighting colonial regimes in Southeast Asia. However, much of its foreign aid (especially in the 1960s) consisted of economic development projects to emerging African nations. But what most upset Americans was both the internal effort to eradicate pro-Western elements and Beijing's identification with the Soviet Union. This convinced many Americans that villains and madmen controlled the new Chinese government. Washington lost sight of the fact that China's massive effort at internal development left few resources available for foreign mischief. Aside from its support for neighboring Communist insurgents, the People's Republic could do little more than cheer on other liberation movements.

Chinese foreign policy had two sides during the 1950s and 1960s. On the one hand, Mao proclaimed the doctrine that all reactionary and imperialist regimes were "paper tigers," doomed to eventual destruction. At the same time, China recognized the actual military and economic superiority of the United States and its allies. Thus Beijing stressed the need for colonial and oppressed peoples to accomplish their own liberation without dependence on outside help. China would resort to arms only in self-defense, to protect its own territory or to protect friendly regimes on its border.

Unlike the rigid stance of the United States, after the Korean War ended China adopted a more flexible approach toward the West. While Washington sought to isolate or topple the PRC, the Communists explored the possibility of an accommodation. During 1954–55, Chinese Premier and Foreign Minister Zhou Enlai invited the United States to begin direct talks aimed at improving relations. Zhou also proposed, to no avail, an exchange of citizens and journalists.

Dulles dismissed several such Chinese initiatives aimed at expanding official and unofficial contacts, denying the possibility of parlaying with such an evil regime. This uncompromising stance was buttressed by the appointment of anticommunist zealots to the top China post within the State Department (Walter Robertson) and to the ambassadorship of Taiwan (Karl Rankin). There could be no peace in Asia, Rankin declared, until the "predatory regime" which had stolen China under the "flag of a Communist conspiracy" was replaced by a real Chinese government. By this he meant the return of all China to Nationalist rule. Such an outlook propelled the United States into a series of military confrontations with China during the 1950s.

In 1955 and especially in 1958 the United States and China came close to war over crises in the Taiwan Strait. The Nationalists retained control over several small offshore islands, the most important of which, Quemoy and Matsu, lay only a few miles off the south China coast. Chiang had stationed large-troop garrisons on these islands, partly to assert his claim to the mainland and partly to further frequent commando operations. In an effort to force a Nationalist withdrawal—which would eliminate a military threat, mobilize morale and destabilize Taiwan—the Communists twice began a blockade and shelling of Quemoy. The most sustained challenge began in August 1958.

The PRC, of course, insisted the island was Chinese territory in which the U.S. had no legitimate interest. Beijing may have intended its challenge to see how far Washington would go in the defense of Taiwan and to test the level of support offered by the Soviet Union, now under the leadership of Nikita Khrushchev. Moscow's half-hearted support of its ally (the Soviets had begun a drive to improve relations with the United States) and the Eisenhower Administration's determined backing of Chiang proved a rude awakening for Mao.

Testifying secretly before the Senate during the first crisis (in January 1955), Dulles stated that the U.S. did not intend to use its own power to restore Chiang's rule on the mainland. Washington had received private assurances from the Nationalist leader that he would not launch a major attack without American permission. At the same time, the Secretary of State revealed that the administration would launch air and sea strikes upon the mainland if any moves against the disputed islands were seen as a threat to Taiwan.

We have got to be prepared to take a risk of war with China if we are going to stay in the Far East. . . . If we are not willing to take that risk, all right, let's make that decision and we get out and we make our defense in California.

Congress followed Dulles's lead by enacting the Formosa Strait Resolution which empowered the President to use force to protect the "security of Formosa [Taiwan], the Pescadores, and related positions and territories of that area." It did not, however, commit American forces to hold any particular island other than Taiwan. Dulles even threatened to use atomic bombs against China.

Behind the scenes, Eisenhower and Dulles worried a good deal about Chiang's motives in stationing so many of his troops on Quemoy. Even the fall of the small island would not directly endanger Taiwan, they reasoned, except that so many Nationalist troops would be lost. American officials began to wonder if that might be Chiang's hidden motive—to stage a defeat requiring that the U.S. rescue his army and get dragged into a war with China.

To avoid such a debacle, Ike and Dulles proposed to Chiang that he voluntarily withdraw the bulk of his forces from Quemoy. Washington would then inform Beijing that no excuse for an armed assault now existed. If in spite of this warning, Chinese troops still attempted to seize Quemoy, the United States would retaliate with a blockade and air strikes against the mainland. This dangerous scenario never came to pass, since Chiang refused to remove his garrison from the offshore island.

A series of adroit American maneuvers during the 1958 crisis finessed the problem. United States navy supply ships were sent to run the Communist blockade of Quemoy and reprovision the hard-pressed defenders. The Chinese, despite threatening rhetoric, carefully avoided attacking the American vessels. The resupplied Nationalist garrison withstood the increasingly erratic shelling, and soon the situation evolved into a standoff. By late 1958 Dulles felt secure enough to visit Taiwan where he informed Chiang to leave well enough alone. Washington would stand by its pledge to protect Taiwan and the most important of the offshore islands, but would not support any major Nationalist campaign against the mainland. Thus the Eisenhower Administration found itself inching toward a sort of "two China" policy. Officially, America recognized the Republic of China on Taiwan as the sole, legitimate regime. In practice, after nearly ten years of denial, Washington seemed almost reconciled to the fact the People's Republic would not be a passing phase. As evidence of this, from the mid-1950s on American and Chinese diplomats in Poland and Geneva engaged in occasional conversations aimed at reducing tensions.

Ironically, it was the Sino-Soviet alliance that suffered the most damage during the 1958 crisis (see also Chapter 8). Up to that point, the alliance represented a marriage of convenience between two traditionally hostile states. Yet, given the reality of China's isolation and desperate need for economic assistance (as well as its vulnerability to a hostile Soviet Union), the benefits of joining the Socialist bloc outweighed the costs.

China's incorporation into the Russian constellation also led to the dubious honor of front-line participation in the Korean War. That involvement, even if partly in China's self-interest, resulted in nearly complete isolation from Japan and the West. In a sense, China had to face the decade of the 1950s politically dominated by its far more powerful and developed ally while isolated and encircled by the world's leading military power.

At least until 1957, however, the bargain still held. China adopted a Soviet model of state organization and followed the Stalinist method of economic and agricultural planning. The payoff for the PRC came from Russia's willingness to transfer a huge industrial infrastructure and technology base to its ally.

Despite this assistance, Mao harbored growing misgivings about the Soviet economic model. He criticized it as urban, elitist and a failure in promoting rapid enough growth. The priority given heavy industry starved the countryside and, he believed, failed to tap the revolutionary fervor of peasants and workers. This chafing under Soviet direction only increased when after Stalin's death his successors began to alter his foreign policy.

The post-Stalin leadership in Moscow had committed itself to improving relations with the United States. Advances in Soviet military and space technology (Sputnik was launched in 1957) provided a badly needed measure of self-assurance to Khrushchev and his colleagues. They now spoke of "peaceful coexistence," the reduction of tensions and a possible limit on the testing and deployment of nuclear weapons. Such talk astounded Mao. He insisted that Soviet technological breakthroughs should make the Socialist bloc more, not less, willing to confront the Western powers. It struck many Chinese leaders as particularly galling that the Russians would soften their stand toward America while Washington maintained its hardline policy toward Beijing. To make matters worse, Khrushchev's failure to consult Mao about a series of major innovations in Soviet domestic and foreign policy seemed a gratuitous insult to Russia's most important ally.

By the late 1950s, the Sino-Soviet alliance showed serious signs of decay. In 1957–58 Mao shocked the Kremlin by rejecting the Soviet model of central economic planning. The Chinese leader announced his "Great Leap Forward" campaign, which was marked by the quick creation of vast agricultural communes and the substitution of revolutionary fervor for careful industrial planning and investment. The whole episode proved an economic fiasco, especially in agriculture where food shortages led to an estimated 20 million deaths in the following years.

Mao's rejection of Soviet models and advice angered the Kremlin leadership for several reasons. It seemed a squandering of the economic aid given the PRC, resulted in the removal from power of pro-Soviet bureaucrats and marked the first shot in Mao's claim to have developed a short cut to modernization. The Maoist model would now compete with the Russian model for influence in both the Socialist and nonaligned blocs of nations. (This is discussed further in Chapter 8.)

By 1960, Beijing and Moscow accused each other of deviating from true Marxism-Leninism. Khrushchev retaliated by withdrawing all Soviet aid and thousands of advisors from China. The widening Sino-Soviet split also ended Russian military assistance, especially in the field of atomic weapons. In fact, after the American atomic threats during the 1953 Korean armistice talks, the 1954 battle of Dienbienphu in northern Vietnam and the 1955 Taiwan Strait crisis, the Chinese began a nuclear weapons program that they believed would deter American pressure and prevent future blackmail. The PRC made a huge commitment of human and material resources to assure development of an atomic weapon. Although the removal of Soviet support represented a particularly acute loss to China's weapons program, Beijing responded by redoubling its effort.

During the early 1960s both the Soviet Union and the United States expressed growing anxiety about China's acquisition of a nuclear arsenal. But even as the two superpowers worried about China's potential, the United States stood on the verge of a new war in Southeast Asia, on China's border.

Selected Additional Readings

On the purge of American China experts, see E. J. Kahn, *The China Hands,* and Gary May, *China Scapegoat,* both cited in Chapter 5; O. Edmund Clubb, *The Witness and I,* N.Y., 1974; David Halberstam, *The Best and the Brightest,* N.Y., 1972; and David M. Oshinski, *A Conspiracy So Immense: The World of Joe McCarthy,* N.Y., 1985.

The China Lobby is discussed in Stanley Bachrack, *The Committee of One Million: China Lobby Politics, 1953–1971,* N.Y., 1976.

The policies of the Eisenhower Administration toward China are discussed in Townsend Hoopes, *The Devil and John Foster Dulles,* Boston, 1974; Robert Divine, *Eisenhower and the Cold War,* N.Y., 1981; David Mayers, *Cracking the Monolith: U.S. Policy Against the Sino-Soviet Alliance, 1949–55,* Baton Rouge, La., 1986; Gordon Chang, *Enemies and Friends: The United States, China and the Soviet Union, 1948–1972,* Stanford, Calif., 1989; J. H. Kalicki, *The Pattern of Sino-American Crises: Political-Military Interactions in the 1950,* N.Y., 1975; and John L. Lewis and Xue Litai, *China Builds the Bomb,* Stanford, Calif., 1988.

On the impact of the Korean War, see the following works: Allen S. Whiting, *China Crosses the Yalu: The Decision to Enter the Korean War,* N.Y., 1960; Burton I. Kaufman, *The Korean War,* N.Y., 1986; Callum A. MacDonald, *Korea: The War Before Vietnam,* London, 1986; and Michael Schaller, *Douglas MacArthur: The Far Eastern General,* N.Y., 1989.

On the connection between China policy and the heroin trade, see

Alfred W. McCoy, *The Politics of Heroin in Southeast Asia,* N.Y., 1972.

On Chinese foreign policy, see Peter Van Ness, *Revolution and Chinese Foreign Policy: Peking's Support for Wars of National Liberation,* Berkeley, Calif., 1970.

7

The United States, China and the Agony of Vietnam, 1950–68

American military assistance to the French colonial war in Indochina began early in 1950 and assumed major proportions
during the Korean struggle. The Truman Administration believed that the Vietnamese nationalists seeking to oust the French
were simply pawns of the "international Communist conspiracy"
and, in particular, puppets of the Chinese. As early as 1945–46
American officials spurned Ho Chi Minh who, as leader of the
Viet Minh insurgents, had appealed to the U.S. for support in his
independence struggle. Even though the Viet Minh had cooperated in the war against Japan and modeled their declaration
of independence on America's, Washington refused to recognize
Ho's Democratic Republic of Vietnam and assisted the return
of French forces to their colony.

In the late 1940s Secretary of State Acheson had disparaged
Ho's credentials with the observation that in colonial areas, "all
Stalinists" masquerade as "nationalists." To be sure, Ho was a
dedicated Communist. Nevertheless, he had devoted his life to
the battle for Vietnamese independence. While a committed
revolutionary, he could hardly be dismissed as a puppet. More-

over, like most Vietnamese, he harbored a great fear of Chinese domination.

Under American prodding, in 1949 France had nominally transferred rule to a Vietnamese puppet emperor, Bao Dai. By all accounts an amiable playboy, Bao Dai had a political following that one cynical American diplomat described as consisting of "a pimp and three prostitutes." This pretext assuaged Washington's guilt about assisting colonialism. In the months preceding the Korean War, the United States began supplying French forces in Vietnam with military and economic aid from a secret fund (the Mutual Defense Assistance Program) designed to "contain Communism in the General Area of China." Aid levels increased rapidly during the next few years and by 1954 Washington was bankrolling the French antiguerrilla campaign to the tune of several hundred million dollars per year. Despite this assistance, the guerrillas proved more than a match for French troops.

In the spring of 1954 the French army (with U.S. logistic support) hoped to engage the Viet Minh in a decisive battle in the valley of Dienbienphu in northern Vietnam. Instead, the guerrillas, assisted by Chinese advisors, trapped the French and stood on the threshold of a major victory. Many observers expected that negotiations at the upcoming international conference at Geneva (scheduled to discuss a series of problems left over from the Korean conflict) would result in France turning over power to Ho's forces.

The Eisenhower Administration feared that the "loss" of Vietnam to communism would breach the containment barrier around China and encourage revolutionary forces throughout Asia. Even though Vietnam was not especially rich, the surrounding parts of Southeast Asia (Thailand, the Philippines, Malaya and Indonesia) were considered economically vital to Japanese and Western European prosperity. Moreover, Eisenhower and Dulles worried that a Communist victory would expose the Republicans to the same charges they had leveled against the Democrats in 1952—that they were "soft" on communism in Asia.

Vice President Richard Nixon, Secretary of State Dulles and the Chairman of the Joint Chiefs, Admiral Radford, urged

Eisenhower to rescue the French garrison at Dienbienphu through air strikes and, perhaps, use of tactical atomic bombs. British reluctance to escalate the conflict, and French misgivings about turning the war over to Washington, convinced Eisenhower to reject this extreme advice. Nevertheless, he remained eager to support anticommunist resistance in Indochina, with or without the French.

In May 1954, as the Geneva Conference began, the French forces at Dienbienphu surrendered. A new government in Paris, led by Premier Pierre Mendes-France and influenced by the loss of popular support for French involvement in Vietnam, declared its determination to quit the war as soon as possible. After prolonged negotiations, the conference released a set of "Geneva Accords" in July. These declared that France would leave Indochina (Cambodia, Laos and Vietnam), that Vietnam would be temporarily divided at the 17th parallel to permit the disengagement of forces (Viet Minh to the north; French and pro-French Vietnamese to the south), and that elections would be held in 1956 to unify the nation. In the interim, no foreign powers were to introduce weapons or troops into the region.

There arrangements angered Ho Chi Minh, who insisted his followers had won the right for immediate control of all Vietnam. He also had reason to fear that accepting even a temporary division might allow the U.S. to replace France as the sponsor of a client regime in the south. Despite his objections, Moscow and Beijing twisted Ho's arm and forced him to accept the Accords. Both Communist powers were eager to improve relations with Washington in the aftermath of the Korean War and did not want a dispute over marginal territory (Vietnam) to interfere.

Secretary of State Dulles attended the conference briefly. His most memorable contribution was a refusal to shake hands with Zhou Enlai. Although the American delegation declined to sign the Geneva Accords, it verbally promised to abide by them. In fact, the United States moved quickly to reverse the verdict of French defeat by accelerating plans to encircle China with a ring of anticommunist, pro-American states. By the end of 1954 Dulles had forged the SEATO alliance and firmed up mutual security treaties with Taiwan, Korea, Japan, Australia and New Zealand. Ho's power base north of the 17th parallel marked a small, but dangerous, breach of the containment barrier. An anticommunist South Vietnamese state seemed the best antidote. Dulles resolved to create one before the scheduled national elections in 1956.

During 1954 the CIA and other U.S. personnel were active in Saigon, creating the framework for a government to replace the French. To many Americans, both in and out of government, Vietnam was a special challenge—an opportunity for the United States to create an Asian regime in its own image. Such a scheme had many apparent virtues. Not only would a pro-American regime in Saigon act as a physical barrier to Chinese-Vietnamese Communist expansion, but it would symbolize a successful political alternative to Communist revolution in the underdeveloped world. A democratic, prosperous, pro-Western and capitalist South Vietnam could be a showcase for U.S. policy in Asia. American leaders probably thought of how well they had succeeded in restructuring defeated Japan, so that now its society appeared democratic, pro-Western and thoroughly anticommunist. The fundamental social and economic differences between Vietnam and Japan—the former a preindustrial, traditional and rural society, the latter an urbanized, modern industrial state—were subtleties lost on the American mind. American planners thought of Vietnam as clay in their hands, to be molded at will, regardless of what the Vietnamese wanted or the Geneva Accords called for.

The concept of making Vietnam a "showcase" of democracy in Asia also fit neatly into the current theory of global strategy. Beginning under Truman and accelerating under Eisenhower, American policymakers posited a world of political "dominoes." According to this theory, a Communist advance in one vulnerable spot would quickly spread and topple over adjacent noncommunist, pro-American governments. Like a row of falling dominoes, the chain reaction was nearly impossible to stop once begun. Thus holding every piece of noncommunist real estate in Asia became vital to American security since its loss might start the dominoes falling. This mechanistic theory completely ignored the actual sources of instability in most poor Asian countries. Where Communist insurgent movements were active, their success or failure was due almost entirely to local support, not

Moscow's or Beijing's control or aid. Pro-American regimes in Southeast Asia and elsewhere were vulnerable because they were unable or unwilling to rectify fundamental social problems. No amount of U.S. assistance could alter the basically corrupt policies of an unpopular regime. It had not worked in China and would not work elsewhere.

Disregarding history, American leaders believed outside reform could be successful if only the United States would intervene earlier and more completely in Asia to stop the spread of communism. Vietnam had the dubious distinction of being Washington's classroom for a public experiment in counterrevolutionary nation building.

The man the Eisenhower Administration tapped to rule South Vietnam was, fortuitously, living in the United States. Ngo Dinh Diem came from a prominent Vietnamese Catholic family (the Vietnamese were overwhelmingly Buddhist) and enjoyed support from a number of American academic and political notables, including Senators John Kennedy and Mike Mansfield, Cardinal Spellman and Supreme Court Justice William O. Douglas. A group of political science specialists at Michigan State University (which received a U.S. government contract to help set up a regime in Saigon) championed Diem and helped convince the CIA and other important groups in Washington to support him as the leader of a new Vietnamese government. Diem, it appeared, was a new and improved Chiang Kai-shek—Christian, anticommunist and pro-American.

By the end of 1954 extensive American economic and military support had enabled Diem to establish himself with a personal army in Saigon. By 1956 he had increased his power over a large part of Vietnam south of the 17th parallel. As the scheduled 1956 elections approached, Diem proclaimed the existence of the "Republic of Vietnam" in the south as an independent nation. Washington quickly recognized its own creation and declared that it would defend South Vietnam's "independence and freedom." Since, as Eisenhower admitted in his memoirs, Ho Chi Minh would probably win any free election in Vietnam, neither Washington nor Saigon would permit a vote.

Thus, as of 1956, the U.S. declared there were two separate Vietnams—Ho's "Democratic Republic of Vietnam" in the north and Diem's "Republic of Vietnam" in the south. This arrangement offended most Vietnamese who lacked any concept of "two Vietnams." The permanent division not only violated the Geneva Accords of 1954 but flew in the face of the prolonged Vietnamese struggle to throw out foreign influence and create an independent, unified nation. Nevertheless, Washington was now committed to preserving Saigon both as a model of nation building and as a barrier to presumed Chinese Communist expansion.

The struggle which soon erupted in South Vietnam in many ways resembled the earlier war against the French. Guerrilla fighters in the south—the Vietcong—began an insurrection against the Saigon regime. As the rebellion spread, leading to increased repression and foreign (U.S.) intervention, the north came to the aid of its brothers in the south. North Vietnamese troops and large-scale aid only appeared later in the conflict, after it had escalated.

Five successive presidential administrations—from Eisenhower through Ford—ignored or denied the nature of the civil war in Vietnam. American leaders—buttressed by fallacious arguments from their national security advisors—insisted that the North Vietnamese and Vietcong were nothing more than proxies fighting against South Vietnam on behalf of China and the Soviet Union. Permitting this aggression to succeed would endanger world peace. To prevent the feared "domino" from falling, the United States committed itself to the defense of South Vietnam.

As a senator in 1956 John Kennedy described Vietnam as the "cornerstone of the Free World in Southeast Asia, the Keystone to the arch, the Finger in the dike." As soon as he became President in 1961, Kennedy's "New Frontier" laid the groundwork for a wider American involvement in Vietnam. Despite his calls to propose new solutions to international problems, Kennedy's foreign policy embraced many existing cold war clichés. While JFK occasionally spoke of the need to improve relations with China, he did not permit members of his administration to pursue innovations. Instead, the major thrust of Kennedy's policies toward the Third World was an effort to expand and perfect "counterinsurgency" warfare. The judicious application of Special Forces (the Green Berets) and CIA covert operations com-

bined with increased military and economic aid to friendly regimes was designed to sweep back the tide of change in the
underdeveloped world. The New Frontier remained convinced
that developing societies must follow the American model or
else be considered hostile.

Kennedy's policy toward Vietnam was bound to exacerbate
the situation and worsen relations with China. JFK chose Dean
Rusk as his Secretary of State, a man with a long history of an-
tagonism toward China. Rusk adhered to the belief that it was
"as essential to 'contain' Communist aggression [in Asia as] in
Europe." During his nearly eight years of tenure under Kennedy
and Johnson, Rusk frequently raised the specter of "one or two
billion Chinese armed with nuclear weapons" as a justification
for American involvement in Vietnam. In his mind, Ho Chi Minh
and the leaders of the People's Republic of China could only be
compared to Adolf Hitler, and their policies to Nazi aggression.

Surrounded by such advisors, prodded by an entrenched anticommunist bureaucracy, and himself ever mindful of Truman's
misfortune at being blamed for the "loss of China," Kennedy
was determined not to abandon the Saigon regime. By 1962–63,
as Diem's position grew weaker, he turned his wrath against
noncommunist critics. Like Chiang, Diem seemed to fear his
liberal opponents (who might be a magnet for U.S. support) as
much as he feared the Communists. During the autumn of 1963
Americans were shocked to see on television gruesome films of
Buddhist monks immolating themselves in protest against Diem's
political and religious oppression. Despite Kennedy's efforts to
shore up Saigon by steadily increasing the level of aid and number of U.S. military advisors (from 800 to 16,000), South Vietnam seemed on the verge of collapse. Not only did this threaten
a Communist advance in Asia, but it loomed as an awesome domestic political setback for the Kennedy Administration. JFK
had no desire to be called the first President to lose a war—
whether or not the charge had any meaning.

To buy some time to shore up South Vietnam, Diem would
have to go. The longer this unstable puppet remained the more
likely the pro-American group in Saigon would lose whatever
hold on power it still retained. By the end of October word had
filtered down from the White House to South Vietnamese army

officers that the U.S. favored the accession of a new regime in Saigon. On November 1, 1963, Diem and his closest aides were slain in a coup, to be succeeded by a line of tin-horn generals. The last of these, Nguyen Van Thieu, fled to Taiwan in 1975.

Kennedy's own assassination three weeks after Diem's death brought no reassessment of American policy in Asia. Like his predecessor, Lyndon Johnson was a committed cold warrior and a believer in the theory of falling dominoes. "We will not permit," he declared, "the independent nations of the East to be swallowed by Communist conquest." Nor was LBJ alone in this belief. Richard Nixon, titular leader of the Republican Party, solemnly intoned his belief that "a United States defeat in Vietnam means a Chinese Communist victory."

Johnson, torn between his desire to fund Great Society economic and social programs at home and to defend the faith abroad, fell into the same trap as his predecessors. Reflecting on his decision to escalate the war in 1965, Johnson told his biographer, Doris Kearns,

> if I left that war and let the Communists take over South Vietnam, then I would be seen as a coward and my nation would be seen as an appeaser and we would both find it impossible to accomplish anything for anybody on the entire globe. . . . Everything I knew about history told me that if I got out of Vietnam and let Ho Chi Minh run through the streets of Saigon then I'd be doing exactly what Chamberlain did in WWII. I'd be giving a big fat reward to aggression. And I knew that if we let Communist aggression succeed in taking over South Vietnam there would follow in this country an endless national debate—a mean and destructive debate —that would shatter my Presidency, kill my administration and damage our democracy. I knew that Harry Truman and Dean Acheson had lost effectiveness from the day the Communists took over China. I believed that the loss of China had played a large role in the rise of Joe McCarthy. And I knew that all these problems, taken together, were chickenshit compared with what might happen if we lost Vietnam.

Johnson's "theory" about Communist aggression and domestic reaction was part self-serving rationalization and part a ménage of misinformation about the nature of the civil war in Vietnam. He cast the giant United States as the victim of a heinous attack by tiny Vietnam. America was the injured party which had no choice but to fight for justice.

This distorted reality became evident in August 1964 during the Tonkin Gulf incident. In a report to Congress, Johnson alleged that U.S. navy destroyers were attacked by North Vietnamese ships while on peaceful patrol in international waters. Congress responded almost unanimously by passing the "Gulf of Tonkin Resolution," an open-ended statement giving Johnson a free hand to resist attacks on U.S. forces in Southeast Asia. With hardly a perfunctory investigation, Congress approved what amounted to a virtual declaration of war against North Vietnam.

Only several years later did subsequent investigations reveal the administration's duplicity. U.S. naval forces at the time of the Tonkin incident had actually been sailing along a strip of the North Vietnamese coast where American ships had recently assisted South Vietnamese coastal raids. Thus the attacks were hardly unprovoked. Even more startling, several American sailors testified that no North Vietnamese attack had occurred. They had only detected some unidentified electronic sightings which were erroneously reported as attacks. Again, the specter of revolution abroad and the Red Scare at home pushed American leaders into a reflex decision to fight in Asia.

Following his election in November 1964 (in which he promised *not* to escalate the war), Johnson saw no alternative but to become more involved in Vietnam. Without an infusion of American military power, the Saigon regime was doomed. By the summer of 1965, though Congress had not formally declared war, the United States initiated a massive bombing campaign in both South and North Vietnam, designed to destroy the power of the insurgents. As this tactic faltered, 500,000 American troops were dispatched to South Vietnam. The dimensions of such a war in this small country defy description. Over the next decade many hundreds of thousands of Vietnamese died, as did over 50,000 Americans. At the height of the airwar more tons of bombs were dropped each month than had been used in all of World War II.

Asked to explain his fixation with victory in Vietnam, Johnson was alleged to have said what his predecessors must have thought: he would not be the first President "to lose a war." But the issue went beyond both LBJ's vanity and Vietnam's particular importance. The war assumed the dimensions of a contest of wills and a proxy battle between Beijing and Washington. In April 1965 LBJ declared:

> Over this war—and all Asia—is another reality: the deepening shadow of Communist China. . . . The rulers of Hanoi are urged on by Peking. . . . The contest in Vietnam is part of a wider pattern of aggressive purpose.

A month later Johnson explained that China had targeted "not merely South Vietnam [but all] Asia" for conquest.

Through 1967 most traditional liberal institutions and politicians voiced agreement with Johnson's vision and policy. In October 1967 Vice President Hubert Humphrey (a war supporter right through his defeat by Nixon in 1968) declared:

> The threat to world peace is militant, aggressive Asian communism, with its headquarters in Peking. . . . The aggression of North Vietnam is but the most current and immediate action of militant Asian communism.

Two years earlier he had told George McGovern that unless the U.S. "stopped the Communists in Vietnam . . . they would take all of Asia."

The *New York Times,* eventually the foremost journalistic forum of antiwar sentiment—and publisher of the *Pentagon Papers*—came late to dissent. The paper had supported editorially the French colonial war in Vietnam and in the early 1960s had prodded the Kennedy Administration to expand the U.S. combat presence in Southeast Asia. Following Diem's death in the 1963 coup, the *Times* expressed relief that the "new Vietnamese rulers are dedicated anticommunists who reject any idea of neutralism and pledge to stand with the free world."

As with so many grandiose American statements on the importance of the war, these totally distorted what many observers knew at the time. Within the Communist camp Vietnam was tied more closely to the Soviet Union than to China. Even the basis of this tie was largely Hanoi's desperate need of modern weapons to combat the Americans. The deep, often ugly, traditional dislike between the Vietnamese and Chinese resurfaced almost as soon as the war in Vietnam ended. The supposedly monolithic allies quickly regrouped their armed forces along each other's borders. By February 1979 China had begun its own Vietnam War.

Oblivious to this and many deeper contradictions, America plunged headlong into the disaster of Vietnam. Between 1965 and 1968 the U.S. carried out the most intensive bombing campaign in human history and committed an army and navy of over half a million men against the guerrilla forces of one of the more economically backward nations of the earth. But technological superiority and promises of imminent victory failed to bring Washington any closer to securing Saigon against its Vietnamese opponents. Within the United States disillusionment grew as did lists of casualties and military appropriations. Soon the immense cost of the war undercut Johnson's plans for the Great Society.* The President, to use his own phrase, was forced to sacrifice "the woman I really loved" (the Great Society) to pay for "that bitch of a war on the other side of the world. . . ." As a growing number of national politicians, scholars, students and draftees voiced opposition to the quagmire of Vietnam, Johnson isolated himself from critics. Increasingly suspicious that the opposition to the undeclared war was disloyal if not treasonous, LBJ ordered the FBI and CIA to monitor and even harass antiwar organizations and individuals.

As the war escalated, so did the likelihood of a direct Chinese-American confrontation in Southeast Asia. In their attacks upon North Vietnam, American planes passed perilously close to China. Several were actually shot down after intruding into Chinese air space. As both a measure of support for Vietnam and a warning signal to Washington, between 1962 and 1968 approximately 300,000 Chinese soldiers went to North Vietnam, 4,000 of whom died. Though not participating in ground combat, they helped operate anti-aircraft weapons and communications facilities. Without question their presence was largely intended to deter the Americans from attempting any invasion of the north such as MacArthur had staged in Korea. Washington, having

---

* The huge military outlays were paid by federal borrowing, a major factor contributing to the inflation and the economic problems of the 1970s.

learned how seriously China would react to any ground attack upon its neighbors, exercised caution. For its part, China's worsening border dispute with the Soviet Union constrained any inclination Beijing may have had to assist Hanoi more directly.

The bloody fighting in Vietnam's jungles enraged a growing number of Americans. Opposition to the war grew not only on college campuses but also in Congress and in the press. Repeated promises that America had turned a corner and could now see "the light at the end of the tunnel" were belied by mounting casuality lists and ever-larger draft calls. Johnson's own optimism was shattered by the Communists' Tet Offensive, launched in February 1968. American military leaders had assured the President and public that the enemy was virtually defeated, that the end was within sight. Yet, during Tet the Vietcong demonstrated remarkable strength throughout Vietnam, actually penetrating the grounds of the "impregnable" U.S. embassy in Saigon, while attacking all the major cities of the south simultaneously. The response of the Joint Chiefs was a call to send more American troops. Clearly, the policy of escalating until the enemy (be they Vietcong or Chinese Communist) left South Vietnam in peace had borne no success. The question was no longer whether one particular military plan or another might eventually succeed. American military power could never resolve the internal political struggle in Vietnam. The foreign forces who would have to leave turned out to be the American crusaders themselves.

On March 31, 1968, President Johnson acknowledged the failure of his policy and announced his decisions both not to seek reelection and to call a limited halt to the airwar over North Vietnam. Although the war in Vietnam would actually continue for several more years (American forces did not withdraw until early 1973, and Saigon received military aid until May 1975), Johnson's decision not to escalate the conflict further had a tremendous impact on domestic and foreign affairs. In their mounting frustration with "LBJ's War," the American people turned away from the Democratic Party and in the November election selected Richard Nixon as President. While he had earlier been a vociferous "hawk" on the war, in 1968 Nixon campaigned on a platform of having a "secret plan to end the war." During the six years of his presidency, Nixon would lead the American nation down many unexpected paths in Asia. None would be more unpredictable than his policies toward Vietnam and China.

Selected Additional Readings

America's tortured involvement in Vietnam is the subject of a growing literature. Among the best studies are George C. Herring, *America's Longest War: The United States and Vietnam, 1950–1975*, N.Y., 1986; Stanley Karnow, *Vietnam: A History*, N.Y., 1984; Archimedes L. Patti, *Why Vietnam? Prelude to America's Albatross*, Berkeley, Calif., 1980; Lloyd Gardner, *Approaching Vietnam: From World War II Through Dienbienphu*, N.Y., 1988; George McT. Kahin, *Intervention: How America Became Involved in Vietnam*, N.Y., 1986; Gabriel Kolko, *Anatomy of a War: Vietnam, the United States and the Modern Historical Experience*, N.Y., 1985; Frances Fitzgerald, *Fire in the Lake: The Vietnamese and the Americans in Vietnam*, Boston, 1972; David Halberstam, *The Best and the Brightest*, N.Y., 1972; Daniel Ellsberg, *Papers on the War*, N.Y., 1972; Doris Kearns, *Lyndon Johnson and the American Dream*, N.Y., 1974; Allen S. Whiting, *The Chinese Calculus of Deterrence: India and Indochina*, Ann Arbor, Mich., 1975; and Neil Sheehan, *A Bright Shining Lie: John Paul Vann and America in Vietnam*, N.Y., 1988.

8

The Long Journey:
Sino-American Détente

In January 1969, as a new administration assumed power in Washington, few Americans still voiced enthusiasm for the war in Vietnam. Some felt the war was justified but unwinnable. Others condemned it as a senseless, immoral slaughter. Whatever the basis of their criticism, most "hawks" and "doves" agreed that the Asian policy of the United States was a shambles. Washington seemed unable either to destroy the Vietcong or to silence the growing peace movement at home. Although a succession of presidents had approved of the war to demonstrate American power and unity, the policy had proved a dismal failure.

Even while President Johnson was expanding the war after 1965, an impressive number of American opinion leaders—journalists, scholars, members of Congress—began to question the conventional wisdom which sanctioned unremitting hostility toward China and communism in Asia. At the same time, many of Chiang Kai-shek's political allies in the U.S. had grown old, disterested and tired of the battle. In this atmosphere of war-weariness, a rethinking of old ideas became possible.

A series of hearings before Senator William Fulbright's Senate

Foreign Relations Committee in 1966 confirmed this trend. Fulbright, originally a war supporter who emerged as a leading war critic, assembled a cross-section of respected scholars and experts on Asian politics who argued that the American government had grossly misinterpreted Chinese foreign policy ever since the Second World War. They questioned Washington's depiction of the PRC as a ruthless, imperialistic power. To a great extent, they said, Chinese behavior was following a traditional pattern, that of reasserting leadership in East Asia, seeking friendly neighbors and demanding respect. Even though the PRC sympathized with the goal of world revolution, and supplied limited assistance to scattered guerrilla groups, there was little real evidence to show that Communist China had tried to conquer Asia. The testimony also asserted that the North Vietnamese–Vietcong struggle to unify Vietnam had its roots primarily in nationalism, rather than in a Communist plan for world domination. While several painful years elapsed before American political leaders accepted these concepts, a new perspective had been offered by those on the fringes of influence. China, it proposed, might have just aspirations in Asia and realistic grievances against American actions. Understanding Communist China was now more crucial than ever, for in October 1964 the People's Republic had exploded its first nuclear device. By 1967 Beijing had developed a hydrogen bomb and in 1970 orbited its first earth satellite.

In many ways it remains a historical irony that the American leader who reestablished a dialogue with China was Richard Nixon, a politician whose entire prepresidential career had been highlighted by relentless opposition to revolutionary movements. Early in the 1950s, Nixon endorsed McCarthy's charge that treasonous diplomats had "lost China." In 1954, while Vice President, he had urged Eisenhower to send American forces to Vietnam; during the crises over the offshore islands in 1955 and 1958 he was most adamant about not surrendering a foot of territory to the Chinese Communists; when debating John Kennedy in October 1960 he had declared: "Now what do the Chinese Communists want? They don't just want Quemoy and Matsu. They don't just want Formosa. They want the world." As spokesman for the Republican Party in 1965 he criticized President Johnson for not doing enough to resist the Chinese and Vietnamese Communists. Since 1949, in effect, Nixon had continually opposed any "softening" of United States policy toward China.

Until he assumed the presidency, Nixon gave little indication that his earlier opinions had changed to any great degree. In an article appearing in a 1967 issue of the influential journal *Foreign Affairs* ("Asia After Vietnam"), Nixon urged that the United States give even greater assistance to its Southeast Asian allies to contain China militarily. He reaffirmed his opposition to granting China diplomatic recognition, U.N. membership or trade privileges. American policy, he argued, should be "to persuade China that it must change: that it cannot satisfy its imperialistic ambitions." In a significant ambiguity, however, Nixon implied that when and if China did change its behavior the U.S. might reassess its own frozen attitudes.

For better or worse the Nixon presidency put U.S. foreign policy on an irreversible course. It marked a belated acceptance of a limited role in Southeast Asia; a realization that the U.S. must live with nuclear parity with the Soviets; a diminished role for America as world policeman; and a determination to bring China into world councils.

Nixon's willingness to pursue new approaches toward China after 1969 reflected an understanding on his part that the politics of Asia were far more complicated than the United States had realized for a generation. Yet, even this realization gained slow acceptance. The failure to achieve victory in Vietnam crumbled one pillar of American policy. But it required the outbreak of virtually open warfare between the Russians and Chinese in 1969 to alter Washington's fixation on the specter of "monolithic communism." More than any other factor, the Sino-Soviet split was the force which drove the United States and China toward a new relationship.

Tension between the Chinese and Soviet Communists had a long and clouded history. As far back as the 1920s, Stalin had opposed Mao's doctrines of peasant revolution. During the Second World War, Mao and Zhou had frequently hinted to Americans that the CCP preferred to keep its distance from Moscow, but that Washington would force them to side more openly with Stalin if it continued to support Chiang. Not only did American leaders reject this course, but, after 1949, they also insisted that the Chinese Communists were slavish servants of the Kremlin.

The Sino-Soviet alliance proved far stormier than most Americans realized. From its inception in 1950, the Chinese harbored many grievances about Russian aid. Although Stalin had granted China several hundred million dollars' worth of credits, he insisted that China pay for the almost $1 billion worth of military equipment it desperately required during the Korean War. Stalin also insisted that the Soviet Union keep its special port, naval and railroad privileges in Manchuria. Only after the long-time Soviet leader's death in 1953 did the new Russian leadership agree to a more generous aid package and the complete abandonment of Soviet facilities in Manchuria.

From the mid-1950s on, Sino-Soviet relations continued to deteriorate. Mao insisted that Moscow not only accept the Chinese as full "partners" in the Communist movement, but must also admit that the Chinese political and economic model of development was especially applicable to the "Third World." Mao's programs such as the Great Leap Forward in 1958 was in direct opposition to the Soviet model of proper development. In 1957 Mao had given a speech in Moscow which declared "the East Wind is prevailing over the West Wind." This symbolized much more than his belief that communism was the wave of the future. In essence, Mao was saying that China's revolutionary experience would become the example for all developing nations, not the program advanced by the already industrialized and European-oriented Soviet Union.

Despite Chinese calls for a Soviet commitment to aid China and other revolutionary movements with greater economic and military assitance, the Soviet leadership refused to budge. Khrushchev and his fellow Russian leaders had, in fact, become more cautious as their nation achieved a more secure military and economic level. Now they advocated "peaceful coexistence" with the United States and other capitalist nations. According to the Chinese, the Russian line betrayed the long-term goals of world revolution. These political and theoretical disputes opened a widening rift between the Soviet Union and the People's Republic of China.

That rift grew even wider when the Soviets, in their effort to improve relations with the U.S., pledged only half-hearted commitment to the Chinese during the Sino-American conflict over the blockade of Quemoy island in 1958. Shortly thereafter, in 1959, Khrushchev gave cautious verbal support (followed by economic aid) to India, then in a protracted border dispute with China. By the early 1960s it seemed as though the Soviet Union had not only drifted apart from China politically but had begun to see it as a military rival. When the long-festering Sino-Indian border dispute led to a brief war in 1962 (now generally blamed on India's refusal to reach a reasonable compromise), the Soviet Union supported the Indians with military and economic aid.

Indeed, as China's relations with the Soviet Union deteriorated in the late 1950s and early 1960s, Russian-American relations began to improve. Eisenhower and Khrushchev had a pair of successful summit meetings before the flap over the Soviet downing of a U-2 spy plane in the spring of 1960 temporarily set back the relationship. Prior to that, Eisenhower told several close advisors that he hoped one byproduct of warmer ties with Moscow would be a worsening of relations between the two major Communist powers.

The Kennedy Administration, from 1961 to 1963, pursued the same path. President Kennedy made several appeals to Khrushchev to cooperate with the United States in restraining Chinese ambitions. By 1963 JFK worried most about China's imminent test of an atomic bomb. In fact, he pushed vigorously for a limited test ban treaty with Moscow in part to bring joint Soviet-American pressure against Beijing's nuclear program. By acting together, he hoped, the two superpowers could compel China not to test its prototype. The Kennedy Administration even gave some thought to a preemptive strike against Chinese nuclear research installations.

Before Kennedy's death in November 1963, he and his advisors acknowledged that the Sino-Soviet "monolith" had, in fact, broken apart. Since 1949 this had been a major goal of America's China policy. Yet, the development did not fit the predicted pattern. Instead of China abandoning its alliance with Russia and seeking support from the West, the People's Republic accused both Washington and Moscow of conspiring to encircle China. Mao condemned Khrushchev's "revisionism" as akin to American capitalism.

American policymakers had little sympathy for China's anti-Soviet complaints. Instead of making common cause with Beijing, the Eisenhower and Kennedy administrations hoped to forge closer links with the Soviet Union. Both powers, they argued, had common interests in curbing Chinese power and pretensions. This attitude underlay growing American intervention in Vietnam, then considered a Chinese "test" of Western resolve.

The dismal prospect of encirclement by both the Soviet Union and the United States propelled Mao toward increasingly radical domestic policies. The Chinese leader utilized the threat by the superpowers to purge domestic policy opponents and to advance many ideas first associated with the abortive Great Leap Forward. From 1962–65 Mao berated the Soviets as "revisionists" and labeled Chinese bureaucrats who opposed him as virtual traitors.

American escalation of the Vietnam War, especially under President Lyndon Johnson, somewhat restrained Mao's plans. However, by 1966, Washington made it clear that it did not intend to invade or destroy North Vietnam or to provoke a war with China, as MacArthur had threatened earlier in Korea. As fear of imminent American invasion faded, Mao launched his "Great Proletarian Cultural Revolution."

The Cultural Revolution lasted a full decade (1966–76), with the most "radical" phase taking place during its first three years. Through this mass political upheaval, Mao hoped to purify Chinese society, advance its development, drive from power allegedly pro-Soviet and procapitalist bureaucrats and, not incidentally, ensure his control over all the levers of power. By mobilizing students, peasants and workers and by organizing the youthful "Red Guards," Mao attacked the entrenched leadership of the Communist Party and state planning bureaucracy. He and his radical supporters purged tens of thousands of bureaucrats and technical experts accused of stifling the spontaneous abilities of the masses. Among the most prominent victims were Liu Shao-chi and Deng Xiaoping. The former would die in prison, while the latter would make a spectacular political recovery a decade later. During the purge, central planning virtually ended, higher education ceased, economic incentives for agricultural and industrial workers were abolished and a primitive egalitarianism became the norm. In the resulting chaos, probably a half million people were persecuted to death while millions of others lost their jobs and standing in society. By 1969, political and economic institutions were in such disarray that Mao had to call on the armed forces, led by Defense Minister Lin Biao, to restore order and administer a wide range of services.

These excesses rekindled American fears of Chinese "hordes" and of the "yellow peril." Certainly, the Cultural Revolution was a harrowing experience, especially for urban and educated Chinese. American policymakers like Secretary of State Dean Rusk justified containment and the war in Vietnam by quoting the xenophobic and nativist rhetoric coming from Mao's radical clique. At the same time, Rusk and others overlooked a basic fact: China's very turmoil reduced to almost nothing its ability to act on the world scene. At one point during the upheaval, for example, China practically severed all contact with the outside world, recalling all but one of its ambassadors from abroad.

In the midst of this chaos, and while a half million American troops still fought in Vietnam, Sino-Soviet tensions took a dramatic turn for the worse. China's 4,500 mile border with the Soviet Union remained poorly marked, and both nations harbored an intense historic territorial rivalry. Ever since Czarist Russian explorers had ventured across Siberia in the seventeenth century, China had steadily lost territory to the Russians. Large tracts were acquired through "unequal treaties" in the nineteenth century. Since the 1920s, the Soviet Union had dominated Outer Mongolia, traditionally part of the Chinese Empire, and kept imperialistic privileges in Manchuria until the mid-1950s. Now that their ideological split had widened into a chasm, China and the Soviet Union accused each other of illegally occupying border territory and planning the seizure of additional land. The Soviets confirmed China's fears by steadily increasing the deployment of troops and equipment in the Far East.

Chinese anxiety increased greatly in August 1968, when Soviet forces invaded Communist Czechoslovakia. That spring, a group of liberal reformers had taken control of the Czech Communist Party and government and started dismantling the Stalinist structures imposed on Eastern Europe after World War II. Soviet leader Leonid Brezhnev denounced this deviation and proclaimed Moscow's "right" to use force to reimpose orthodoxy on any wayward Communist regime. The implication for China was obvious.

In March 1969 Chinese and Soviet armed forces clashed near the islands along the course of the Amur and Ussuri rivers. That summer, following additional skirmishes, both nations deployed substantial forces in the area. The Soviets brought up approximately thirty-five divisions armed with nuclear weapons and transferred bomber units from Europe. Reports soon circulated that the Soviet Union might launch a preemptive nuclear strike against Chinese millitary facilities, just as the United States had weighed such an option in 1963. Suddenly, China faced the combined wrath of two hostile superpowers while wracked by internal disarray and lacking any significant foreign allies. Mao responded publicly with a homily, ordering the Chinese people to "store grain and dig tunnels deeply" as a precaution against invasion by the "#1 enemy," the Soviet "social imperialists," or the nearly as threatening capitalist imperialists. Mao's heir apparent, Lin Biao, was personally identified with this "dual adversary" approach toward foreign policy.

By the time Richard Nixon assumed the presidency in January 1969, simplistic assessments of Chinese foreign policy had given way to more sophisticated reevaluation. Nixon and his National Security Advisor, Dr. Henry Kissinger, realized that the Sino-Soviet conflict and the reverses already suffered by the United States in Vietnam altered radically the past positions of China and America. Washington no longer assumed it could impose its military will upon East Asia; China had lost its major foreign ally, had failed in its radical development program and stood vulnerable between the Soviet Union and the United States.

Nixon's consummate political opportunism coincided perfectly with Henry Kissinger's interest in balance of power politics. Both reasoned that, in light of the Soviet threat, China might be willing to make concessions to the United States in order to reduce tensions and marshal its limited strength against the Russians. By conceding to China a greater role in Asia and the world, America might gain increased leverage over a nervous Soviet Union. In a break from the classic "bipolar" cold war, the two American leaders envisioned a "multipolar" world in which the United States, the Soviet Union, Japan and Western Europe all enjoyed spheres of interest. Often called "détente" (literally a reduction in tension), this policy represented an accommodation to the fact that in the nuclear age all powerful and established nations must coexist peacefully or risk destruction. The United States had not abandoned its opposition to radical social change in general, but would acknowledge that China and the Soviet Union had legitimate security interests that did not necessarily collide with those of America. At the same time, Washington hoped to exploit the opportunity of the Sino-Soviet split to play off Moscow and Beijing against one another.

Improved contacts with China promised additional benefits for the Nixon Administration. The Soviet Union might adopt a more cautious foreign policy and agree to limitations in strategic arms in order to reduce the possibility of a Sino-American alliance aimed against Moscow. Similarly, Beijing might modify its policies to minimize Soviet-American cooperation. Nixon and Kissinger hoped that in their effort to court Washington's favor, both Communist powers would also assist the United States in negotiating a compromise settlement of the Vietnam War. Since both supplied many forms of assistance to Hanoi, they were in a strong position to press North Vietnam to adopt a more flexible policy. These considerations impelled Nixon and Kissinger to seek improved relations with China soon after taking office.

Chinese policy mirrored, in significant ways, Washington's assessment. Mao and the contending "radical" and "conservative" factions around him did not suddenly fall in love with the United States. However, all were realistic enough to see that a reduction in tensions with America would permit China to counter more effectively the acute Soviet threat. In agreeing to throw overboard the most radical ideology of the previous decade, Mao moved away from Lin Biao and closer to the position advocated by Zhou Enlai, that China adopt a classic balance of power approach to world affairs. Almost as soon as Nixon took office, the Chinese began signaling their desire to improve relations with the United States.

The decision by Nixon and Kissinger to pursue a new relationship with China faced a peculiar problem in Washington. Ever since 1949 all planning and policies regarding China were conditioned by the fact of Sino-American hostility. The policy formulating staffs of the State Department, National Security Council, CIA, and Defense, Treasury and Commerce departments had spent twenty years trying to "contain" Chinese communism and interfere with the internal and foreign policies of the PRC. Dozens of military agreements, trade sanctions and propaganda machines were all arrayed against China. As China expert Michel Oksenberg (appointed to the National Security Council staff by President Carter) wrote, throughout the government "vested bureaucratic interests developed around a hostile policy towards China; no bureaucracy had an interest in improving relations with China. . . . The McCarthy era showed what could happen to an individual within those hostile structures who might argue that our national interest was not well served by all of this." In pursuit of change Nixon and Kissinger had almost no choice but to form a "cabal" against vested anti-China organs inside the U.S. government—organs Nixon himself had helped create.

The Great Turnaround

Not surprisingly, both Washington and Beijing found it difficult to reverse twenty years of unremitting hostility. Continued American participation in the Vietnam War and the feeling among Mao's more radical followers that no compromise with America was possible or justified compounded the problem. Although Nixon and Kissinger had already decided upon a gradual Vietnam withdrawal, they were unprepared to abandon Saigon suddenly and risk a domestic backlash. Their behavior might be compared to the lawman in a frontier fable: they would back out of the saloon with both guns blazing.

Hoping to leave the South Vietnamese regime with some temporary breathing space, termed "a decent interval," Nixon and Kissinger actually approved an expansion of the war against the Communist forces in Southeast Asia. In March 1970 neutralist Prince Sihanouk of Cambodia was overthrown in what was probably a CIA-assisted coup. His successor, General Lon Nol, received increasing amounts of U.S. aid in an ultimately futile attempt to preserve his rule. Outraged by this reescalation of the war, Mao personally denounced America's action in Cambodia, calling upon the "people of the world" to "unite and defeat the U.S. aggressors and all their running dogs."

Washington then secretly expanded the Vietnam War into neighboring Laos in the spring of 1971, hoping to destroy Communist sanctuaries there. Zhou Enlai responded to this challenge by flying to Hanoi to publicly renew China's pledge of support against the United States. China, he asserted, would be the "reliable rear area," helping the revolutionary struggles of Southeast Asia against attacks by American imperialism.

In light of these events, both the hostile rhetoric and military confrontations of the past seemed unabated. Yet, important changes were taking place in the perceptions that Beijing and Washington had of each other. Despite the new involvement in Cambodia and Laos, American ground troops were being gradually withdrawn from Vietnam. By May 1971 Nixon had almost halved their number from the 1968 level. Meanwhile, China witnessed the ominous buildup of Soviet conventional and nuclear forces all along its northern border. The Chinese leadership saw this as a much more immediate threat to their nation's security. American containment, it seemed, was being overshadowed by Soviet encirclement. The Chinese increasingly denounced Soviet "social imperialism" as an even greater threat than American imperialism. This new threat prompted China to begin a quiet approach toward Washington.

Soon after Nixon's election, Chinese officials suggested publicly that "peaceful coexistence" should be pursued by America and China. Then, at a reception, a Chinese diplomat told an American that the two nations ought to resume their suspended ambassadorial discussions. (Since 1955, occasional talks, first in Geneva, then Warsaw, had been held between U.S. and Chinese ambassadors.) Although Nixon agreed, the Chinese suddenly canceled the proposed Warsaw meeting at the last moment. Apparently, the Communist leadership was itself divided on what approach to take to the United States. The Warsaw talks, moreover, had limited value since both parties assumed the Russians "bugged" the meetings. Then, in July 1969, the State Department announced a relaxation of the restrictions on American travel to China. Henceforth, students, scholars, doctors and scientists would be issued passports specially validated for China. Since the PRC still barred most Americans—explaining that Washington's action fell short of acknowledging Beijing's legitimacy—the act was largely symbolic. Nevertheless, the announcement was the first sign of an American policy change in many years. About the same time, the 7th Fleet reduced patrolling in the Taiwan Strait.

Chinese-Soviet tensions remained a powerful catalyst for change. In March 1969, Soviet and Chinese troops fought two battles along the Ussuri River. If a wider war developed, the Chinese had a very limited ability to match Soviet strength. This fact made improved relations with Washington a vital requirement of Chinese security. By January 1970 Chinese officials again suggested resumption of ambassadorial talks with Washington and two meetings were quickly held before the Cambodian coup of March 1970 temporarily stopped progress.

A few months later, during the summer of 1970, China sent renewed signals that it desired to resume a dialogue with the United States. Because the Warsaw talks were no longer an appropriate forum for discussion, the Chinese relied on symbolic gestures and messages carried by go-betweens, who included private Americans and leaders of nations on good terms with China. In July China released from prison an American Catholic bishop who had been held since 1958. In August American journalist Edgar Snow received an invitation for an extended visit to China. Snow's 1938 book, *Red Star Over China*, had catapulted the then little-known Mao and CCP to world fame, and he was widely known as a "favorite" American among the Chinese leaders. While in China Snow was accorded the unusual privilege of interviewing both Mao and Zhou and actually stood beside Mao in reviewing the October 1 National Day parade.

Within China, the leadership itself appeared divided over how to proceed. Mao's most radical supporter and heir apparent, Lin Biao, seemed opposed to détente with Washington. Other officials rejected the idea that relations could be improved while the United States remained committed to the defense of Taiwan. Nevertheless, between August and September 1970, Mao and Zhou's more moderate policy prevailed. These men understood that China could not possibly deter a Soviet attack if Washington remained an active enemy. Liberating Taiwan was an issue which could be postponed for later solution.

The victory of the "moderates" cleared the path for new openings. Mao told Edgar Snow during a December 18, 1970, interview that Nixon's personal history of anticommunism should not block improved relations, that "at present the problems between China and the U.S.A. would have to be solved with Nixon. Mao would be happy to talk with him, either as a tourist or as President." In an incident of historical irony, word of Mao's startling invitation to his old enemy was presented to the American people in an article Snow published in *Life* magazine. The former vehicle for the China Lobby had now become a messenger of quite a different sort. Ironically, the more liberal *New York Times* refused to publish an earlier version of Snow's article. The White House learned of Mao's remarks to Snow almost immediately and did not have to await their publication.

During late 1970 Nixon and Kissinger grew increasingly frustrated by the inability of U.S. military offensives in Cambodia and Laos to "soften" up the North Vietnamese negotiating position. In a flanking move, designed in part to scare Hanoi, Nixon decided to step up the pace of his approach toward China. In late October, during a news conference, Nixon made reference to the "People's Republic of China." This marked the first time an American President had publicly used the real name of the Chinese government: implicitly it acknowledged the legal existence of that regime. During the same period of time Pakistani President Yahya and Romanian President Ceausescu served as intermediaries, carrying messages between Washington and

Beijing. Zhou Enlai, in a conversation with a Romanian official, hinted that U.S.-PRC relations might be established without a formal U.S. break with Taiwan.

President Nixon eagerly responded to and encouraged the Mao-Zhou policy line. The President's address to Congress on February 25, 1971, provided a deep clue that something important was brewing. That Richard Nixon expressed the following thoughts was all the more remarkable. He deplored the twenty-two years of Sino-American hostility, stating:

> In this decade, therefore, there will be no more important challenge than that of drawing the People's Republic of China into a constructive relationship with the world community. . . . We are prepared to establish a dialogue with Peking. We cannot accept its ideological precepts or [its] hegemony over Asia. But neither do we wish to impose on China an international position that denies its legitimate national interests.

Nixon went on to reaffirm America's commitment to the defense of Taiwan and explained that he did not yet favor the admission of China to the U.N. Nevertheless, he promised:

> In the coming year I will carefully examine what further steps we might take to create broader opportunities for contacts between the Chinese and American peoples, and how we might remove needless obstacles to the realization of these opportunities. We hope for, but will not be deterred by a lack of, reciprocity. . . .

The President's words were quickly followed by a decision on March 15, 1971, to remove all remaining passport restrictions on travel by Americans to China, reversing a twenty-year-old policy. Americans would no longer be required to apply for a special stamp which China claimed insulted its sovereignty. The Chinese responded almost at once to this signal. An American table-tennis team, currently in Japan, was quickly issued an invitation to compete in China. The Nixon Administration immediately gave its blessing to the idea. The visit gave birth to the phrase "ping-pong diplomacy."

The team of young American athletes was accompanied by an entourage of U.S. journalists when they arrived in China in April 1971, ending the information blockade which limited communication between the two countries since 1949. The importance which the Chinese gave to the occasion was highlighted when Premier Zhou greeted the visiting team, telling the Americans that "your visit to China on invitation has opened the door to friendly contacts between the people of the two countries." On the same day Zhou greeted the American athletes, Nixon announced that he was preparing to abandon the general trade embargo which had been imposed on China since the Korean War.

Nixon's initiatives were made possible, in part, by a new mood in the United States. As informal contacts with China became more common, few Americans stood up to denounce the perfidy of dealing with "godless Red China." Most political leaders, the media and a large majority of the public seemed ready to accept a change. President Nixon, moreover, had a tremendous advantage over all his predecessors. He was the first President since 1949 who did not have to fear being attacked by politician Richard Nixon for being "soft on communism"! His anticommunist credentials were clean. The receptiveness he found both in America and among Chinese leaders encouraged him to proceed with more formal contacts.

The visit of the American ping-pong team initiated a policy of "people-to-people" contacts between Americans and Chinese. Soon a number of delegations of American students, scholars and journalists were invited to China. Among the guests were several American diplomats and scholars (including John Service and John K. Fairbank) who had been accused of disloyalty for their accurate reporting of Chinese politics during World War II.

However useful these exchanges were, the problem of establishing formal political contact still remained. The Nixon Administration sought to breach the barrier by accepting Zhou Enlai's April invitation to send Henry Kissinger on a secret mission to China. Kissinger's mission had to be kept under wraps for several reasons. No one knew what fruits it might yield. The Chinese feared provoking a Russian reaction and arousing the ire of their own radical factions. Nixon still harbored some doubts about how conservative Americans would react to his diplomatic venture. Furthermore, Washington was proceeding with Kissinger's mission without any consultation with its Japanese allies.

By mid-1971 the close partnership between Japan and the U.S. which had prevailed since the Korean War had begun to show strains. Increasingly, the two nations were becoming trade rivals and finding it difficult to agree upon how to deal with China. The Nixon Administration's disdain for Tokyo was demonstrated by the manner in which the White House undertook a unilateral decision to devalue the dollar in relation to the yen. While this act would have a serious effect on the Japanese economy, Nixon publicly announced the devaluation without bothering to consult Japan. Adding insult to injury, the action was taken on the anniversary of Japan's World War II surrender, August 15, 1971. This action, when combined with the American decision to ignore its ally when dealing with China, confirmed Japan's suspicion that it was a very secondary concern of American Asian policy. The President succeeded in adding another new English word to the Japanese vocabulary: "Nixon Shock."

The Kissinger Mission

Early in July, accompanied by three close aides, Henry Kissinger flew from Pakistan to Beijing. He arranged the trip in utmost secrecy, feigning sickness to win a few days out of the spotlight while on a foreign tour. The Kissinger-Zhou conversations proved frank and useful. Zhou wanted the U.S. to acknowledge Taiwan as part of China, a province whose fate should be decided by the Chinese. He expected Washington to break relations with Taiwan and end its defense commitment to the Nationalist regime. Kissinger declared that the U.S., while not willing to abandon Taiwan immediately, would be happy to establish an intermediate form of diplomatic relations with the PRC. U.S. military ties to Japan, Korea and the Philippines posed no problem, since China now preferred to see them maintained as a barrier to the Soviets. On July 10, Zhou Enlai formally invited Nixon to visit China, a sign that the preliminary talks had been successful.

On July 15, 1971, Richard Nixon stunned the world by going on television to announce that Henry Kissinger had just returned from a week-long visit to China. The initial talks had proved so productive, Nixon explained, that he would accept an invitation to visit China early in 1972. The American public reacted with excitement and approval to an announcement that promised to speed termination of both Sino-American hostility and the seemingly endless war in Vietnam.

Ironically, Mao appeared to have a more difficult time selling the Nixon visit than did the President. The more radical faction in China, led by Lin Biao, vigorously opposed the prospect of détente. Between July and September 1971, a major power struggle erupted between the "moderates," led by Zhou Enlai and supported by Mao, and Lin Biao's "radicals." Chinese officials have never fully explained the policy advocated by Lin, accusing him instead of personal disloyalty to Mao and the Chinese Communist Party. Lin was rumored to have favored a policy of improving relations with Moscow rather than turning to Washington for support. Undoubtedly, many other domestic issues, not just the Nixon visit, separated the moderate and radical factions in China. Whatever the case, in September Lin disappeared and was later reported killed in a plane crash. Chinese officials claimed he had attempted to assassinate Mao and seize power. After this plot failed, Lin and his followers allegedly fled in a doomed effort to reach the Soviet Union. Although we may never know how much of this story is true, the power struggle was clearly decided in favor of the moderates who had invited Nixon to China. Kissinger visited Beijing a second time in October to confirm arrangements for the President's trip.

An interesting footnote to Kissinger's October mission was his encounter with former diplomat John Service, also in China on a visit. Apparently, one of Kissinger's aides thought it might be useful for the President's National Security Advisor to speak with Service, who during World War II had had extensive contact with Mao and Zhou. When the two Americans were introduced, however, Kissinger seemed ignorant of Service's unique experiences and ended the meeting after some perfunctory remarks. His behavior suggests that even the highest American officials were still unprepared to take seriously those diplomats who had campaigned for Chinese Communist-American détente twenty-five years before Nixon and Kissinger.

The impending Chinese-American summit had an immediate impact upon world politics. Obviously, the United States could no longer actively campaign to bar China from U.N. membership. But in an effort to save a seat for Taiwan, Washington announced belated support for a "two China policy." The PRC, it now argued, should gain a seat on the Security Council while Taiwan should be permitted to retain a seat in the less important General Assembly. China, as well as many other nations, objected to this compromise as a continued slight to the PRC. In October 1971, the U.N. membership finally voted to expel Taiwan completely and grant sole recognition to the People's Republic. In 1972 Japan established full diplomatic relations with China (after having long deferred to U.S. wishes that it *not* do so) and by 1988 more than 122 other countries had followed suit.

China's admission to the United Nations in late 1971 symbolized its formal reentry into the community of nations. The isolation of the post–Korean War period had finally ended, and now China eagerly sought new forms of contact. Among other things, the Chinese leadership hoped that normal political relations with the United States, Europe and Japan would yield trade and technological benefits. Since 1949 China had either "gone it alone" economically or relied on Soviet assistance. The latter was no longer possible and in order to overcome their relative backwardness, Chinese leaders were now prepared to import foreign technology. Détente with the West and Japan would make possible more rapid modernization of the economy and increase military security—vis-à-vis the Soviet Union.

The Nixon Visit and Its Aftermath

President Nixon's departure for China on February 17, 1972, was surrounded by a degree of pomp, circumstance and "hype" unsurpassed since Dorothy and Professor Marvel prepared to fly by balloon from Oz to Kansas. Plans for the four-day-long journey (scheduled so that the President would always be landing or taking off during prime TV time and would reach his destination without jet lag) were programmed precisely. The Chinese and American governments arranged for an advance team of reporters to precede the presidential plane so that live TV coverage could be flashed via satellite to the United States. Though space was limited, a last minute decision included Mrs. Nixon's personal hairdresser on the roster of Air Force One.

As Nixon deplaned in Beijing on February 21, the flair of meticulous public relations enhanced the real drama of the event. His enthusiastic handshake with Zhou Enlai symbolically compensated for the snub John Foster Dulles had shown Zhou at the Geneva Conference in 1954. The reporters accompanying the American delegation provided the first sympathetic impressions of Chinese life seen by a mass audience in the United States. Citizens of the People's Republic, despite their very different politics and culture, appeared to be human beings, not just "blue ants" or a "yellow horde."

Once in China, the Nixon-Kissinger entourage enjoyed a crowded schedule of intense negotiations and playful sightseeing. Almost as soon as they arrived, Mao invited them to a private audience, signifying his approval for the summit meeting. This meeting consisted largely of an exchange of pleasantries and reference to broad concerns. The substantive negotiations were conducted by Zhou Enlai and Jiao Guanhua over the following four days. Nixon alternated between jaunts to the Great Wall and intricate discussions on the many points of Sino-American conflict.

On February 27, 1972, as the week-long presidential visit neared its end, Chinese and American leaders issued the "Shanghai Communiqué." This carefully worded document articulated the new contours of the Sino-American relationship. Both parties agreed that "countries, regardless of their social systems, should conduct their relations on the principle of respect for the sovereignty and territorial integrity of all states." Tensions would be relaxed by expanding nongovernmental "people-to-people contacts" and mutually beneficial bilateral trade. Both governments expressed the hope for the further improvement of their relationship since "the normalization of relations between the

President Richard Nixon and Chairman Mao Zedong seal a new relationship, February 1972. (National Archives)

two countries is not only in the interest of the Chinese and
American peoples but also contributes to the relaxation of tension in Asia and the world."

Although the affirmative, friendly tone of the joint statement
represented a real breakthrough, major issues still separated the
two nations. Each side insisted upon a separate declaration concerning Taiwan. "The Chinese side reaffirmed its position: the
Taiwan question is the crucial question obstructing the normalization of relations. . . . Taiwan is a province of China. . . ."
Accordingly, China had a right and a duty to "liberate" Taiwan
by any means it chose without outside interference. To normalize U.S.-China relations, Washington must sever its ties with
Taiwan and remove its forces from the island.

The position stated by the United States appeared as something of a mirror image. It acknowledged that "Taiwan is part

Chairman Mao receives President Nixon and Henry Kissinger in Beijing, February 1972.

of China" but insisted that the U.S. would only withdraw its military forces from the island "as the tension in the area diminishes" and when the two rival regimes reached a peaceful settlement. Without some form of assurance from the PRC that no invasion was planned, the U.S. would not abrogate its 1954 mutual defense treaty with Taiwan.

Of course, these contrary assertions were not new. Now, however, both governments seemed determined to proceed with Sino-American détente despite their remaining differences over Taiwan. Though the Communist leaders would not admit it openly, they were prepared to defer the question of Taiwan to the future. Nixon and Kissinger seemed convinced that with the end of the Vietnam War approaching, the reduction of tensions in East Asia would permit a gradual U.S. military disengagement from Taiwan. Since China lacked the naval and air power required for an invasion of the island, the military security of Taiwan seemed assured for the foreseeable future regardless of Chinese claims. (In his private comments to Chinese leaders—

according to those who saw the transcript—Nixon actually promised to establish full diplomatic ties with China and sever relations with Taiwan after the 1972 election.)

In May 1973, following several more Kissinger trips to China, the two nations agreed to establish "liaison offices" in their respective capitals. These unofficial embassies served as an important forum for ongoing political talks. In the aftermath of the Nixon visit other changes occurred in the Sino-American relationship. Initially, trade between the two nations soared. Mostly this consisted of Chinese purchases of American cereal grains. China had little besides handicrafts to export to the United States. Although China's purchases from the U.S. rose to $900 million in 1974, the total soon declined. When it became clear that Washington would not quickly establish full diplomatic relations, the Chinese shifted their purchase of grain to other exporting nations.

The creation of liaison offices proved to be a plateau in the new Sino-American relationship. Following this, both countries seemed uncertain of their future course. Yet, much had already been accomplished. The Chinese had ensured that Moscow would think very hard before undertaking any military moves against China, while Washington had established a framework for the post-Vietnam era in East Asia. The dialogue with China, and that nation's growing trade, cultural and political contacts with the West and Japan, were actually far better ways to stabilize Asia than the maintenance of hostile regimes on China's borders. Nevertheless, domestic political turmoil on both sides of the Pacific slowed the pace of détente.

President Nixon's mounting involvement in the Watergate scandal by the spring of 1973 prevented any dramatic moves toward closer relations. Unwilling to risk antagonizing his conservative supporters who maintained a fondness for Taiwan, Nixon broke his secret promise to the Chinese to establish formal diplomatic relations once he was reelected. Gerald Ford's presidency, from August 1974 to January 1977, was largely a caretaker administration. When the accidental President did travel to China in December 1975, little of the Nixon-visit drama remained in the air. Kissinger and Ford declined to move forward toward a full diplomatic relationship with China, fearing such a move would jeopardize sensitive negotiations with the Russians on arms limitations.

The new relationship between Beijing and Washington had an indirect effect upon ending the war in Vietnam. Originally, of course, American leaders had justified intervention in Southeast Asia as a struggle to "contain" Chinese expansion. Now, given the more tolerant view of China, and considering China's preoccupation with the "Soviet threat," there seemed little danger of armed Chinese expansion in Asia. In fact, Washington now hoped that Chinese power would help to offset Soviet influence in Asia and elsewhere. These factors totally undercut America's position in Vietnam, while the war itself only inhibited closer Sino-American relations.

Terminating American involvement in Vietnam, however, proved a very difficult task for the Nixon Administration. For one thing, détente with China and the U.S.S.R. marked a policy of accommodating the realities of Chinese and Soviet power. It did not signify the end of American opposition to regional revolutionary movements, or termination of aid to anticommunist regimes. During the early 1970s Nixon and Kissinger engineered a successful coup against the Allende regime in Chile and stepped up military aid to Iran and South Vietnam. Even as American forces withdrew from Southeast Asia, Washington continued to believe that its policy of "Vietnamization" would allow the noncommunist forces in South Vietnam to hang on for a "decent interval."

During the summer and autumn of 1972 (as Nixon prepared to meet the challenge of antiwar candidate George McGovern), U.S. and North Vietnamese negotiators devised a compromise formula to end stalemated peace talks. The U.S. declared a willingness to pull out all remaining ground and air forces from South Vietnam within four months in exchange for an in-place cease-fire (leaving North Vietnamese and Vietcong troops in control of large parts of the south—something Nixon had pledged never to do) and the return of all U.S. POWs. Hanoi dropped its insistence that the U.S. depose the Thieu regime in Saigon as a prelude to a cease-fire. Instead, it would settle for an in-place truce, the rapid departure of all American forces and a promise that some form of coalition political structure would soon be created in the south.

Although Nixon announced a virtual peace agreement just before the 1972 presidential elections, he backpeddled shortly after his overwhelming electoral victory. He required more time to beef up Saigon's forces and to demonstrate to Hanoi that they ought not to overrun the south immediately after the American withdrawal. During December 1972 Nixon ordered the U.S. air force to conduct a massive bombing campaign against the North Vietnamese capital. The "Christmas Bombing" coincided with a huge airlift of military equipment to Saigon. The message contained in these acts was twofold: Hanoi was shown how Washington might react to any early offensive against the south; the Thieu regime in Saigon was assured that it could afford to accept the cease-fire agreements since it had acquired a vast new stockpile of arms.

The final peace agreement signed in Paris on January 13, 1973, closely resembled the agreement both sides had approved in October. The few changes actually called for a more rapid U.S. departure from the south. Even more incredible were the contents of a secret letter sent by Nixon to Hanoi. In it he promised North Vietnam almost $5 billion of postwar economic aid, with no strings attached! (Nixon and Kissinger denied this until Hanoi later made the letter public.)

In practice, the Paris Peace Agreement proved an impossible document. In the hours before it went into effect both Communist and anticommunist forces went on an offensive to seize new territory. Departing U.S. forces transferred title to a vast amount of military equipment, violating a pledge that the U.S. would only replace old weapons, not give Saigon additional arms. Furthermore, several thousand American military personnel were quickly reassigned as "civilian advisors" to the Saigon army, thus remaining in Vietnam.

After discounting all the inflated rhetoric, this "peace with honor," as Nixon referred to it, represented little more than an American withdrawal. All parties understood that the rival Vietnamese factions would soon resume their battle for national unification. Nixon's hope, it seems, was that a huge infusion of military aid to Saigon, combined with a continuing threat against the north, would prevent the collapse of the South Vietnamese regime for a "decent interval." By then, perhaps, no one would blame the disaster on him.

A brief interlude of scaled-down fighting followed the American withdrawal as both sides braced themselves for a final confrontation. Early in 1975 Vietcong and North Vietnamese forces launched an offensive which tore apart the Saigon army. American-trained and -equipped forces fled the battlefield, often dropping their weapons (guns, planes, tanks) for the enemy to capture. Neither Washington nor American representatives in Vietnam would accept the debacle about to engulf them. Little preparation for an orderly evacuation took place. When the end came late in April 1975, thousands of hysterical Americans and Vietnamese clawed their way to the roof of the embassy in Saigon to be rescued by helicopters as the city fell. The U.S. left Vietnam with as little grace and honor as it came with.

Fortunately, despite the gruesome spectacle of Saigon's fall, America did not experience a repeat of the "Who Lost China?" inquisition. Perhaps the fact that seven presidents, Democratic and Republican, had been involved in the Vietnam crusade since 1945 mitigated most partisan recrimination. Not suprisingly, the disgraced ex-President, Richard Nixon, tried to blame his political enemies for the outcome in Southeast Asia. In his 1978 *Memoirs*, he still claimed he had won "peace with honor," but that the Democratic Congress had squandered victory (by reducing aid to Saigon) after his resignation. During the 1980 presidential campaign, and several times following his election, Ronald Reagan described the Vietnam War as an "honorable" venture that should have been fought through to victory. But his rhetoric seemed aimed mostly at convincing Congress and the public to support a large defense budget. He never pursued the theme.

Most Americans were apparently content with, or resigned to, the view expressed by President Gerald Ford in 1975, as the last "choppers" lifted embassy staff from Saigon. The war was over, he counseled. The United States should look ahead and not apportion blame. No one seemed interested in arguing that Vietnam was "ours to lose." In fact, far from hastening to shore up some new containment line in Southeast Asia, by June 1977 the United States allowed the moribund SEATO alliance to pass out of existence with no publicity. The formal containment of China had finally ended.

Selected Additional Readings

The following books discuss the evolution of Sino-American relations during the Nixon presidency: John Gittings, *The World And China, 1922–72*, N.Y., 1974; Robert Sutter, *China Watch: Toward Sino-American Reconciliation*, Baltimore, 1978; Richard M. Nixon, *RN: The Memoirs of Richard Nixon*, N.Y., 1978; Henry Kissinger, *The White House Years*, Boston, 1978; Tad Szulc, *The Illusion of Peace: Foreign Policy in the Nixon Years*, N.Y., 1978; Seymour Hersh, *The Price of Power: Kissinger in the White House*, N.Y., 1983; and Craig Dietrich, *People's China: A Brief History*, N.Y., 1986.

9

The Politics of Normalization

The Crisis of Post-Maoist China

The end of the war in Vietnam coincided with a series of major political changes inside China. Since the late 1930s the top leadership of the Communist Party had been drawn from a relatively small circle of long-lived individuals, headed by Chairman Mao Zedong. As old age took its toll (no fixed terms or retirement age existed), senior officials began to fall from power. Purges during the Cultural Revolution accelerated the process. On Taiwan, Chiang Kai-shek, a leader of the same generation, died in 1975. The next year, first Premier Zhou Enlai, then Mao, died as well.

In many ways, these two leaders represented contrasting factions within Chinese politics. Zhou, long head of the administrative arm of government, emphasized careful planning, order and expertise as the key to progress. He had also led China's tentative forays toward better relations with the West. Mao, always more of a romantic and visionary, had rejected many of these notions since the late 1950s. In the Great Leap Forward and especially during the Cultural Revolution, Mao championed grand ideological campaigns and internal political struggle as the best way to mobilize China and speed its development. The increasing enfeeblement of both men during the 1970s (Zhou suffered from cancer, Mao from Parkinson's disease) provoked a conflict over the succession and the future direction of the People's Republic.

For many years the CCP had been rent by a schism pitting "moderates" (who favored careful planning and reliance on technical expertise) against "radicals" (who proclaimed revolutionary fervor as the key to development). The terms were inexact and difficult to apply, since many individuals adopted a radical stance on some issues and a moderate approach on others. Even Mao wavered, sometimes advocating precise, cautious planning while at other times calling for mass mobilization to triumph over technical and material obstacles. Up to the mid-1970s, moderates generally favored central economic planning and the promotion of heavy industry in accord with the Soviet model. They stressed the importance of higher education, rapid industrial growth and technological modernization as keys to development. Zhou and his disciple, Deng Xiaoping, typified this group.

Radicals comprised a more diverse group, stressing the primacy of ideological purity over economic performance. They criticized reliance on foreign technology and denounced central planning for stifling the spontaneous creativity of the masses. Borrowing foreign ideas or methods, or relying on material incentives, struck them as abhorrent. They championed total egalitarianism and proclaimed class struggle as the only permissible path to progress. A strong antipathy toward the outside world permeated their rhetoric.

Despite these historic differences in attitude about the outside world, in the early 1970s both moderates and radicals generally agreed on the necessity of improving relations with the United States, if only to deter the immediate Soviet threat. There were, however, a few radicals, notably Defense Minister Lin Biao, who rejected this approach. Some evidence suggests he tried, in vain, to persuade Mao to abort the opening to Washington in 1971 and patch up differences with Moscow. When the Chairman rejected his advice, Lin probably sensed that his favored position as heir apparent had lapsed. This may have prompted his alleged coup attempt, which reportedly led to his failed escape to the Soviet Union, and his death.

Mao's willingness to follow Zhou's more moderate advice in a pinch showed his own flexibility. As earlier, the Chairman continued to juggle both factions adroitly. However, as his health and mental acuity deteriorated, the balancing act proved more difficult.

During the Cultural Revolution, Mao's wife, Jiang Qing, emerged from relative obscurity to become a leading exponent of radical ideas. She seized control of Chinese cultural life and tried to make all artistic expression conform to a rigid ideological mold. Gradually, she and three comrades (the so-called Gang of Four) tried to gain total control of government policy.

After suffering a partial eclipse during the Cultural Revolution, Premier Zhou Enlai made a comeback by the early 1970s. Although suffering from a fatal cancer, he maneuvered to arrange a moderate line of succession to himself and Mao. Lin Biao's death late in 1971 eliminated a major rival. Afterward, Zhou campaigned to rehabilitate high officials disgraced during earlier purges. Chief among these was Deng Xiaoping, named a Vice Premier in 1975.

Zhou's death early in 1976 removed Deng's chief patron. Mao succumbed to radical pressure and his own misgivings by repurging the Vice Premier, but he declined to appoint a radical candidate to fill Zhou's job. Instead, Mao named a relative nonentity, Hua Guofeng, as Premier in charge of the governmental apparatus. Although he benefited from the purges of the Cultural Revolution, Hua seemed more of a centrist and opportunist than a confirmed radical.

The real showdown came after September 9, 1976, when Mao died at the age of eighty-three. In subsequent weeks, his widow and her allies tried to grab power but were frustrated when Hua and moderates in the party, government and army staged a counter coup. On October 6 the Chinese press announced that the Gang of Four—Jiang Qing, Zhang Chunquiao, Yao Wenyuan and Wang Hongwen—were under arrest. Following their downfall (later they were tried and sentenced to long prison terms), Hua Guofeng capped his meteoric rise by assuming the role of Mao's successor as Chairman of the Communist Party.

Hua's succession proved short-lived. His lack of a broad power base in the party or state bureaucracy made his legitimacy dependent on his links to Mao. Although he acknowledged the need to approve modest economic reforms and to abandon the radical postures of the Cultural Revolution, Hua showed little inclination to terminate the policies pursued by Mao from 1966–76. He blamed past problems on the excessive zeal or corruption of Mao's radical supporters rather than on the policies themselves or on structural defects in the Communist system. Hua sought to restore aspects of the pre-Cultural Revolution political-economic system (such as central planning) but opposed any fundamental change in the way the party and state apparatus functioned.

This led quickly to new problems. For example, in 1978 Hua endorsed an ambitious modernization program. But the party leader failed to coordinate the new approach with needed reforms in the nation's basic industrial or agricultural policy or in China's economic orientation to the outside world. Without these innovations, the modernization drive bogged down.

Meanwhile, Deng bided his time in genteel "retirement," cultivating plans for a dramatic overhaul of the Communist system. A remarkably skillful coalition builder, the twice-purged Vice Premier developed a wide network of supporters while waiting for Hua to stumble. By 1978, senior members of the party, army and bureaucracy compelled Hua to reappoint Deng as Vice Premier. Although the party Chairman retained his post for a few more years, no one doubted who really dominated the political process. Indeed, having isolated opponents and rewarded allies, Deng had so expanded his bases of support in the party, government and army that by 1982 he emerged as the undisputed leader of China. Two protégés, Hu Yaobang and Zhao Ziyang, became the party's General Secretary (the post of Chairman was abolished) and government Premier, respectively. The hapless Hua Guofeng had to settle for a low-level sinecure.

Sadly, China continued to suffer the effects of the Cultural Revolution. People distrusted the party and government, yearned for stability and demanded an increase in living standards. The nation's factories were filled with obsolete technology and produced insufficient or shoddy products. Dead-wood functionaries, as well as radicals promoted during the Cultural Revolution, retained a stranglehold on the bloated but indolent central planning bureaucracy. Farmers had few incentives to produce more food, as the state simply took the surplus with inadequate payment. Institutions of research and higher education, plundered by the Cultural Revolution, remained in shambles, with an entire generation suffering the effects. Without some startling innovations, China seemed likely to fall further behind the rest of the world.

Deng surprised friend and foe by rejecting both paths of development (Soviet-style central planning and Maoist radicalism) followed since 1949. An eclectic reformer, he decried these two approaches as failures unsuited for China's future needs. Downplaying the importance of dogma (it made no difference, he quipped, if a cat were black or white, so long as it caught mice), he argued for pragmatic solutions to material problems. Economic growth, not class struggle, he insisted, must become China's priority.

Although Deng and his allies had no firm blueprint for revitalizing China, they proved eager to replace revolutionary rhetoric with various ideas to restore stability, loosen political controls, reform the bureaucracy and provide material incentives to workers and peasants. Their primary economic goal was to create a more efficient system capable of sustained growth and of providing rewards to ordinary Chinese. To accomplish this, they began to decollectivize agriculture and industry, relying less on central planning and more on market mechanisms. The large collective farms were subdivided into family plots; peasants could contract to sell a portion of their produce to the state and were permitted to market the surplus for profit. This "household responsibility system" resulted in large production gains and the virtual restructuring of the countryside.

In industry, the government steered investment toward light manufacturing and consumer production, giving peasants and workers more to buy with their money. Factory managers and workers gained greater leeway in running their plants and more responsibility for both profits and losses. Individuals were encouraged to start small-scale businesses, especially in the service sector. These reforms quickly improved the quality of life for most Chinese.

The party and government did not abandon control of the economy, however. They retained modified central planning mechanisms, especially in the heavy and strategic industrial sectors. But instead of simply commanding production, the state would rely on a combination of incentives, prices and market forces to steer agriculture and industry.

With encouragement from national leaders, Chinese economists became increasingly bold in proposing ways to invigorate industry. Some suggested eliminating state ownership by selling shares of stock to private shareholders and groups such as schools, municipalities, workers' cooperatives, etc. Control by groups concerned with profitability and efficiency, these economists suggested, would revitalize sluggish industry, promote overall prosperity and lay a foundation for greater political democracy. Any such program would take China far from the socialist path.

China's reform leadership concluded early on that modernization could not be accomplished without expanding economic relations with the rest of the world. The acquisition of vital modern technology and capital required a new "Open Door policy," whereby foreign contact would be increased while trade, investments and loans from abroad would be encouraged. Deng blamed much of China's stagnation since the 1960s on Mao's romantic notion of autarky, or economic self-reliance. The contrast between China's relative backwardness and the rapid growth of such Asian export-oriented societies as Taiwan, South Korea, Hong Kong and Singapore could not be more stark.

China's two-way international trade in 1970 totaled $4.6 billion. By 1975, as the worst chaos of the Cultural Revolution receded, foreign trade rose to $15 billion. By 1978 the figure reached $20 billion and by 1988 approximately $75 billion. Japan quickly emerged as Beijing's biggest trading partner, accounting for a fourth of the two-way trade. The United States accounted for about $13 billion of this total. The bulk of Chinese exports to America consisted of textiles. Initially, most American sales were of grain. As Chinese agriculture improved, Beijing purchased more machinery and technology from the United States.

In order to acquire advanced technology from the West and Japan, China encouraged foreign investments in modern factories by establishing special economic zones and designating many cities and regions as model areas for development. In these localities, foreign factories were given special privileges to operate. Increasingly, China borrowed money from foreign banks to finance long-term growth. Although many bottlenecks to development remained, the Chinese domestic and foreign economy of the 1980s was a far cry from that championed by Mao. Rates of growth during the past decade remained consistently high. As of 1988 the U.S. had $3 billion invested in joint ventures in China.

Deng also pioneered a plan to streamline the bloated party, government and army bureaucracies. Instead of purging overage and underqualified hangers-on, he pensioned off many senior officials with honorific titles and a retirement income. Younger, better trained replacements understood that they must demonstrate technical ability, not just political orthodoxy. Under this plan, the army would shrink by twenty-five percent, emerging as a smaller but more professional force. During the 1980s the military's share of the budget fell by more than fifty percent.

The Communist Party, Deng insisted, should meddle less in economic decisions than was traditionally the case. In its place, government administrators and technical experts would exercise the authority formerly reserved for political activists. New restraints were also imposed on party intrusion into personal affairs. A new constitution and legal code, even if crude by Western standards, imposed a rule of law and due process on Communist Party activities. Predictable order, if not American-style civil liberties, became more common.

In politics, the bonds of Maoism were loosened more slowly. Although some local elections gave citizens a chance to select candidates for various minor posts, the Communist Party retained its monopoly of power. A great deal of diversity was permitted in art, culture, music and literature. Chinese could easily purchase foreign books and magazines, listen to foreign radio programs and watch Western television shows. Ordinary

Chinese were freer to express their personal beliefs, dress as they chose, start small businesses and exercise more control over their own lives. Hundreds of thousands of American and other tourists visited China annually in the 1980s, with relatively few restrictions imposed on their local contacts.

However, this freedom did not include the right to organize opposition political parties. In the late 1970s and again in 1986, student demonstrations demanding greater political freedom were harshly suppressed. Periodically, Chinese leaders warned against the evils of "bourgeois liberalism" and "spiritual pollution" from the West. Although Deng promoted the ideal of greater individual initiative in the economic sphere, he joined with many traditionalists in limiting the scope and nature of poltical liberalization. The Communist Party showed no inclination to give up its political monopoly.

At the same time, Chinese reformers acknowledged the need to train a new generation of experts to run the country. Given the virtual cessation of higher education and scientific research in the years from 1966–76, this presented a major obstacle. Thus Deng encouraged thousands of Chinese students to go abroad for college and post-graduate study, mostly in science and engineering. By the late 1980s, over 41,000 Chinese were enrolled annually in American universities. But the popularity of foreign study created a problem common to many developing countries, a "brain drain," as many students extended their time abroad. In fact, during 1988, the Chinese government threatened to curtail the program (especially in the U.S.) unless more students returned.

As in other countries, various factions and interest groups contend for power in China. Many economic reforms have proceeded by fits and starts, as advocates of more daring change have been restrained by moderates who have preferred to go slowly. Yet, something of a consensus emerged by the end of the 1980s. Deng succeeded in institutionalizing what he and his allies called "China's second revolution."

China Policy and American Politics, 1976–80

Just as the succession crisis in China following Mao's death affected domestic and foreign policy, the Watergate crisis and the political demise of President Nixon altered the pace of American policy. Nixon had promised to normalize relations with China after his reelection in 1972. However, as his administration succumbed to the Watergate scandal, he grew more cautious, and following his resignation under threat of impeachment in August 1974, America's China policy was put on hold. President Gerald Ford seemed reluctant to undertake any major initiative before the 1976 election. Moreover, he feared that recognition of China might anger the Soviets and thus prevent a Strategic Arms Limitation Treaty (SALT) with Moscow. Unenthusiastic about Nixon's successor, Chinese leaders openly criticized continued American efforts at arms control and related negotiations with the Soviets. They urged Washington to take a tougher line against Soviet "hegemonism" and fulfill past promises to normalize relations with the PRC.

Jimmy Carter, elected President in 1976, initially found reasons for delaying recognition as well. While he agreed with the goal of normalizing relations, Carter, like Ford, did not want to endanger the prospect of achieving deep cuts in the Soviet and American nuclear arsenals. The Carter Administration also pushed a pair of foreign policy initiatives which further postponed negotiations with China.

The first initiative was aimed at improving ties with Vietnam, in part to gain cooperation in settling unresolved cases of missing American soldiers, but also to discourage both Vietnam's expansionism in Southeast Asia and Hanoi's dependence on Moscow. Unfortunately, the Vietnamese demanded extensive reconstruction aid (promised by Nixon in 1973) as a precondition to diplomatic relations. When Carter balked at such prior payments, the talks stalled. China, which now condemned its Communist neighbor as a Soviet proxy, bitterly criticized the initiative.

Carter's second foreign policy venture was the long-delayed effort to secure Senate approval for a Panama Canal Treaty (designed to restore gradually Panama's control of the water-way). This also worked against any dramatic approach toward China. Long a symbol of American dominance of the Western hemisphere, control of the canal became a major domestic political issue. A coalition of Republican and Democratic Senators, as well as Republican presidential hopeful Ronald Reagan, criticized the proposed treaty as a betrayal of the national heritage. To maximize support for the treaty, Carter opted to delay any diplomatic break with Taiwan, much to the dismay of the PRC.

In fact, during 1977–80, the question of how to handle Taiwan proved to be a particularly thorny issue for the administration. Secretary of State Cyrus Vance visited China in August 1977 to explore a compromise solution. Beijing had always insisted upon three criteria for normalizing relations. Washington must derecognize Taiwan, terminate its military presence on the island and abrogate its 1954 mutual security treaty with the Nationalist regime. Vance proposed that normalization be modeled on the formula adopted by Japan in 1972. Tokyo and Beijing had established full diplomatic relations under an arrangement which permitted Japan to maintain an "informal" liaison office in Taiwan. This ostensibly private mission (and its Taiwanese counterpart in Tokyo) was staffed by "retired" diplomats empowered to conduct diplomatic, economic and cultural business.

The U.S. case, however, had unique complications. Unlike Japan, Washington maintained a formal defense treaty with Taiwan, sold weapons to the Republic of China and had pledged, publicly, to assure the island's security. American officials feared that if they unilaterally abrogated these defense commitments, with no reciprocal pledge from China to avoid the use of force, U.S. security arrangements with Japan, South Korea and the Philippines might be jeopardized. When China declined to make any pledge, Vance's mission ended without an agreement.

By the spring of 1978, a number of international developments changed the terms of the debate in Washington and Beijing. Senate passage of the Panama Canal Treaty alleviated Carter's concern about a political backlash at home. In August, China concluded a friendship pact with Japan. The agreement, under discussion since the two Asian nations had established diplomatic ties in 1972, promised a further increase in bilateral trade, perhaps to the disadvantage of American businesses. When Deng visited Tokyo in October, he made a great show of meeting Emperor Hirohito, for decades a figure denounced by China as the symbol of Japanese militarism. By embracing Japan's nominal World War II leader, Deng signaled Beijing's acceptance of the East Asian status quo. China also ceased its criticism of American defense arrangements with Japan and South Korea.

As part of an overall effort to ease tensions in Asia, and to persuade China's neighbors not to support the Soviet Union, Chinese regional policy softened markedly after 1978. Beijing wooed such Southeast Asian states as Burma, Thailand, Malaya, Singapore, the Philippines and Indonesia by ceasing support for numerous small Communist insurgencies. China also scaled down its involvement in Africa where for years it had promoted a large foreign aid program. Both moves signaled China's decision to concentrate on internal development and to accept the current world system.

In May, in something of a sentimental gesture to American friends, the Chinese invited the surviving members of the original Dixie Mission and their families to revisit Yenan. A round of speeches and toasts celebrated the mission's abortive effort during World War II to bring about U.S.-Chinese Communist cooperation. A Chinese spokesman noted that Beijing still awaited formal recognition by Washington, but "could not wait forever."

Shared anxiety about Soviet expansionism helped break the impasse. Traditional Vietnamese-Chinese rivalry, dating back a thousand years, resurfaced in the wake of Hanoi's 1975 victory in Indochina. During 1978 Vietnam moved closer to the Soviet Union, outraging China. When Hanoi expelled several hundred thousand ethnic Chinese from Vietnam (part of an exodus of millions of Southeast Asians in the decade following the end of the Vietnam War), the dispute assumed ugly racial overtones. China denounced Vietnam as a Soviet "pawn" and Moscow's "forward post" for Asian conquest—terms reminiscent of U.S. charges a decade earlier—and cut all economic ties. Soon, the two neighbors charged each other with territorial violations and began sporadic cross-border shooting.

Soviet behavior also aroused new worries in the American government. During 1978, Soviet and Cuban military involvement increased in a number of regional disputes, especially in northern and southern Africa. Zbigniew Brzezinski, Carter's National Security Advisor, convinced the President to downplay the importance of any SALT agreement with the Soviets. He advocated a strategic alliance with China as a more effective way of restraining Russian expansion. Somewhat crudely, Brzezinski described this strategy as "playing the China card."

When the National Security Advisor visited Beijing in May 1978, he assured Chinese leaders that President Carter shared their view of the "common Soviet threat" both globally and in Asia and desired to work out a compromise solution regarding Taiwan. This convinced Deng, at the time nominally second in command but already emerging as China's de facto leader, of Washington's good faith. During the following months the United States informed both Beijing and Taipei that America would consider imposing a temporary moratorium on arms sales to Taiwan as part of a normalization agreement with China. At the same time it reserved the right to sell Taiwan limited defensive armaments in the future. This policy of even-handedness, Washington hoped, would meet with some approval in both camps.

Although unwilling to accept such terms in public, Deng and his colleagues were prepared to tolerate an ongoing U.S.-Taiwan security relationship. The symbolism of "liberating" Taiwan paled when compared to the problems China faced with its Communist neighbors. In November 1978 Vietnam and the Soviet Union signed a friendship treaty. The following month Hanoi invaded Kampuchea (Cambodia).*

---

* Since 1975, the Khmer Rouge under Pol Pot had ruled Kampuchea with an iron fist. A combination of brutality and incompetence led to the death of several million people. In the tradition of Southeast Asian politics, the anti-Vietnamese Khmer Rouge found an ally in China—even though China had abandoned the Maoist principles motivating Pol Pot. Vietnam, which traditionally coveted influence over its Indochinese neighbors, justified its invasion of Kampuchea, and subsequent creation of a puppet regime, as a humanitarian rescue mission directed against the vicious Khmer Rouge. The Vietnamese occupation led to a protracted guerrilla war in which the United States supported the resistance movement which included the remnants of the Khmer Rouge. Both China and the United States justified their actions as designed to counter a Soviet-Vietnamese threat to Southeast Asia.

After the 1978 Congressional elections had passed, Washington and Beijing initiated intensive discussions to work out the details of a normalization agreement. On December 15, 1978, President Carter announced that the United States and the People's Republic of China "have agreed to recognize each other and to establish diplomatic relations as of January 1, 1979." Washington recognized Beijing as the sole legal capital of China. Nevertheless, Carter explained, the United States would maintain "cultural, commercial and other unofficial relations with the people of Taiwan" through nongovernmental organs. Speaking in a relaxed manner, the President explained his action as an opportunity to resume the "long history of friendship" between the American and Chinese people and to strengthen world peace.

The details of the arrangement revealed mutual compromises. Carter announced the abrogation of the U.S. defense treaty with Taiwan, effective after a required one-year period. The American government asserted that it expected the Taiwan issue to be "settled peacefully by the Chinese themselves," while Americans maintained unofficial business, cultural and political ties to the island. Washington pledged to stop arms sales to Taiwan for at least one year. However, it continued to reserve the right to resume defensive arms sales to Taiwan after the moratorium.

The Chinese, who had always balked at accepting such an arrangement, proved flexible. At an unprecedented news conference before foreign journalists, Hua Guofeng (still, nominally, at the helm in Beijing) explained that while China did not consider such sales legitimate, they would not be permitted to stand in the way of full Sino-American relations. Perhaps the most important evidence of Chinese determination to overcome obstacles came with the announcement that Deng Xiaoping would celebrate the restoration of relations by visiting the United States at the end of January 1979. In a typical quip, the first Chinese Communist leader to journey to Washington declared he "wanted to visit America before going to see Marx."

The public, press and most politicians in the U.S. greeted the renewed diplomatic ties with overwhelming approval. Some extreme conservatives, like Arizona's Senator Barry Goldwater, accused the President of a "cowardly act" that "stabs in the back the nation of Taiwan." He and a small group of Senators filed a

"Welcome to Peking." (Tony Auth, *Philadelphia Inquirer*)

suit in federal court that challenged the President's authority to terminate a defense treaty without Senate approval. (The courts sustained Carter's action.) Actually, several Senators who joined Goldwater's legal action favored recognizing China, but simply wanted to assure greater security for Taiwan or assert the Senate's role in abrogating a treaty. Most Republican officials (with the notable exception of Ronald Reagan) accepted the Carter policy as the logical extension of the process begun by Richard Nixon.

A pair of symbolic actions by two American private institutions conveyed popular support for normalization. First, the Coca-Cola Company announced that it, too, was establishing ties to China. Soon, the citizens of Beijing and Shanghai would have the chance to consume the "real thing." *Time* magazine also sanctioned Carter's deal. Moving ever farther from its pro-Nationalist stance, the journal featured Deng Xiaoping as "Man of the Year" for 1978. No Chinese leader since Chiang Kai-shek, forty years before, had so graced *Time's* cover.

Deng began his nine-day, whirlwind tour of the United States

During his early 1979 visit to the United States, Vice Premier Deng Xiao-ping dons a ten-gallon hat at a Texas rodeo. Some weeks later, he ordered Chinese troops to invade Vietnam. (UPI/Bettman Newsphotos)

at the end of January. His public statements combined praise of America with verbal attacks on Soviet "hegemonism." While Carter sidestepped the invitation to endorse these attacks on Moscow, he hailed the "new and irreversible course" in Chinese-American relations. The two leaders signed agreements to expand a wide range of contacts. During Deng's tour across America, audiences in China were treated to a virtual nonstop advertisement of the riches of U.S. material life. The feisty tourist enjoyed himself thoroughly. At a Texas rodeo he donned six-shooters and a ten-gallon hat, mugging for the photographers. A decade earlier, when Nikita Khrushchev asked to visit Disneyland, security concerns blocked the trip. No such inhibitions applied to the Chinese Communist leader. He toured the Magic Kingdom and had the thrill of dancing with a life-sized Mickey Mouse. What better evidence could an observer find of America's "tilt" toward China!

Two events, one domestic, the other in Asia, brought this party to an end. In March 1979 China launched a brief invasion of Vietnam, designed, Deng declared, "to teach Vietnam a lesson" about the risks of collaborating with Moscow and invading Kampuchea. The short, inconclusive border war proved costly for both sides. Washington responded in a low-keyed way, with President Carter urging all parties to cease fighting. America would no longer act as the "policeman of Asia."

Although China did not object to Washington's attitude toward the renewed fighting in Vietnam, simultaneous action in Congress outraged Beijing. During the first months of 1979, a coalition of liberal and conservative representatives cobbled together the "Taiwan Relations Act." Senators Barry Goldwater, S. I. Hayakawa and Jesse Helms (on the right) and John Glenn (in the liberal camp) still felt that President Carter had failed to win assurances from China that protected Taiwan's security. While the conservative legislators thought mainly in terms of safeguarding an old anticommunist ally, others, like Glenn, worried about the stability of the region and U.S. economic interests.

One of their considerations was the fact that, in normalizing relations with the PRC, the U.S. no longer considered Taiwan a sovereign state. Yet, Taiwan enjoyed extensive trade and cultural ties with the United States. America would, in time, probably resume arms sales to the island as well. Other uncertainties surrounded the mechanism for establishing liaison offices, such as the "American Institute" on Taiwan and the Taiwanese "Coordinating Council on North American Affairs"—in effect the new, informal embassies. Assuring Taiwan's eligibility to participate in a variety of ventures with American citizens and the U.S. government depended on new legislation. The authors of the Taiwan Relations Act hoped to accomplish these goals. Despite the participation of conservatives, they did not seek to roll back the relationship with Beijing.

They did, however, include wording in the new law which reiterated America's determination to sell defensive weapons to Taiwan so long as a threat of invasion continued. The act asserted that "the future of Taiwan [should] be determined by peaceful means" and that the U.S. would "resist any resort to force or other coercion that would jeopardize" the island's well-being.

In spite of what Carter and the supporters of the act expected, China reacted angrily both to administration and Congressional policy. Beijing objected to what it labeled continued interference in its internal affairs. If, as Washington agreed, Taiwan was part of China, Americans had no business telling the PRC how to handle its renegade province. Chinese leaders insisted they retained the right to use any means to unify their country. Perhaps part of Beijing's response was posturing, an effort merely to warn the U.S. against too close a relationship with Taiwan. Alternatively, some of the rhetoric might have been directed at appeasing nationalist sentiment within China.

The lingering dispute over Taiwan, and disagreement over strategic cooperation against the Soviet Union, continued to complicate Sino-American relations throughout the remainder of the Carter presidency. In the immediate aftermath of normalization, however, Beijing and Washington reached a series of agreements that settled financial problems dating from the Korean War. American property seized by the PRC in 1950–51 totaled about $200 million, while the U.S. government had frozen $76 million in Chinese bank accounts. Outstanding claims in American courts presented various barriers to trade and contracts. In the spring of 1979, the two governments agreed to a formula to settle all claims. In August Vice President Walter Mondale met Chinese leaders and announced the elimination of many restrictions on the transfer of advanced technology to China. This soon led to a marked increase in bilateral trade.

But National Security Advisor Brzezinski criticized this emphasis on economic links, arguing that Washington should seek closer military and strategic cooperation with Beijing. Secretary of State Vance continued to insist that good relations with China should not be premised on anti-Soviet cooperation, especially while Washington and Moscow still had arms limitations under discussion. Most China experts in the State Department agreed that Brzezinski's single-minded effort to build an anti-Soviet coalition represented an unstable foundation for long-term policy. Soviet actions in the Third World soon provided new ammu-

nition for Brzezinski's call to "play the China card." Late in
1979, Russian troops invaded Afghanistan to rescue a faltering
Communist regime. This first foreign deployment of Soviet combat forces outside of Eastern Europe, near a region whose oil
resources were vital to the West, led to sharp American retaliation. President Carter withdrew the draft SALT treaty from
Senate consideration, ordered an embargo on grain and technology sales to the Soviet Union, and canceled American participation in the upcoming Moscow Olympics.

The Soviet invasion frightened the People's Republic, which
denounced it in even harsher tones than had the United States.
Beijing characterized the Soviet move as a "grave threat" to the
"security of Asia and the whole world." Deng suggested that
Washington must coordinate retaliation against Russian expansion.

The growing political turmoil in Iran magnified the impact of
the Afghan invasion. An Islamic fundamentalist government had
already replaced the pro-American Shah. Then, in November
1979, student radicals stormed the U.S. embassy in Teheran and
took more than fifty Americans hostage. Washington's inability
to free its citizens and the apparent chaos in the Persian Gulf
raised the specter of a possible southward thrust by Soviet forces.

In January 1980, President Carter dispatched Defense Secretary Harold Brown to Beijing. He informed the Chinese of
America's willingness to sell nonlethal military equipment to
China, to provide a satellite ground station which would provide military intelligence data on Soviet activities and to assist
Chinese military retaliation if Vietnamese forces in Kampuchea
threatened Thailand. Chinese and American officials also agreed
to coordinate support for Afghan guerrillas and to assist Pakistan, which served as a base for anti-Soviet Afghan activities. At
one point, Chinese officials allegedly broached the idea of some
sort of formal military "alliance" directed at the Soviet Union.

Glib talk of a Sino-American military pact faded almost as
quickly as it began. China reacted with anger and distress to
Carter's decision in January 1980 to resume selective weapons
sales to Taiwan, following the one-year moratorium. Although
the decision was not unexpected, the PRC reissued its protest
that such sales represented interference in Chinese internal af-

fairs. At the same time, Deng and his colleagues concluded that American strategists like Brzezinski and Brown expected to use China as a "front-line state" in any confrontation with the Soviets. The U.S., they feared, would urge China to stand up to the Soviets in Asia, while Washington limited its own efforts to token assistance. Beijing had little interest in such a partnership.

Although the Carter Administration was ready to sell nonlethal military equipment to China, Beijing quickly discovered the expense of acquiring advanced Western weapons systems. Since Deng had resolved to trim military expenditures, little money could be spared for a major arms buildup. The Chinese also lacked the advanced technical infrastructure to coproduce, maintain or even utilize many modern defense items. Yet, partly for reasons of pride and partly to scare the Soviets on the cheap, China pressed the United States to announce its *willingness* to sell the PRC advanced weapons and military technology.

By late 1980, a host of domestic and foreign problems beset the Carter Administration. Inflation, largely due to skyrocketing oil prices, had rocked the American economy. The intractable hostage crisis in Iran, and the U.S.'s abortive effort to rescue the hostages, made Carter appear weak and vacillating. Challenged on the left by Senator Edward Kennedy and on the right by Ronald Reagan, Carter's reelection prospects dimmed rapidly.

The Chinese worried over the prospect of tying themselves to an unraveling American administration. They also doubted whether they could count on future support from Carter's likely successor, Ronald Reagan. The former movie actor and California governor denounced all Communist regimes and shocked Chinese sensibilities by voicing a proposal to restore formal diplomatic ties with Taiwan. Reagan's victory in November 1980 left Deng and his colleagues justifiably fearful that America's China policy stood on the verge of another abrupt turn for the worse.

Selected Additional Readings

Jimmy Carter, *Keeping Faith: Memoirs of a President*, N.Y., 1982; Cyrus P. Vance, *Hard Choices: Critical Years in America's Foreign*

Policy, N.Y., 1983; Zbigniew Brzezinski, *Power and Principle: Memoirs of the National Security Adviser, 1977–1981*, N.Y., 1983; Orville Schell, *In the People's Republic: An American's First Hand View of Living and Working in China*, N.Y., 1977, and *Watch Out for the Foreign Guests: China Encounters the West*, N.Y., 1980; Fox Butterfield, *China Alive in a Bitter Sea*, N.Y., 1982; Robert Sutter, *The China Quandary: Domestic Determinants of U.S. China Policy, 1972–82*, N.Y., 1986, and *Chinese Foreign Policy: Development After Mao*, N.Y., 1986; Jay and Linda Matthews, *One Billion: A China Chronicle*, N.Y., 1983; Jonathan D. Pollack, *The Lessons of Coalition Politics: Sino-American Security Relations*, Santa Monica, Calif., 1984; and Harry Harding, *China's Second Revolution: Reform After Mao*, Washington, D.C., 1987.

10

Toward the
Twenty-First Century

During the 1980 presidential election campaign Republican candidate Ronald Reagan bitterly criticized the way Jimmy Carter normalized relations with China. Denouncing the compromises reached in December 1978, Reagan declared that a "two China policy," i.e., recognizing formally both the PRC and the Republic of China on Taiwan, was "something very much worth exploring." The candidate went on to say:

> I want to have the best relations and have the Republic of China, the free Republic of China, know that we consider them an ally and that we have official relations with them . . . that liaison office [the American Institute on Taiwan] is unofficial . . . I would make it an official liaison office so that they had a governmental relation [with the U.S.].

When asked if Washington should recognize Taiwan as an independent nation if it declared itself separate from the mainland, Reagan said, "Yes, just like a lot of countries recognized the thirteen colonies when they became the United States."

Up to this point, China had generally avoided comment on domestic American politics or the presidential race. Now Beijing warned that Reagan's position, "if carried into practice, would wreck the very foundation of Sino-U.S. relations." China also criticized the U.S.'s decision to resume limited arms sales to Taiwan in 1980.

Following Reagan's inauguration as President in January 1981, the direction of China policy became an open question. In Beijing, leaders feared the new administration might rush to implement its campaign promises. In fact, China did not rank high on Reagan's list of foreign policy concerns. The conservative activists in the State and Defense departments and National Security Council focused public attention—and the President's energy—on the program of massively rearming the American military, opposing revolutionary movements in Central America and supporting anticommunist forces in Poland, Afghanistan and southern Africa. Many of Reagan's advisors appreciated China's opposition to the Soviet Union and sympathized with Deng's modernization program. After all, it marked a profound change in orthodox Communist ideology and promised to make China both a better trading partner and stronger barrier to Soviet expansion in Asia. At the same time, a feeling lingered among administration ideologues that they should shun overly close ties with any Communist regime and that they owed some special obligation to the veteran anticommunists on Taiwan.

Hoping to capitalize on the new atmosphere in Washington soon after Reagan took office, Taiwan requested approval to purchase advanced fighter planes. At first, the President delayed responding, then confused the issue by suggesting that he favored selling weapons to *both* Taiwan and China in order to improve relations with the rival regimes. Reagan ignored protests from home and abroad that such moves were utterly contradictory.

The situation improved, a bit, during the summer of 1981 when Secretary of State Alexander Haig visited Beijing. The diplomat informed his hosts that Washington would remove many restrictions still preventing China from buying advanced American technology. In addition, the United States would consider selling China, "on a case by case basis," lethal weapons. Nevertheless, Haig's haughty style of publicly announcing his decisions, even before informing his hosts, angered Chinese leaders. President Reagan compounded the insult by telling the press that his feelings about Taiwan, despite Haig's visit, had not changed.

During the first two years of the Reagan Administration, Secretary Haig tried, with only limited success, to soften the President's stand. Unfortunately, other influential officials felt that although China needed American protection and assistance, the United States had no need or obligation to win China's goodwill. They made little effort to remove bureaucratic roadblocks in the way of high technology trade. As a result, few of the promised military or computer sales to China went through.

Chinese disillusionment during the early 1980s contributed to an atmosphere in which otherwise trivial incidents took on disproportionate significance. Beijing howled in protest when a popular tennis player defected to the United States, and it expressed defiance when a U.S. court ruled that China must make full payment to American speculators holding Ch'ing Dynasty railroad bonds. Certainly the U.S. would have been equally outraged if French citizens holding Confederate Civil War bonds won a suit in Paris ordering Washington to honor the debt. As it turned out, the U.S. court's decision was later overturned.

By the end of 1981, Beijing adopted an openly critical stance toward aspects of American policy and insisted that *any* weapons sales to Taiwan would violate China's sovereignty. Early in 1982, the Reagan Administration announced its decision on such sales. It called for continued U.S.-Taiwanese coproduction of model F 5E fighter planes on the island, but prohibited sales or coproduction of the more advanced F 5G aircraft. Washington reasserted the right to sell whatever weapons it chose to Taiwan, but promised to refrain from selling the most advanced models as long as no grave military threat existed.

Confronted by the Reagan Administration's tough line, the PRC felt compelled to back away from its threat to downgrade relations with Washington if the U.S. continued to arm Taiwan. Beijing decided to interpret the decision as an implied American promise to end, eventually, U.S. arms sales. Chinese negotiators worked behind the scenes to come up with a mutual agreement

that allowed both sides to "save face." On August 17, 1982, the
United States and the People's Republic issued a joint communiqué declaring, in part:

> The U.S. Government states that it does not seek to carry out a
> long-term policy of arms sales to Taiwan, that its arms sales to
> Taiwan will not exceed either in qualitative or quantitative terms,
> the level of those supplied in recent years . . . and that it intends
> to reduce gradually its sales of arms to Taiwan, leading over a
> period of time to final resolution.

Now President Reagan could claim, with some justice, that he
had compelled China to accept American arms sales to Taiwan
for as long as Washington deemed necessary. China, in turn,
pointed to the pledge to limit and eventually end such sales.

The compromise thus promised to reduce, for the near term,
a major impediment to stable Sino-American relations. Bilateral
ties began to improve during 1982 and even more so when Defense Secretary Casper Weinberger visited China in the fall of
1983. Promising to overcome past bottlenecks, the Defense chief
announced streamlined procedures for high technology sales.
Communist Party General Secretary Hu Yaobang then visited
Japan where he praised the American ally and made light of recent friction with Tokyo over Japanese rearmament and efforts
by Japanese politicians to justify the invasion of China in the
1930s.

But just as the situation stabilized, the President provoked a
sharp exchange with China by again praising Taiwan as a formal American "ally." The depth of Chinese anger came through
late in 1983 when Hu Yaobang sent a private threat (through
this author, then visiting China, as well as through other channels) to cancel President Reagan's upcoming preelection junket
to China unless "he kept his big mouth shut." The tension abated
early in 1984 when Chinese Premier Zhao Ziyang visited Washington and received assurances that the President would contain his loose tongue.

That spring, Ronald Reagan finally traveled to the People's
Republic. He shunned his familiar anticommunist rhetoric and
anachronistic praise of Taiwan. Instead, the President and Mrs.
Reagan played dutiful tourists at historic sites, bought antiques,

visited a farmer's market and announced with glee that China had discovered the virtues of capitalism. Following the President's reelection in 1984, and throughout his second term, he devoted remarkably little attention, in public or private, to any aspect of China policy. Instead, he and his inner circle concentrated their diplomatic effort on arms negotiations with the Soviet Union and on the web of intrigue which became the Iran-Contra scandal.

The Taiwan Factor

In the years following Chiang Kai-shek's death in 1975, the situation on Taiwan changed dramatically. The Generalissimo's son, Chiang Ching-kuo, succeeded his father and began to transform the political and economic system. Wisely rejecting a "fortress mentality," the younger Chiang strove to assure Taiwan's survival by building its economic strength. Through adroit diplomacy Taiwan maintained strong commercial and informal diplomatic links with nearly all the one hundred or more nations that formally recognized the People's Republic.

Since the late 1950s land reform, stress on light manufacturing, and American and Japanese assistance had laid the basis for prosperity. By promoting the export of textiles, footwear and consumer electronics, the small, resource-poor island gradually emerged as a regional "economic mini-superpower." From the late 1960s on, economic growth averaged more than nine percent annually. Per capita income increased twenty-fold from the 1950 level, reaching over $5,000 by 1988. Low unemployment and a relatively egalitarian distribution of income reduced social tension between the native Taiwanese and the mainlanders who dominated the island after 1949.

Under the younger Chiang, the political process opened a bit. Taiwanese were allowed to play a larger role in it, and some modest opposition activity was tolerated. Since the mid-1980s small opposition parties have been permitted to compete in local elections. A few opposition members even won seats in the island's legislature, although it remained under firm KMT control.

In order to avoid the political turmoil which beset authoritarian regimes in South Korea and the Philippines, Chiang initiated some important reforms. In 1986 he lifted martial law, which had been in place for thirty-eight years. More flexible, if still stern, laws permitted greater freedom of speech, assembly and press. Verbal attacks on Beijing decreased, and family members were permitted to visit relatives on the mainland. Before his death in January 1988 Chiang Ching-kuo moved to block succession by members of his family (either his son or stepmother, Madame Chiang, who, in her nineties, returned to Taiwan in 1987 from self-imposed exile on Long Island) and seemed determined to leave behind a legacy of reform.

President Lee Teng-hui, Chiang's successor, symbolized a passing both of generations and of origins. Born on Taiwan and educated in the United States (with a Cornell Ph.D. in agricultural economics), Lee resembled the new breed of Asian technocratic politicians found in Hong Kong and Singapore. As a native Taiwanese, he could reach out more easily to the eighty-five percent of the population who had lived on the island for centuries before the 1949 influx from the mainland. Also, despite the fact that mainlanders continued to dominate the Nationalist Party, army and security apparatus, many Taiwanese had risen to powerful positions. Increasing rates of intermarriage and broad-based economic growth reduced tensions further.

Even following its modest liberalization, Taiwan could hardly be considered democratic. It remained a crime either to advocate Taiwanese independence or to question the goal of national reunification. The legislature was still controlled by aged members, most of whom were elected on the mainland before 1949 or appointed by the government to fill openings. Beginning in 1988 President Lee forced senile or incompetent legislators to resign and replaced them with locally elected members. Of course, continued KMT control of political campaigns, the media and electoral rules meant that no dramatic changes would occur in the immediate future.

Economically, Taiwan has amassed one of the world's largest foreign currency reserves. In 1988, they totaled more than $75 billion, second only to Japan. The American trade deficit that year with the tiny island totaled about $20 billion, also second only to Japan. Some three-fourths of Taiwan's exports are sold in this country, often under the brand names of American distributors (e.g., General Electric, Wilson, Mattell).

The severance of formal diplomatic relations with the United States has had little impact on economic or cultural ties between the two countries, in which everything from investments to tourism has flourished. The largest single group of foreign students in the United States comes from Taiwan. Nearly three-fourths of them choose to remain in America after completing their education. This has created the same kind of "brain drain" that worries Chinese Communist leaders.

Although a state of war nominally exists between Taiwan and China, since 1987 family members from Taiwan have been permitted to visit mainland relatives. During the first two years of this program, more than 500,000 Taiwanese made the pilgrimage home. Trade links, mostly through Hong Kong, reached the $2 billion level by 1988. Still, Taiwan's leaders reject the notion of any formal political contacts or direct negotiations with Beijing. They are prepared to talk about reunification, but only on their own terms. However, in 1989 Taiwanese officials began, for the first time, to attend international meetings held in China.

Since the early 1980s China has alternately threatened and cajoled Taiwan. Beijing has proposed several formulas for peaceful reunion in which Taiwan would be classified as a special administrative region with autonomy over its economy, culture, etc. Deng Xiaoping even suggested retention of separate military forces. In effect, "one China" with "two systems" would emerge.

Apparently frustrated by Taiwan's refusal to negotiate, in 1988 Deng threatened to consider a "small-scale military operation" if peaceful approaches failed. China also declared its determination to intervene with force under any of four circumstances: (1) domestic turmoil on the island; (2) any Taiwanese proclamation of independence from the mainland; (3) Taiwan's entry into a military alliance with the Soviet Union; or (4) Taiwan's deployment of nuclear weapons.

When not threatening Taiwan, Communist authorities have tried wooing it by playing the "Chiang card." After four decades of vilifying the former Nationalist leader, and despite the fact that since his death in 1975 his name has lapsed into near oblivion on Taiwan, Beijing has decided to make Chiang's hometown a national shrine. The Communist government has rebuilt his villa (bombed by the Japanese in 1939) in the town of Xikou in east China, restored his family's graves and opened the former home of his son, Chiang Ching-kuo, as a tourist site. By paying homage to the main villain in the annals of Communist history, Chinese officials hoped to convince Taiwanese to be more enthusiastic about reunification.

And yet, while Taiwanese tourists have visited the village in large numbers, the town's sanctification has not had a marked political impact. Significantly, the affluent Taiwanese are more impressed by the low-wage rates of local workers and have decided to open several factories in the area to benefit from cheap labor costs.

Indeed, Beijing has expressed some anxiety about the Nationalist regime's recent loosening of political control. China has come to realize that the Taiwanese majority, as distinct from the mainland elite, has less interest in any sort of reunification. Thus, when Chiang Ching-kuo died, Communist leader Zhao Ziyang sent an effusive condolence, praising Chiang's determined opposition to Taiwanese independence. He urged Chiang's successors to reaffirm the principle that Taiwan remains part of one China.

But in spite of the Taiwan regime's ritualistic pledges to "Recover the Mainland," after forty years of separation much of the vigor has gone out of the promise. Many people in and out of the government see the mainland as a large, but not particularly desirable, piece of real estate. The new attitude has left many in both China and Taiwan uneasy. Prominent business people allied to the ruling group on Taiwan have said privately that the economic gap separating the two societies has grown so large and the mainland is so comparatively poor that "we don't want it back. But how can you say that?"

In casual discourse, most Taiwanese no longer denounce political leaders in Beijing as "Communist bandits." They have become "mainland authorities." Instead of describing their own country as the Republic of China, they refer to it as Taiwan.

The prospect of reunification appears to many on the island as a frightening burden.

Part of this anxiety stems from the increased levels of trade and familial contact between the two societies since the late 1980s. The more contact there is, the less Taiwanese seem to covet the mainland. In fact, so many Taiwanese consider China poor and dirty that they react angrily to official KMT ideology about the duty of recovering the lost nation. Officials in Beijing are aghast at this turn of events and have stressed their determination to unify the homeland regardless of preferences on Taiwan. Ordinary Chinese now look to Taiwan as a model of prosperity and even liberalization, to the chagrin of Communist authorities.

Taiwan's links to the United States appear quite strong for the foreseeable future. Both American political parties share a belief in peaceful reunification and both support continued sale of defensive arms. In 1988 these sales totaled at least $700 million. In order to assure Taiwan's security while diminishing Sino-American friction, Washington has encouraged U.S. arms manufacturers to sell military production technology to the island. Thus, in the coming years, Taiwan will become nearly self-sufficient in building aircraft, tanks, ships and short-range missiles.

The United States has drawn the line on nuclear proliferation. It pressured Taiwan to sign the international treaty giving up all rights to construct or use atomic weapons. In March 1988, when the Reagan Administration uncovered evidence of a secret project on Taiwan that was capable of producing weapons-grade plutonium, it insisted that the work cease. Although Taiwan complied, this remains a sensitive problem.

Hong Kong and Macao

China has negotiated successfully for the return of other "lost territory," notably British Hong Kong. In 1984 Great Britain reached an agreement to return, by 1997, its entire colony to Beijing. Unification will occur in stages, so as not to upset the booming economy. China, of course, hopes to benefit from the colony's dynamic commercial infrastructure. Meanwhile, private enterprise and other unique features of the Hong Kong's pluralistic system would be guaranteed for up to fifty years. In 1987 Portugal, which ruled the tiny enclave of Macao for some four hundred years, reached a similar arrangement to relinquish control to China.

These generous arrangements (China could have seized both colonies at will) reflected the PRC's determination not to kill the goose that laid a golden egg (Hong Kong) and represented a test case for impressing Taiwan. If the reunion goes well and Hong Kong's diversity and prosperity survives, this success may provide the catalyst for settling the larger question of Taiwan.

The United States, China and the World Community

Within the last two centuries, Western leaders as diverse as Napoleon and Franklin Roosevelt have predicted China's emergence as a "Great Power." Until recently, this prediction had little basis, as China remained too weak, disorganized and backward to count for much in world affairs. But once China emerged from the chaos of dynastic disintegration and revolutionary upheaval, it could no longer be dismissed as either the "sick man of Asia" or a satellite of some larger power.

Increasingly, the overriding priority of economic development has driven Chinese foreign policy in recent years. In 1985 General Secretary Hu Yaobang and Premier Zhao Ziyang told an assembly of China's ambassadors that "economic diplomacy" stood at the center of the nation's relations with the outside world. Foreign policy would serve the "greatest national interest": modernization.

In order to devote its full energy to modernization, the People's Republic has required a peaceful and stable international environment. In 1984 Deng Xiaoping noted that "China needs at least twenty years of peace to concentrate on our economic development." In practice, this has meant adopting a policy of "omni-directional peaceful co-existence." Thus China has moved to improve relations with all its neighbors and past rivals, including even Vietnam: by 1989 Beijing and Hanoi began to discuss ways of settling their dispute over Kampuchea and restoring more normal ties.

For nearly a decade (1971–81), Beijing sought a closer strategic relationship with the United States. At first, it hoped for American support as leverage against the Soviet Union. Later, China urged the U.S. to play a more active role in challenging Soviet activities in Asia and the Third World. Discovering by the early 1980s that the United States had its own priorities, China feared ending up as an American pawn in the competition between Moscow and Washington.

After reassessing their basic interests and goals, Chinese leaders have abandoned the strategy of trying to profit from Soviet-American rivalry. Beijing has, in effect, accepted the legitimacy of the current international economic and political system, disavowed the Maoist critique of the world order and dropped calls for "people's wars" against the superpowers. China has practically eliminated its support for revolutionary movements abroad and has joined most major international organizations. Instead of confrontation, it recommends cooperation between advanced and less developed countries.

China now attempts to deal with most international issues on a pragmatic, case-by-case basis. In 1986 Premier Zhao explained that Beijing would make diplomatic decisions based on the "merits of each case" and would not determine "closeness with or estrangement from other countries on the basis of their social systems and ideologies."

In practice, China has generally supported America's post-Vietnam policy in Asia, especially toward Indochina and Afghanistan. Implicitly, at least, Beijing accepts the benefits of U.S. military deployments and bases in the Pacific, Japan and the Philippines. In fact, like most Asian states, it much prefers a substantial American military presence in the region to unilateral Japanese rearmament. China has even privately admitted some common interest in preserving, for the time being, the status quo in Taiwan and South Korea. China condemns what it sees as unbalanced American support of Israel and South Africa. It denounced with great bitterness the Soviet Union's military buildup in Asia, intervention in Afghanistan and support for Cuban military activity in southern Africa.

China's effort to fulfill its modernization program will, almost certainly, increase its stake in keeping the regional and international system stable. Domestic economic progress and political liberalization could eventually ease reunification with Hong Kong and perhaps Taiwan.

Despite exaggerated rhetoric that China could become a great economic power in the coming decades, any change is likely to be incremental. By even the rosiest estimates, China will remain a relatively small player in the world economy through the beginning of the next century. In recent years, growth in two-way trade has been rapid, but China still accounts for less than two percent of current world commerce. Optimistic projections suggest a doubling of this level, to about four percent, by the year 2000.

Americans pay a great deal of attention to well-publicized but essentially trivial economic developments. For example, in 1987 China opened a large Kentucky Fried Chicken restaurant opposite Mao's mausoleum in Beijing. The two-story franchise, shaped like a large bucket, features the likeness of Colonel Harlan Sanders facing the austere monument to the dead revolutionary. But aside from the ironic juxtaposition, the franchise represents, quite literally, only a "drop in the bucket." American industry is just not likely to find a huge China market for fried chicken or consumer products in general.

It can, however, expect to sell high technology items, agricultural technology and specialized services. The growth in China's foreign trade will probably have its greatest impact on Japan and Southeast Asia. The United States will benefit economically from these developments, but the "China Market" will not prove any panacea.

China will seek to bolster its trade with, and adopt models from, the dynamic economies of North- and Southeast Asia. As Beijing becomes less concerned with its strategic position between the Soviet Union and United States, it will naturally focus more on regional issues. Japan's remarkable emergence as a center of global economic power has sometimes obscured the progress achieved by newly industrializing states nearby, especially Taiwan, Singapore, South Korea and Hong Kong. India and Pakistan also play a growing economic, political and military role in the Asia-Pacific region. China's search for stability and economic modernization will almost certainly prompt closer relations with these societies.

By the end of the 1980s, the intense hostility and vitriolic rhetoric of the Sino-Soviet split began to mellow. This reflected both China's greater concentration on economic affairs and changes in Soviet policy. Early in 1989, Soviet and Chinese foreign ministers announced plans for a summit conference between Soviet President Mikhail S. Gorbachev and Deng Xiaoping. Scheduled for May, it would be the first meeting between leaders of the two nations since the frosty Khrushchev-Mao summit in 1959. Deng characterized the upcoming summit as an opportunity to "close the page on the past and open up the chapter on the future."

Nevertheless, Soviet and Chinese officials emphasized that their countries would not resume the close alliance which existed during the 1950s. In an obvious effort to reassure the U.S., Japan and others, the Russian and Chinese foreign ministers stressed that improved Sino-Soviet relations would not come at the expense of any other nation.

The signs of improved ties coincided with efforts by the two major Communist powers to settle old disputes. They announced a plan to reduce tensions along their borders by informing each other of military movements and by establishing a commission to demarcate contested territory. Fulfilling long-standing demands of the Chinese, the Soviets started to withdraw troops from Outer Mongolia and from elsewhere in the Far East. Early in 1989 Soviet forces departed from Afghanistan, a move pleasing to both Washington and Beijing. Also, after years of inflexibility, Soviet-allied Vietnam began removing troops from Kampuchea and participating in an effort to form a coalition government there. Hanoi pledged to withdraw Vietnamese troops by the end of 1989. Gorbachev impressed many Asians by offering to remove Russian naval forces from bases in Vietnam if America gave up its Philippine bases. Apart from that offer, most of the Soviets' actions fulfilled conditions previously imposed by China and the U.S. for proof of change in Soviet behavior.

Thus, both domestically and internationally, the goals of Moscow and Beijing seemed to move in a new harmony. Each of the Communist states began adopting forms of a market economy and increased political pluralism. Each required a peaceful regional and international environment to achieve internal restructuring. The U.S. could draw comfort from the fact that, unlike the situation in the 1950s, the restoration of normal relations between China and the Soviet Union did not imply greater hostility toward America. However, improved ties would alleviate a major cause of China's initial tilt toward the U.S. in the early 1970s. China no longer would require American insurance against a Soviet military threat and thus would follow a more independent course. More than ever, successful American diplomacy in East Asia would require cooperation between the United States and a wide range of Asian nations.

Beyond the Reagan years, the prospects for continued peaceful relations between the United States and the People's Republic of China appeared hopeful. China's commitment to modernization has given it every incentive to behave in ways compatible with U.S. security interests in Asia. However, several possible sources of international tension exist on the horizon. China, Japan, Vietnam, Taiwan and the Philippines all assert competing claims to several small island chains in the South China Sea. These tiny outcroppings, such as the Spratly Islands, have significance because whichever country controls them can lay claim to ocean-bed mineral and petroleum resources and fishing rights along the continental shelf.

China, like several of its neighbors, also fears reassertive Japanese nationalism and militarism. Several times in recent years leading politicians in Tokyo have publicly defended such pre-World War II actions as the colonization of Korea and invasion of China. At one point, the Education Ministry proposed that school children be taught that Japan's invasion of China was nothing more than an "advance," presumably for the good of civilization. Although Tokyo relented when confronted with angry protests throughout Asia, these incidents raised questions about how some Japanese officials interpreted the past and envisioned the future.

Given the relative decline in American influence and Japan's dramatic economic growth of late, some commentators in both countries have called for Tokyo to shoulder greater military responsibilities in East Asia. This might include sharing American defense costs in the region or, perhaps, expanding Japan's own military force. Although barred by its constitution from resorting to war, Japan fields a substantial "self-defense force" and already boasts the world's third largest military budget, over $30 billion by minimum estimates. Nevertheless, the U.S. Congress in 1988 passed a resolution calling for Japan to triple its defense outlays. Chinese, like other Asians who suffered under Japanese occupation, worry about the behavior of a heavily rearmed Japan. If indeed Tokyo were to increase its defense spending, whether on its own or under American prodding, it would probably alienate the very countries Washington hopes to protect.

Other Issues

One little noticed area of growing Chinese-American contact is immigration. Between the 1880s and World War II, of course, virtually all Chinese were barred from migrating to the U.S. The tiny quota of 105 per year, granted in 1943, was the worst sort of tokenism. Immediately following the war, Congress passed the so-called War Brides law of 1946, permitting spouses and children of American service people to enter this country. Several thousand Chinese and Japanese came in under these provisions.

When Congress got around to writing a comprehensive new immigration law in 1952, it actually worsened the opportunities for most people desiring to immigrate. The McCarran-Walter Act was permeated with anticommunist rhetoric and made no secret of the desire to bar "indigestible blocs" unsuitable to the "American way of life." However, in a nominal effort to prove that America treated all groups equally, Congress allowed that 100 persons per year from every Pacific Basin country could enter the U.S. Yet, ethnicity rather than nationality remained at the root of this quota. For example, any person with one Asian parent was classified as Asian. So a Peruvian citizen with a Chinese mother was, for immigration purposes, classified as Chinese and subject to the tiny quota.

During the next dozen years, Chinese benefited from a series of special refugee programs designed primarily to provide shelter to Europeans and Cubans fleeing Communist regimes. Presidents Eisenhower and Kennedy used a procedure called "parole" to suspend immigration quotas and allow large numbers of Hungarians, Poles, Germans and Cubans into the U.S. Several thousand Chinese from Hong Kong were included in these programs.

The real change in policy occurred in 1965 when Congress, affected by the civil rights movement, eliminated the national origins quota system. The new immigration law put all countries on an equal basis. A cap of 170,000 immigrants from the Eastern hemisphere could enter the U.S. annually. Any single country could send a maximum of 20,000 per year.

Within these totals, the law gave preference to close family members of persons living in the U.S. or to people with desirable job skills. Race and ethnicity were no longer factors in eligibility. Between 1965 and 1989, at least eleven million people entered America as legal immigrants. Asians benefited more than any other group from this liberalization. Even discounting for the one million Southeast Asian refugees admitted since 1975, over forty percent of the post-1965 immigrants came from the Asia-Pacific region. This included about four million people from China, Hong Kong, Taiwan, South Korea and the Philippines. Chinese and other Asians now make up sizable minorities in many American states and cities. Moreover, they have diffused into American society at all levels.

A matter of concern in Sino-American relations is the fact that China has already emerged as the third largest nuclear power, behind the United States and Soviet Union. Currently, it is working to improve the survivability and mobility of its missile force. Beijing possesses two nuclear missile submarines and plans to deploy several more. These weapons, China insists, are designed solely to deter attack, not to intimidate any other nation. In the past, Beijing ignored concerns over nuclear nonproliferation (is rumored to have helped Pakistan try to build an atomic bomb) and criticized Soviet-American arms control agreements. Both Washington and Moscow must work to ensure Beijing's collaboration in future arms reduction treaties. In 1988 China indicated greater concern with limiting the spread of atomic weapons and endorsed the Reagan Administration's agreement with Moscow to reduce intermediate range nuclear missiles.

Less reassuring has been China's willingness to plunge into the stormy world of large-scale arms sales to warring countries. Both to gain influence and earn hard currency, in the late 1980s China began selling several types of short and intermediate range missiles to Iran, Syria and Saudi Arabia. This has increased tensions in the already overarmed Middle East. Of course, China points to both the United States and the Soviet Union as far bigger arms merchants.

In the future, certain disputes may well continue to cause friction between Washington and Beijing. Concern over human rights, for example, has already prompted the U.S. Congress to object to China's harsh suppression of Tibetan independence protests during 1987–88; the PRC in turn complained of U.S. interference in its domestic affairs. Moreover, China has charged that American trade regulations unfairly limit textile exports to the United States. Beijing is also likely to continue criticizing the "brain drain" of Chinese students who elect to stay in America. Should the United States encourage Taiwan's desire for reunification on its own terms or for independence, that issue might again flair up as a source of grave trouble.

During the years of the Reagan Administration, U.S. officials frequently condemned Chinese population control measures—which sought to limit family size to one child and, Washington charged, pressured women to have abortions. While the Chinese denied the allegation of forced abortions, they insisted Americans had no business telling them how to control birth rates. The issue receded by 1989 as "Right to Life" advocates lost ground in Washington and as China relaxed the one-child rule. However, several Chinese women have sought asylum in the U.S. on the grounds of fleeing forced abortions.

Still, China's burgeoning population (just over one billion in 1989) will put great pressure on its agricultural and industrial economy. One sign of relaxed population policy is already apparent. Cities have experienced a dramatic population gain since the mid-1980s, both through rising birth rates and in-migration. Some demographers predict that by the mid-1990s thirty-five or forty percent of Chinese may live in cities, double the number who did as recently as 1980.

The United States will have to accept an ambivalent strategic relationship with China. The People's Republic will seek friendship with America, but avoid any appearance of subservience or alliance. For its part, the U.S. should remain supportive of Chinese economic modernization and encourage trade and technological transfers. While facilitating the exchange of people and ideas, it must shun the temptation to pressure China to adopt American political norms. Foreign pressure would likely backfire and encourage xenophobic nationalism.

Several ugly incidents in early 1989 showed that a form of racism and hostility toward foreigners lurked close to the surface of Chinese society. University students in several Chinese cities demonstrated against and assaulted hundreds of African scholarship students for allegedly molesting Chinese women. Even though prejudice against dark skin has had a long history in Chinese culture, many observers felt that the violence revealed broader frustration among Chinese elite youth. Foreign students, travelers and business people in China have enjoyed material privileges which few Chinese could ever hope to realize. Primitive conditions were the norm even in China's best universities. (Chinese students lived six or eight to a small room, without heat, running water, adequate electricity or decent food.)

Although the Africans came from some of the world's poorest nations, as compared to Western countries and Japan (or even China), even they seemed pampered. It appears that large numbers of Chinese students acted out of both racism and frustration at their own poor living standards to attack the weakest and least respected foreigners. In some ways, this resembled violence directed at missionaries during the era of foreign military domination. It also sent a message to Chinese leaders that they must deliver quickly on promises of higher living standards or risk alienating an entire generation.

A handful of American officials have, since the early 1970s, become adept in managing policy toward China, but the U.S. government is nevertheless plagued by a chronic shortage of mid-level career bureaucrats who qualify as China specialists. Whether serving in an embassy or in the State Department, most Foreign Service officers rotate every two years. This provides littel incentive or opportunity to become familiar with the language, history, culture and politics of their assigned nation. The problem is especially severe regarding China, since few people entering government service have any relevant training in the Chinese language or history.

In fact, one academic specialist, serving temporarily on the China policy desk in the State Department, found that, throughout the government, her colleagues' ignorance of Chinese history bordered on the insensitive. For example, in 1987 she received a call from the Department of Commerce's China section. In a show of goodwill designed to promote trade, the Commerce Department planned to hold a ceremony in Washington to "commemorate the U.S. victory in the Boxer Rebellion and wanted to know which Chinese they should invite, mainland or Taiwan?" Politely but firmly, the specialist explained that neither side would appreciate an invitation to celebrate what all Chinese considered a humiliating defeat at the hands of Western imperialism. The project, fortunately, was scrapped. Still, it revealed the inadequate attention paid, at all levels of government, to staffing agencies with qualified personnel.

When dealing with the PRC, the United States must keep in mind that Chinese politics is still characterized by factionalism between full-blown reformers and those determined to limit the scope and pace of change. Late in 1986, pressure from political liberalization resulted in large student demonstrations in Beijing and other cities. Those fearful of loosening the Communist Party's grip utilized the protests to attack party General Secretary Hu Yaobang, allegedly a supporter of the demonstrators. Hu's idiosyncratic behavior (a penchant for designer suits and garish Hawaiian shirts, appeals for Chinese to use forks instead of chop sticks, and a spontaneous invitation for 3,000 Japanese students to visit China) led some of his associates to refer to him as "the clown."

Meanwhile, some conservative party leaders were displeased at Hu's efforts to consolidate power by placing allies in key positions. Military officials objected to the prospect of Hu replacing Deng on the Central Military Commission. Deng himself may have been angered when Hu urged his mentor to follow through on his oft-stated promise to retire fully.

Besides these factors, Deng feared that public disorder would endanger both economic reform and the principle of party control. Deng thus decided to appease the go-slow faction by forcing Hu's ouster as party leader (he was relegated to a minor post) and expelling from party membership several prominent intellectuals identified with the student protests. Within a year, Premier Zhao Ziyang replaced Hu as General Secretary, and Li Peng, a Soviet-trained engineer, stepped into Zhao's shoes as Premier. Though ostensibly semiretired, the aged Deng still pulled the most powerful strings behind the scenes. When foreign dignitaries like George Bush or Mikhail Gorbachev planned to visit China in 1989, Deng remained the man to see.

For the first time, the four major powers of the Pacific Basin—the United States, China, Japan and the Soviet Union—appear to be on a parallel rather than a collision course. Orthodox Maoism and Stalinism have been discredited, prompting the Communist states to experiment, at least for a time, with new economic and political models. Japan has emerged as a global economic power courted by the other three Pacific giants. The U.S., which has seen its relative economic influence decline, has become ever more deeply involved with the Pacific Basin economy.

The maturing American relationship with China in the last decade of the twentieth century must now take into account a widening network of regional interests. The reduction of military tensions among the U.S., China, Japan and the Soviet Union highlights the growing importance of the Asia-Pacific area in the world economy. By weighing carefully the competing interests of the region, the United States may finally achieve the peaceful balance it has sought to promote throughout this century.

Selected Additional Readings

Alexander M. Haig, Jr., *Caveat: Realism, Reagan and Foreign Policy*, N.Y., 1984; Orville Schell, *Discos and Democracy: China in the Throes of Reform*, N.Y., 1988; Harry Harding, ed., *China's Foreign Policy in the 1980s*, New Haven, Conn., 1984; and Samuel S. Kim, ed., *China and the World: New Directions in Chinese Foreign Relations*, Boulder, Colo., 1989. See also the books by Harding, Pollack and Sutter listed in Chapter 9.

Epilogue

The death in January 1989 of Emperor Hirohito—the last active leader of the World War II era—brought symbolic closure to a time when Washington, Tokyo and Moscow fought to control China's destiny. As one of his first official acts, President George Bush (who served during the mid-1970s as de facto ambassador to China) decided to attend Hirohito's funeral in February and to visit Beijing as well. His meeting with Chinese officials was brief, representing a courtesy call more than a serious summit. The most notable event occurred when police barred China's leading dissident, Fang Lizhi, from attending a banquet at the American embassy. Fang and his supporters expressed disappointment that U.S. officials did nothing to help him.

In mid-May, however, the summit conference between Mikhail Gorbachev and Deng Xiaoping took place in a very different atmosphere. A month before, on April 15, 1989, former Communist Party General Secretary Hu Yaobang died of a heart attack. His death sparked a massive wave of student demonstrations, boycotts and marches in Beijing and other cities in which protestors praised Hu as a martyr to democracy and demanded implementation of political reforms. This "democracy movement" called for a more open press and the end of corruption and special privilege among the party elite. Beside students, the movement appealed especially to urban workers, intellectuals and civil servants—groups which had benefited less than others from economic reform and who felt excluded politically from the still closed circle of Communist leadership.

When Gorbachev arrived in China, his presence breathed new vigor into the flagging protest movement. The reform-minded Soviet leader emerged as a symbol of new Communist political thinking, and demonstrators filled Tiananmen Square, holding signs pleading that he intercede on their behalf with China's officials. Crowds surrounded the Great Hall of the People (where the summit took place) and carried placards reading, "Give Us Democracy Or Give Us Death." To the embarrassment of his hosts, Gorbachev's entire schedule had to be rearranged around the demonstrations, forcing cancellation of his tour of the Great Wall and the Forbidden City.

By May 16–17, over one million demonstrators virtually took control of central Beijing. Factory workers, civil servants and even police and soldiers rallied with students to demand democratization. Many came to show solidarity with 3,000 hunger strikers who pledged to fast unto death (they relented), citing Martin Luther King, Jr., and Gandhi as models. The protest movement called more and more for the retirement of Deng Xiaoping and Premier Li Peng, accusing them of blocking democratic reform.

Officially, Deng held only one government post, chairman of the commission overseeing the armed forces. Unofficially, however, he was still the key power broker. Li Peng, who had been informally adopted by Zhou Enlai in the 1930s after his parents' death, enjoyed Deng's patronage. Like his mentor, Li actually supported economic reform and opposed any return to Maoist orthodoxy. But also like Deng, Li feared that rapid political liberalization threatened to undermine central control by an entrenched oligarchy and might lead to chaos.

In contrast, Communist Party General Secretary Zhao Ziyang emerged as an unexpectedly strong advocate of political reform. He met with students in Tiananmen and called publicly for an open dialogue with the regime's critics. Deng and Li rejected his approach and forced Zhao from power.

The intransigence of Deng and Li sparked increasingly large demonstrations throughout the country. The heavy foreign news coverage (which coincided with the Sino-Soviet summit) enlivened the protests and, temporarily, deterred hardline leaders from ordering violent repression. Demonstrators attracted foreign, especially American, sympathy by erecting models of the Statue of Liberty rechristened the "goddess of democracy," in front of TV cameras.

By May 20 Premier Li Peng had had enough. He declared martial law, limited news coverage and ordered military units to disband the crowds in Tiananmen. Beijing's populace intervened, stopping troop convoys by means of nonviolent sitdowns. When military commanders hesitated to attack civilians, the central leadership seemed to falter. Then, on June 4, heavily armed troops and tanks attacked the 10,000 to 20,000 students still holding out in Tiananmen. Several thousand were reported to have died in the square and surrounding neighborhoods in a brutal massacre. It appeared as if Deng, Li and hardline allies in the military had crushed the reform faction and had initiated a purge of those crusading for political liberalization.

During the first stages of this period of turmoil, American leaders kept an advisedly low profile. President Bush appealed for moderation on both sides, expressed broad support for democratic reform and praised the principle of nonviolent protest. Any strong criticism of Chinese authorities or specific encouragement of the students, he feared, would be taken as unwarranted foreign meddling. Washington also believed that while many Americans empathized with calls for internal reform, a victory for either faction in China was not likely to have much affect on foreign relations.

Following the June 4 assault on the unarmed students, however, U.S. officials criticized the violence forcefully. The American embassy in Beijing even granted asylum to Fang Lizhi and his wife, Li Shuxian. The Chinese government charged Washington with interference in its internal affairs and compared American actions to the plots hatched against China by John Foster Dulles in the 1950s. China's harsh repression of dissidents and criticisms of alleged foreign interference may thus bring a new period of strain in Sino-American relations.

Although Mikhail Gorbachev's Soviet reforms inspired the democracy movement in China, the summit meeting barely touched on domestic politics. Gorbachev declared that the Soviet Union must shoulder a large part of the blame for the three decades of Sino-Soviet hostility. Deng commented that cold war tensions had been partly responsible for the break between Moscow and Beijing. As Soviet-American relations improved, one source of friction had abated. Quoting from one of his favorite American movies, Deng declared that Sino-Soviet hostility was "gone with the wind."

But even as China applauded the reduction of Soviet forces in the Far East, as well as the withdrawal of Soviet troops from Afghanistan and the progress toward a political settlement in Kampuchea, Beijing emphasized its independence from Moscow. Ships from the U.S. 7th Fleet, which for twenty years shielded Taiwan, received an invitation to visit Shanghai on the same day as the Soviet leader. When American officials suggested a postponement to avoid embarrassing anyone, the Chinese insisted that the fleet's visit should take place as planned. In the end, a one-day delay was arranged.

Ever since President Nixon's visit to China in 1972, Washington has regarded the triangular relationship of the U.S., Soviet Union and China as the stable foundation of superpower relations. The likelihood of Soviet-Chinese rapprochement, most observers feel, will not alter that fact. As ties between the two major Communist states improve, the military resources freed are not likely to be turned against the West or Asia. Chinese and Soviet development plans both anticipate economic cooperation with the dynamic states of Asia, including Japan, South Korea and Taiwan.

Throughout four decades of the cold war, the United States struggled to block Chinese and Soviet involvement in Asia. As its fears of monolithic communism have waned, however, the United States now believes that such involvement, as well as its own, may become the key to peace and prosperity in the region.

Index